QUANTUM CREATIVITY
WAKING UP TO OUR CREATIVE POTENTIAL

Perspectives on Creativity
Mark A. Runco (ed.)

QUANTUM CREATIVITY

WAKING UP TO OUR CREATIVE POTENTIAL

AMIT GOSWAMI
UNIVERSITY OF OREGON AND
INSTITUTE OF NOETIC SCIENCES

WITH MAGGIE GOSWAMI

HAMPTON PRESS, INC.
CRESSKILL, NEW JERSEY

Printed in the United States of America

Library of Congress Cataloging-in-Publication Data

Goswami, Amit.
    Quantum creativity : waking up to our creative potential / Amit Goswami with Maggie Goswami.
       p.   cm. -- (Perspectives on creativity)
    Includes bibliographic references and indexes.
    ISBN 1-57273-226-1 (hardcover). -- ISBN 1-57273-227-X (pbk.)
    1. Creative ability. 2. Creative thinking. 3. Quantum theory.
I. Goswami, Maggie. II. Title. III. Series.
BF408.G64 1998
153.3'5--dc21   98-42483
                                                  CIP

Cover design and figure illustrations by Lucas Plumb

Hampton Press, Inc.
23 Broadway
Cresskill, NJ 07626

To our children

Shankar Goswami
Mimi Goswami-Hill
Eric Weeks
Benjamin Weeks

and to all children of the present and the future
may they explore the creative possibilities

CONTENTS

PREFACE

My first adult experience of creativity occurred a year after I came from India to Western Reserve University in Cleveland, Ohio, as an instructor and post-doctoral researcher in theoretical nuclear physics. I was working hard on research into a new kind of interactive phenomenon concerning atomic nuclei, but to no avail. That day I had discussed with my mentor my umpteenth idea on the subject only to see him poke such serious holes in it that it no longer held together even in my prejudiced eyes. After that I had retired to the Snakepit, the basement cafeteria. I was nearly ready to quit when the solution suddenly came to me with such clarity that I knew it was right. I ran upstairs to my mentor who immediately saw its potency. I still remember the joyful haze in which we spent that afternoon.

I continued my research in nuclear physics for ten more years after that incident, solved a great many problems, and wrote quite a few scientific papers; but the joy of that day seemed to elude me. Gradually, I became a little cynical. I assumed, like most of my colleagues, that all scientific research is creative, but that creativity is not necessarily joyful. People who reported such joy probably exaggerated; my own memorable experience was perhaps due to a beginner's naive exuberance. I assumed that creative work brought only the mature satisfaction that I felt each time I succeeded in solving a tractable problem and writing another paper to further my career.

Then a major life change was precipitated by a divorce and the loss of a research grant, followed by remarriage and the abandonment of nuclear physics. I wrote a textbook on basic physics and then a book, with the help of my wife Maggie, that explored the physics of science fiction. At some point I changed my research field to the interpretation of quantum mechanics. Quantum mechanics, this century's new paradigm of physics, is used mostly to calculate the movement of submicroscopic objects (such as atoms, nuclei, and elementary particles) but actually holds for all material objects.

Quantum mechanics rose over the horizon in the twenties, and ever since, this new physics has threatened to overthrow the prevailing worldview of science which is based on the idea that everything real is made of matter--any phenomenon that looks nonmaterial is illusory. But we are thwarted by paradoxes when we try to explain quantum phenomena while holding on to strict materialism. It is these paradoxes that I set my mind to resolve.

After years of trepidation and false starts, one evening during a discussion with a friend, I realized that the resolution of the quantum paradoxes is to break away completely from the current materialist paradigm, the foundations of which quantum mechanics had irreparably damaged. A new foundation composed of the idea that consciousness--not matter--is the ground of being would give rise to a reinvigorated science capable of exploring beyond its previous boundaries into exciting new territory. I also noticed that this discovery filled me with the same intense joy (perhaps even more intense) that I had experienced in the Snakepit.

As I fleshed out this new consciousness-based paradigm of science, I realized that developing an integrated approach to creativity, an approach that inspires and admits everyone to creative endeavor, was going to be of paramount importance for the new paradigm. Creativity is a phenomenon that is looked upon with suspicion by materialists, according to whom everything that happens now is causally related to the past and nothing truly new is possible. My personal experiences had already told me otherwise. Therefore, I welcomed the challenge to expose the limits of materialism and to transcend them.

Soon I met a colleague, Leonora Cohen, whose special research interest was creativity. Nora and I founded a creativity research group at the University of Oregon (where I work) and began having regular research meetings. Soon after, a behavioral psychologist, Shawn Boles, and an anthropologist, Richard Chaney, joined the group. The larger group dissipated over the next year or two, but Nora, Shawn, Richard, and I formed a bond that was strengthened when we signed a contract to write a joint book on creativity. Although the book was never completed (our differences in approach were too great to find common ground), I learned a tremendous amount from this collaboration about the existing theories and data regarding the phenomenon of creativity.

Shawn and I did agree about an important aspect of handling and classifying the diverse data on creativity. We both thought that creative work must be classified in two basic categories, one that is closer to problem solving (akin to technological invention) and another that is a discovery of deeper truth. Many of the differences of view in creativity research arise because the issues of only one of these two different classes of creativity are addressed.

Somewhere along the line I also recognized that spiritual growth is "inner" creativity as contrasted to creativity in the arts and the sciences which is "outer" creativity.

Meanwhile, Nora organized two research conferences on the theories of creativity. There I met many exponents of creativity research and witnessed the deep division that exists among them. However, developing a complete synthesis of the disparate ideas of creativity had to wait until the new consciousness-based paradigm was developed and the definitive book on it written and published. When that book (The Self-Aware Universe) went to the printshop, I was finally free to work on the integration of the various ways we think of creativity and how we approach it, both personally and socially. This book is the result of that work.

I began the book with the clear vision of the necessity for a proper classification of all the diverse phenomena that are uniformly labeled as creativity. As I wrote the book, I also saw the need to emphasize an integrated approach to all these different types of creativity. When we recognize consciousness as the central theme of the universe, it becomes clear that all creativity is subjective; in fact, creativity is our lifeline to consciousness. Then we begin to see that each of the different types of creativity has a role to play in embracing our full potential. And yes. We see clearly that creativity is not restricted to geniuses; all of us have the potential to be creative, and at any age.

Traditionally, the West has favored outer creativity over inner, and the East, inner over outer. Past societies have ignored invention as a way of achieving social change; present societies emphasize invention far too much because of their consumer orientation. But such polarization keeps us from achieving our full potential. These polarized ways to harvest creativity will not be sufficient to meet the tasks of the next millennium.

So the theme of the book, in the final reckoning, is the creative song, with all its different harmonies emphasized. When we sing this music of creativity, using whichever harmony is appropriate for the demands of a particular creative moment, then our individual simple verses become part of the all-inclusive cosmic multiverse--the united verse that we call the universe.

Besides the people already mentioned who played important roles in my research, I am grateful to Paul Ray, Howard Gruber, Kathy Juline, Robert Tompkins, Shawn Boles, Jean Burns, and Ligia Dantes for thoughtful readings of the manuscript. Thanks are also due to Ann Sterling, Michael Fox, and Anna St. Clair for helpful comments. Maggie's help with the editing was crucial and all but one of the poems at the end of the chapters are the products of our joint collaboration. The help of Don Ambrose, Joe Giove, and Nan Robertson with the figures is gratefully acknowledged. We also want to thank our friends for being there during the arduous process of writing: Geraldine and Ed Black, Mike Coan, Phil Gill, Stuart Over, Joanne Crandall, Henry and Hope Swift, Tera St. Johyn, Larry and Janie Brown, Hugh and Ruth Harrison, just to name a few. We thank you all.

PART ONE

AN INTEGRAL VIEW OF CREATIVITY

"Welcome to the annual creativity teaching fair," the young man at the gate says to you as he admits you. Inside, you see many buildings in a variety of sizes. Is each of them a school for teaching creativity? Why so many schools? You think to yourself, why not browse and see what you find? One can always learn more about creativity.

The first building that interests you looks like a church; inside sits a priestly person, serene in contemplation. When he opens his eyes, you ask him what he has to teach about creativity. He says, "I don't teach creativity. How can you teach something that is new, a creation *ex nihilo*? Creativity is like picking a flower from heaven, God's garden. Creativity is God's gift to a chosen few. It comes from divine inspiration."

You respect his sincerity, and he may have a point; but divine inspiration seems a little vague and outdated as a motif for creativity in this scientific age. You move on.

The second building you enter looks like a computer-game park. Lots of people are playing. Well, they may have the right idea, you think. Creativity is supposed to be play. Somebody explains in response to your inquiry, "Creativity is problem solving by combining old ideas to make something new and shiny. Computers can do it. By studying how computers creatively solve problems, you learn to solve problems better and thus find your creativity."

"But I am not a computer. I am not made of silicon," you protest.

1

"No matter. Haven't you heard of a Turing machine? A computer is a device that carries out a bunch of algorithms to achieve a final result. The specific hardware does not make any difference. Your hardware is organic, and you call it a brain. So what else is new? You are still a Turing machine. Have you ever written a poem?"

"I have, but not very good ones," you reluctantly admit. "In fact, that's part of the reason I am here to learn about creativity. Maybe I will produce better poems that will get deserved attention, at least from my significant other."

"Well, here is a poem written by a computer." The man hands you a poem written by *Arthur* ("That's automatic record tabulator but heuristically unreliable reasoner," the teacher explains). You recognize that some of the early lines originated in the minds of famous poets, but the last lines seem vague and therefore impressive:

There was a time when moorhens in the west
There was a time when daylight on the top
There was a time when God was not a question
There was a time when poets
Then I came (Boden, 1990, p. 1)

"I don't understand these last lines, so they must mean something subtle. Poetry is supposed to be ambiguous, so I suppose this qualifies. I never knew that computers could write poetry." Your interest is piqued.

"Not just poetry," the teacher enthusiastically responds. "Computers can draw like regular artists, solve scientific problems, prove theorems of geometry. If that's not creativity, what is?"

You are ready to try out one of the machines, but another thought stops you. "Creativity comes with anxiety and ecstasy. Even I know that. A few times when I have been creative there was a lot of anxiety which ended in a lot of ecstasy when the insight came. My subjective experiences were crucial to the shape of the final product. But even if a computer can write a poem, does it feel these emotions? Does it have subjective experiences that guide its work? And what about intuition?"

"There you go again. The old argument about emotions, feeling, intuition, and all that. Forget subjectivity! A scientific theory of creativity has got to be objective. Besides, have you been inside a computer to know that they don't feel or don't intuit?"

But that answer only aggravates you emotionally, and you decide not to take his training after all. He is too busy to mind, it seems.

At your next stop, you are surprised with the lack of fanfare. One man is sitting at a desk; if other people are around, they are not making themselves conspicuous. After hearing your experience with the computer scientist, the man says, "Well I have a very different view. I don't disagree that there is a mechanical, more objective, type of creativity, which I call secondary creativity. But creativity at its highest, primary creativity, is subjective. It involves our transpersonal self" (see Maslow, 1968).

You interrupt. "What is transpersonal self?"

"It is your self beyond ego," says the man.

"How do I find it?" You are curious.

"By joining the journey of self-actualization. How better can I explain it? Stay with me for awhile."

But you have no time, you explain. "Sorry, fella."

You next stop at a building that looks like a magician's parlor on the inside. Strange cards vaguely resembling the Tarot are displayed prominently.

"Can I help you?", a woman asks.

"Might as well. I was told that you have creativity to teach me," you respond with not a little curiosity.

"Creativity is mystery, it is magic. Who can teach it? But the magic may be within you. I can help you learn to explore it. In fact, if you are with me for awhile, I guarantee that you will learn the magic of creating thought vibrations in your head that can materialize anything—a poem, a piece of sculpture, or a song."

That sounds familiar to you. "Didn't Bishop Berkeley say something like that? The sound of a tree falling in the forest remains in potentia until an observer stumbles onto the scene and has the thought vibration, I hear the sound of a falling tree. Is creativity like that?"

In answer to your question, the woman is impatient. "It's nothing like that. Don't philosophize or escape into trendy clichés. There is no rational explanation of creativity. It's all mystery. You become part of the mystery and just do it."

Unfortunately, too much mystery always mystifies you, and so you escape. But not far. Soon a man stops you. "What are you looking for, my friend?", he asks.

"I am looking for creativity," you answer.

"It's a vain search, don't you understand?" the man responds. "You are already creative. All your acts are creative. Everything in the world is an act of creativity."

"Maybe so. But thinking in this way is not very useful. It does not make me happy. Some acts make me really happy, joyful. Those are the ones I like to call creative. And I'd like to learn the trick of how to do such acts all the time."

"You are suffering from a great delusion. You are discriminating between illusory acts of the world: this is good, this is bad; this is creative, this is not. When you don't discriminate, you find perpetual happiness."

Maybe so, but such undiscriminating perpetual happiness does not interest you. You move away and enter the nearest building. Soon a woman stops you and smiles. "What are you escaping from?", she asks. You tell her about your last encounter.

"There is truth in what that man claims, you know. Creativity is illusory; it has to be," says the woman.

"Why?", you challenge defiantly.

"Why? Because of Newton's laws, that's why. Everything is determined by the physical laws that Newton discovered. We don't deny that there is an appearance of creativity in the world, but that's because some physical systems are unpredictable. They respond to little triggers that are impossible to keep track of. We call them chaotic systems."

"Are you saying that my creative thoughts, my anxiety, and my ecstasy are all appearances because there is a chaotic system in my brain that responds to little nuances in seemingly unpredictable ways? And that, in truth, all my behavior is quite determined?"

"Yes," the woman says simply and firmly.

You feel a little demoralized. If creativity is only appearance, why bother to investigate it any further? Voilá! The answer appears on a building with a big banner: Chemistry for Better Creativity. You've got to check that out.

"We give you a little pill, the creativity pill; it's the one sanguine contribution of science to creativity research," proclaims the person in the building.

But you object. "I can't believe that the purpose of scientific research on creativity is to create a pill that gives us instant creativity. Everybody knows that there has to be some agony before creative ecstasy."

"Bull. Outdated. Things don't have to be painful in order to be joyful. You can have it all, and you deserve it. Say to yourself, I am worth it, and take this pill. You will see."

"I don't like the idea of taking a pill," you manage to say, overcoming a moment of temptation.

"You are nothing but the dance of atoms, my friend. Why not add a few atoms to make the dance more exotic, which is what you call creativity," the man insists.

But you stubbornly refuse the pill. As you move on, a sign attracts your attention—Find Out If You Are Creative: Take Our Test. What is this all about?

The people attending the booth are all eager to give you the test. "Of all the tests that have been devised for diagnosing creativity, ours is the best," they boast.

"I don't know," you hesitate. "I don't think of creativity as a disease that can be diagnosed."

"It's not like that. What is true is that either you have the right traits for creativity, or you don't. If you have the right traits, you can be creative. If not, tough luck. So take the test. It will save you a lot of agony."

"And also keep me from a lot of ecstasy if the test isn't valid. No, thank you." In truth, you are a little scared of taking the test. Maybe later, when nobody is watching, you will surreptitiously pick up one of their tests and take it in private.

At the next building, a woman sympathizes with you. "You poor soul. Having to listen to all those mechanists and mystics! The mechanists say, in one form or another, that creativity does not exist because we are all mechanical, determined machines. The mystics either mystify creativity or treat creativity and everything else in the world as illusory preoccupations resulting from our ignorance. Fortunately, there is a better way."

Now you are all ears. Maybe you have found your destination, the end of your quest, the oasis in the desert.

The woman further explains. "The answer is holism. Obviously, the mystics have a grain of truth when they say creativity is mystery. It is impossible to dissect creativity into computer programs that show you how. On the other hand, to say that the mystery is beyond our material prediction and control is equally untrue. Creativity is a holistic phenomenon."

"What does that mean?", you ask, puzzling over her words.

"We are looking for an organizing principle that is responsible for all creative behavior in nature, including ours. As you can see, this building is empty except for some preliminary position papers; we don't teach yet. When we find our organizing principle, we will begin teaching in a big way," she promises with a big smile.

It is easy to talk about organizing principles, but finding them is another matter, you complain to yourself. You voice your concern. "I do not understand organizing principle. You guys are so vague! Only the computer people and maybe the chaos theorists seem to have something concrete to say to me. All the rest of you are all sound and no substance."

The woman looks you straight in the eye and recites:

They say you are a classical machine,
your self is a mirage;
you have no freedom, no purpose in being,
no transcendence.
Your creativity is behavioral—
simple Pavlovian conditioning.
Do you lack special brain circuits?
Without them you are hopeless.
You don't buy that? Then creativity must be chance
or maybe chaos. You are a creative chaos machine.
Now, does that sound better?

All of a sudden she connects with you, and you smile sheepishly. "I get your gist. I am not saying I believe that I am a computing machine or a chaos machine. But still it would be nice if you had something concrete to offer," you murmur apologetically.

"Patience," says the woman in benediction.

Suddenly in front of you are two Teutonic gentlemen. You must have been lost in thought and inadvertently walked into another building. Oh, why not?

"So what's your idea of creativity?", you ask the two gentlemen.

"Creativity is the outpouring of the unconscious. Da Vinci represses the memory of his mother and her smile. Out comes Mona Lisa with her famous smile from Da Vinci's brush," says one of the men.

"It's not like that at all," the other fellow objects. "Creativity is the gift of the collective unconscious that transcends our personal unconscious of repressed memories."[1]

"But what is unconscious? How do we know we have an unconscious?", you ask, not a little scornfully.

"It's difficult to explain in a marketplace. Maybe your psychiatrist will explain it to you."

"And charge me a bundle! No, thank you," you mutter as you walk away.

I stop you at the exit. "You seem disappointed," I comment.

"How can I help it?", you ask. "Most of the people in there who touched my heart seemed so vague about what creativity is—God's

---

[1] The reader may notice similarities between the views of these men and those of Sigmund Freud and Carl Jung on creativity.

gift, organizing principle, unconscious. I am not sure if anybody knows what those things mean. Some people insisted that creativity is only for people with certain traits. Okay, I will admit I was scared to take their test, but I don't think that my creativity depends on how I fill out a questionnaire! Only the computer guys seem to have anything concrete on creativity. They showed me things that are seductive to my brain, but to believe that computer art is creative and, by implication, that we are computers is a bit too much! What about our subjective experiences? If they mean nothing, how can anything anybody says help me be creative? Nobody seemed to have any integral vision of creativity. One guy said that we are nothing but the dance of atoms."

"One who wants to dance with the wolves is not a mere dance of atoms," I say. "Your intuition is right. We don't have to succumb to computerism just because computer scientists are the only ones so far to have developed concrete models of creativity. The creativity they talk about is only a pale version of the real McCoy. They have been using too narrow a lens to see the splendor of creativity. You have to look through a wider scope, a new worldview that quantum physics is giving us, to find integral creativity."

"How do you know?" You are trying to sound hopeful.

"Read my book and find out," I reply.

1

THIƧ IƧ THE MOUNT THE CREATIVE RIDEƧ: THE QUANTUM, THE QUANTUM, THE QUANTUM

The world responds to our questions. Sometimes the response is creative, other times not. But progress always begins with questions.

What questions do we ask about creativity—the act of discovery or the invention of something new? Many of us experience ourselves as having some creativity. Some of us feel creative when we work at an easel, painting a picture. Some of us are creative at the piano or on the dance floor. Some of us write poems in the early dawn. Some of us feel creative when we understand a theorem of mathematics after days of study. But few of us are a Michelangelo, Mozart, Martha Graham, Rabindranath Tagore, or an Einstein. Accordingly, our foremost questions are likely to be about our own creativity. How can we be more creative? Is the scope of our creativity necessarily limited, or can we reach all the way to the stars?

But our interest is not only self-centered. The creativity of our society also concerns us. Can we devise an educational system that will help our children grow up to be more creative, productive adults?

Further back in our minds loom questions about the relation of our creativity with our own self-development. We remember being creative as children. We ponder how most of us come to lose the sense of wonder that enchants our childhood experiences, settling into an adulthood dominated by mundane routine in a stale world. At those times

9

we may ask, Is adult creativity reserved for a chosen few, the so-called geniuses like Einstein and Michelangelo? Are geniuses inherently different, or is it possible that with the proper developmental opportunities any of us could have been a genius—or maybe still can be? The physicist Erwin Schroedinger did his most important creative work (the discovery of quantum mechanics) when he was 40. He also wrote a definitive book on biology when he was 55, a book that inspired an entire generation of scientists. Can any of us sail the creative seas at any age?

Why does the creative process involve so much agony (imagine Michelangelo agonizing over how to paint the ceiling of the Sistine Chapel) and anxiety (for which Woody Allen's neurotic image is an archetype)? Yet, who can doubt that there is ecstacy in the creative process in those moments of great creative insight (the image of Archimedes dashing naked into the streets of ancient Syracuse and shouting Eureka! comes to mind) and that there is great satisfaction in finishing a creative product?

The truth is, we become most alive when we are creative. Our creative moments are the greatest moments of our lives. We cherish creativity so much that we become alive even when we participate in or witness other people's creative acts. But even knowing that creativity is our greatest joy, we squander much of our life in endless repetition of learned tasks and their variations. Why don't we spend all our waking hours in the pursuit of creative acts? Can we? How can we and others live our lives with creativity as the center?

Why do people judge a particular act to be creative but not another one? Is the value of a creative act relative to what people think? During Van Gogh's lifetime, there was hardly any recognition of his art. Does this mean that he was not creative then but became creative (posthumously) only when people recognized the value of his art?[1] If that sounds ridiculous, then how do we assign an absolute value to a creative act?

Is creativity all a matter of clever and intelligent reasoning? Or, are those oft-repeated claims of the primacy of spontaneous intuition and insight true? If so, where do these intuitive and insightful ideas come from? What purpose does creativity serve?

Do these questions have answers? Yes, but currently there are many disparate answers and no consensus agreement. The purpose of this book is to show that recent progress in science is giving us satisfying answers that are integrative and personally helpful and should eventually lead to a consensus.

---

[1]The answer is an implicit yes in some social theories of creativity; see Weisberg (1993, pp. 84-88).

Here, in brief, is the central theme of this book. Our creative ideas are the results of the play of consciousness, which is the only real play. However, the shadows (memories) of these creative ideas in our minds give rise to conditioning—a tendency to repeat. Conditioning sets up a seductive shadow play, making the world appear to be a play of opposition: creativity and conditioning, good and evil, consciousness and matter, and so forth. If we can penetrate this oppositional camouflage, even to some extent, the questions of creativity find satisfying personal answers that lead to useful and effective strategies for becoming ever more creative.

The good news is that such an idea is no longer mere philosophy but can be and, in this book, is substantiated by science, with the help of a revolutionary development in physics called quantum physics.[2] Quantum physics is the physics of the twentieth century that has replaced Newton's "classical" physics. The word *quantum* means a discrete quantity; a quantum of energy is a discrete, indivisible bundle of energy. But quantum physics involves much more than discrete energy bundles.

Classical physics is *algorithmic* (an algorithm is a logical step-by-step procedure based on continuity). In classical physics, a knowledge of the "initial conditions" of an object (its position and velocity at some initial time) and of the forces acting on it enables us to calculate all its future (and past) movements by a continuous application of the algorithms that Newton's laws provide. This has given rise to the philosophy of determinism: All motion of all objects is forever determined, given the initial conditions. The future is determined by the past. There is room for only limited creativity in this philosophy—creativity based on a rehash of the past.

But quantum physics has ushered discontinuity and indeterminacy into the arena of physics. From the get-go, quantum physics involves discontinuous quantum leaps for which no algorithm can be given. When an electron jumps from one atomic orbit to another, its motion is discontinous; it never goes through the intervening space (Figure 1.1). Can you imagine jumping from a high curb to the street without passing through the space between? Yet this is what electrons do. And if there are several orbits available, we cannot predict which orbit the electron will jump to. Neither can we tell when it is going to leap. With no complete algorithm—no complete determinism—in the quantum world, a window of opportunity is opened for true creativity, for what is truly new.

---

[2]For popular expositions of quantum physics, read Wolf (1981), Herbert (1986), and Goswami (1993a).

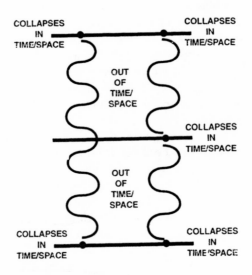

Figure 1.1. The atomic orbits can be thought of as the rungs of a quantum ladder. The electron pops out of an upper orbit and pops into a lower one discontinuously.

Physicists, dealing with many electrons at a time, make do with statistical algorithms to make quantitative predictions in quantum physics, but the subtlety of the situation remains. The truth is, quantum physics regards matter as wavelike. The weirdness of the electron—its quantum-leaping ability—comes from its wave character. Waves spread out and are at many places at the same time, as is revealed when we speak, creating sound waves; the sound can reach several people at the same time. Sound waves also go around obstacles, as when we speak from behind a corner and our friends still hear us, a property called *diffraction*. Similarly, when we send a beam of electrons through a crystal (which is a three-dimensional grid of atoms), the electrons do not appear in a single blob (as when you pour sugar through a sieve) but instead make a diffraction pattern—a distribution of light and dark spots—on a photographic film, confirming their wavy secret (Figure 1.2).

And the behavior of a single electron wave is even more enigmatic. When a single electron appears on the photographic film as shown in Figure 1.2, it is found to appear always at some single spot

Figure 1.2. Electrons make a diffraction pattern when passed through a crystal, a pattern that shows the wave nature of electrons.

(though not necessarily where it might be expected), not spread all over; it is only the totality of all the electrons that makes the diffraction pattern. You may think, perhaps the wave is a property of the entire beam, not of the single electron. To test this possibility, a physicist in the early days of quantum physics set up a diffraction arrangement with a very weak source of electrons, so weak that on the average only one electron passed through the crystal at any given time. Then he left for a trip. If the wave property of the electron was a property of the entire beam, the diffraction pattern would have given way in favor of a single continuous blob. But when the physicist returned after a few days, he found a diffraction pattern. Each electron goes around the atomic obstacles of the crystal to classically forbidden places, very wavelike, but always appears on the film at one spot, very particle-like. The location of the spot randomly varies from electron to electron, cumulatively forming the diffraction pattern when enough electrons have collected on the film.

The interpretation of this experiment is crucial for founding a new worldview that centers on creativity. We have to realize that, before measurement, an electron exists in a realm of possibility, the possibility of appearing at many places. Our looking (the measurement) collapses its wave of possibility into one actual event at one particular place on the photographic film.

Our looking affects the electrons. In an anecdote cited by Sarah Whitfield, the impressionist artist Rene Magritte once went into a store to buy some Dutch cheese. As the storekeeper started to get some for him from the display window, Magritte insisted that he would rather have a piece cut from another cheese ball in an inside case. "But they are the same cheese," exclaimed the storekeeper. "No, madam," said Magritte. "The one in the window has been looked at all day by people passing by." Quantum reality seems to agree with Magritte; looking changes things.

What does all this have to do with creativity? Electrons and all submicroscopic objects, and by implication all material objects built of them, are waves of possibility; the algorithmic mathematics of quantum mechanics determines the probability for each of these possibilities to manifest. And consciousness, in the process of observation, chooses which possibility is going to manifest in a particular event; this choice is discontinuous, nonalgorithmic (Von Neumann, 1955). This choice can be creative; consciousness can use this choice to manifest its purposive, creative play.

Yet the macroworld is overwhelmingly Newtonian and deterministic. This is explained by the correspondence principle: For large masses, quantum behavior often approximates classical behavior. The possibility structure is quite limited for most macro objects—we find the cosmos out there and the cabbages and the cobwebs down here exactly where we expect them—and this gives them the appearance of classical algorithmic continuity and deterministic behavior. And it is a good thing, too. We use the macro as a measuring-aid apparatus to amplify the microquantum possibilities (similar to how we use a hearing-aid apparatus) and to record the actualities of our choice. Only because these records have classical fixity can we share them with others and reach consensus.

Back to consciousness and creativity. The point is this: Consciousness uses matter and mind to perform its play. This should not be surprising: just think of yourself at your word processor. Ordinarily, this play is classical; it better be, we need the deterministic orderliness of things mundane to appreciate what is truly creative. However, when matter and mind engage with consciousness in their quantum aspects, then creativity is possible. In their quantum aspects, the brain and the mind consist of possibilities from which consciousness can create the forever new. When the quantum aspects of the brain and the mind are suppressed, conditioned behavior prevails.

Admittedly, this is a controversial view of quantum mechanics because it invites consciousness into the arena of supposedly objective science (Goswami, 1989, 1990, 1993a; see also Blood, 1993; Herbert, 1993; and Stapp, 1993). Although many physicists think that the problem of interpretation of quantum physics is still open and that an objective interpretation will be found someday, it is a fact that the search for an objective interpretation has remained fruitless for more than seven decades.[3]

The situation reminds me of a story. A woman goes to a fabric store and orders 50 yards of material for her wedding dress. When the shopkeeper expresses surprise, she says, "My fiancé is a quantum physicist who would rather search than find." The fact is that a complete paradox-free interpretation of quantum physics is available, albeit based on consciousness. It is time to give up the unproductive search and seriously consider a consciousness interpretation.[4]

In objective science, a phenomenon like creativity with clear subjective underpinnings goes largely untreated in its fullness; the subjective aspects of creativity are dismissed and become fraught with controversy because consciousness itself is looked on as an epi- (secondary) phenomenon of the brain with no causal power. In the following chapter, a fantasy debate is designed as a guided tour through various controversial ideas on the nature of creativity. In subsequent chapters, I show how all the controversy can be resolved, how all the disparate ideas on creativity can be integrated within the new view.

CREATIVITY AND THE PREPARATION FOR THE NEXT CENTURY

We live in an age in which the forces of separateness, objectivity, and a materialist, determined-machine mentality still dominate our thinking. Is our creativity simply an apparent epiphenomenon of the dance of the atoms in the brain, or is creativity the derring-do of a consciousness with freedom of choice? Fortunately, the power of the quantum world-

---

[3]For a review, see Goswami (1993a, Chap. 6).
[4]A consensus that consciousness is essential to interpret and understand quantum mechanics is gradually coming into vouge, according to the physicist Henry Stapp (1993).

view is emerging. In this situation it is imperative to understand creativity, one phenomenon that the determined-machine view can never fully explain. Yet in creativity lies our primal joy; in creativity we find our utmost satisfaction.

Unfortunately, modern industrial/technological societies, and our high-tech one is no exception, breed mediocrity and consumerism. The following dialogue, taken from Bernard Shaw's play, *Heartbreak House*, could very well take place between modern yuppies:

Ellie: A soul is a very expensive thing to keep: much more so than a motor car.
Shotover: Is it? How much does your soul eat?
Ellie: Oh, a lot. It eats music and pictures and books and mountains and lakes and beautiful things to wear and nice people to be with. In this country you can't have them without lots of money: that is why our souls are so horribly starved.

What starves our souls far more than lack of money is the lack of creativity. And when soul starvation occurs on a massive scale, truly creative people and their avant garde acts come to be regarded as dangerous to the society as a whole. The creative ones then become "outsiders;" when this happens, as the author Colin Wilson (1957) has noted so powerfully, it generally signifies the decay of that particular culture. On the other hand, when creativity thrives and creative people are not looked on as strangers in a strange land, when creativity is at the pinnacle of social respect, societies pulsate with vitality. How shall we regard ourselves at the threshold of the 21st century? The creativity researcher John Gowan (1977) has expressed my sentiments with these eloquent words:

Heretofore we have harvested creativity wild. We have used as creative only those persons who stubbornly remained so despite all efforts of the family, religion, education, and politics to grind it out of them. In the prosecution of this campaign, men and women have been punished, flogged, silenced, imprisoned, tortured, ostracized, and killed. . . . If we learn to domesticate creativity—that is, to enhance rather than deny it in our culture—we can increase the number of creative persons in our midst by about fourfold. That would put the number and percent of such individuals over the "critical mass" point. When this level is reached in a culture, as it was in Periclean Athens . . . and our own Federalist period, there is an escalation of creativity resulting and civilization makes a great leap forward. We can have a golden age of this type such as the world has never seen, and I am convinced that it will occur early in the twenty-first century. But we must make preparations now. (p. xx)

In this book, apart from definitions, classifications, theories, and mechanisms, we are going to talk about these preparations for the new century and about how to build a creative society. My vision is that the manifestations of the theory of quantum creativity developed in this book, both individually and societally, will be a major ingredient of these preparations.

The genie of our creativity is bottled up for most of us—to liberate the genie is to become a genius. It is a certainty that understanding what creativity means, what role creativity plays in our self-development, and how our creative process works will assist many to scale the barriers between us and our natural creativity and its joy. Can your creativity express itself as potently as Einstein's? It's up to you; there is no need to limit your potential by thinking of yourself as a classical computer.

This book puts creativity at the center of human existence with the hope that it will inspire unlimited and unmitigated creativity at the center of your life. I summarize the essence of this chapter in the form of a poem:

Questions about creativity?
Your questions are firefly glimpses
of the soul calling you.

Do you hear the lapping of possibility waves
on the shore of your mind?
Then look through the quantum window.
Face to face with your self,
the quantum leap will take you by surprise.

2

CREATIVITY, WORLDVIEWS, AND INTEGRATION

I begin with a question. Why depend on theories and worldviews? Can we not determine all we want to know about creativity from empirical data on creative acts and the people who perform these acts? Or perhaps we should heed the architect who used to say, "Architectural design is like sausage making; it is best not to ask too many questions about what goes into it."

Alas, it is not that simple. Einstein once reminded Werner Heisenberg (one of the co-discoverers of quantum mechanics) that we cannot do physics without theory. The questions we choose for empirical study are always implicitly guided by the theories and worldviews we hold. Thus we are better off acknowledging the role of theory explicitly. So it is with creativity—we cannot understand creativity without theory. For too long in the field of creativity, we have been doing empirical research without the guidance of any consistent and powerful theory. We need theory to guide the empirical research and—vice versa—the theories we develop must be consistent with the data.

So I return to the question of theory building and the disparate worldviews that theories apply to the questions of creativity. What are these worldviews?

THE MATERIAL REALIST WORLDVIEW AND THE MECHANISTIC CLASS OF CREATIVITY THEORIES

The dominant worldview today is based on the metaphysics of material realism (also called physical or scientific realism), which has shaped modern science and Western culture for the last 300 years:

- What is real consists of matter and its correlates, energy, and fields of interaction. The fields of interaction are local, propagating through space and keeping within the speed-of-light limit that Einstein established. Everything that is not clearly material (such as subjective experience) is a secondary phenomenon (epiphenomenon) with no causal power and is reducible to matter and its interactions.
- The behavior of objects is independent of subjects (us) and is determined, machine-like, and subject to prediction and control, by means of the laws of classical physics that Isaac Newton laid out in the 17th century.
- The mind is a Newtonian machine, an epiphenomenon of the brain, that is completely determined by antecedent local causes, and its dynamics are algorithmic. Causal continuity is assumed in human behavior, limiting what creativity can represent. For example, creativity cannot be anything *really* new because all current things are determined by things that already were.

Nevertheless, some theorists find it intriguing, even challenging, to attempt to develop theories of creativity under the constraint of the worldview of material realism. They assert that in spite of determinism, there may occasionally be a surprise emergent element in complex systems such as us, and it is this unpredictable (or not easily predictable) element that we call *creativity*—an appearance of newness that is important to the human condition. These theorists thus investigate creativity by examining possible emergent and surprise elements of our genetic endowment and environmental conditioning and by employing brain-as-computer models of our thought processes.

Objectivity reigns supreme in the search for the mechanism of creativity. Consciousness is regarded as an epiphenomenon of matter without causal power, and talking about consciousness (or the unconscious) is avoided in the discussion of creativity. All subjective elements of creativity are assumed to be appearances. Such appearances may be due to (a) hidden algorithms in the brain-mind's computer, (b) chance, or (c) the play of chaos dynamics—a dynamics of systems that are supersensitive to changes in initial conditions.

As a result, for better or worse, of this insistence on objectivity, the theories we get from mechanists are concrete, well-defined, and subject to prediction and control. And we get tangible results from these theoretical efforts—computer programs that can write a poem or draw a piece of art. The creativity researcher Pat Langley, for example, has written a program that can even discover a scientific law (Langley, Simon, Bradshaw, & Zytkow, 1987)! Controversial to be sure, but impressive, isn't it? Unfortunately, the mechanistic theories present a constricted view of creativity in which there is no causal role for consciousness or subjectivity. The computer models leave out important developmental questions. All mechanistic models deny questions of creativity that relate to transcendence, purposiveness, or a causally efficacious consciousness.

THE ORGANISMIC WORLDVIEW AND THE ORGANISMIC CLASS OF CREATIVITY THEORIES

Another worldview employed in creativity theorizing is called *organismic:*

- The consideration of the whole organism is important for studying human phenomena, in general, and creativity in particular.[1] Instead of breaking up the system into components and reducing creativity to a mere cacophony of mechanisms, organicists emphasize the importance of the symphony of the whole organism—this idea of holism is a fundamental ingredient of the organismic worldview.
- Human phenomena like creativity (and the phenomena connected with organisms, in general) must involve more than mechanistic, causal explanations; they must involve purpose. In addition to the push of antecedent cause, creativity needs the pull of purpose; thus creativity is seen in terms of what is called *teleology*—final cause.
- We must shift the emphasis from structure or being to becoming. Not becoming in the sense of the continuous modification of behavior, in which becoming ends with conditioning, but becoming as a discontinuous, creative unfolding of purposiveness of the universe and of the individual.

---

[1]For a comparison of materialist and organismic theories of creativity, see Overton (1976); see also Cohen (in press).

Organismic theories address some of our concerns regarding the connection of creativity with the development of the self. For example, the creativity researcher John Briggs (1990) theorized that adult creatives are those who learn early to see nuances, the subtle relationships behind the working of the universe. This is what the child Einstein did, according to this thinking, which led to all the wonderful creative discoveries of adult Einstein. Once when as a child Einstein was ill in bed, his father brought him a compass. Seeing the needle respond to the earth's magnetic field gave Einstein the hint that the universe may similarly be reaching out to him.

Yet organismic theorists are reluctant to bring consciousness in all its facets (e.g., a causally potent self) into the discussion of creativity. A material basis of reality is often implied, and this injects inconsistency in the philosophy. For example, because matter is assumed to be deterministic, driven by antecedent causes, what is the basis for teleology—an additional drive of final causes?

THE MONISTIC IDEALIST METAPHYSICS AND THE IDEALIST CLASS OF CREATIVITY THEORIES

The third worldview that contributes to the theories of creativity is the monistic idealist worldview, variously known as the *perennial philosophy, Platonism,* and *Vedanta* (in India):

- Consciousness is the ground of all being, including matter and mind.
- Within one undivided consciousness, there is an apparent division: a transcendent world of possibilities (potentia) from which arises the immanent world of manifestation. In Christian symbology, the transcendent realm is called *heaven, earth* is the immanent realm, and they both arise from the *Godhead* (consciousness).
- Creativity is fundamentally a phenomenon of consciousness (the self) discontinuously manifesting *really* new (previously unmanifested) possibilities from the transcendent domain, and it cannot be explained by the mechanics of matter alone. Sometimes creativity is referred to as a marriage between heaven and earth, a marriage that takes place in the arena of our subjectivity.

Thus in the idealist[2] worldview, the universe is creative because consciousness is creative. There is transcendence in creativity because consciousness is transcendent. The evolution of the universe that we see, from matter through life to self-consciousness, is regarded as the manifestation of the creative purpose of consciousness.

Within this worldview, one can speak of the importance of the unconscious for creativity, as Freud (1961, 1963) and Jung (1971a) did. The unconscious is potentia, it is the unmanifest that nevertheless affects the manifest. One can also speak of creativity as a search for self-actualization—the urge to know the true nature of our consciousness. This was Abraham Maslow's (1968) great contribution to the psychology of creativity. Thus, the idealists fully address much about what we want to know about the subjective aspects of creativity.

Unfortunately, many ideas are left vague, for example, transcendence. In the idealist literature, at best we find paradoxical statements about what transcendence is including statements such as:

> The kingdom of God is within you
> It is also without you. (Guillaumont et al., 1959, p. 3)

> It [consciousness] is within all this
> It is outside all this. (Nikhilandanda, 1964)

Understandably, such statements are not completely satisfactory to the modern, linear, rational, scientific mind. The idealist theories are also short on concreteness and verifiability.

WHITHER INTEGRATION?

Clearly, all three groups have something relevant to say about creativity. The realists are concrete, which is helpful in dealing with the more mechanical aspects of creativity; in addition, realist theories are verifiable. Organismic theorists introduce the important issues of purpose and the development of the self into the equation. And idealists introduce consciousness, which obviously must play a role in subjective aspects of creativity. But in the absence of any integrative worldview, the three kinds of theorists are locked in incessant debate with no synthesis on the horizon.

---

[2]In this book, idealist always refers to monistic idealist. This caution is needed because some philosophers, notably Bishop Berkeley, have developed idealism as a dualist philosophy that distinguishes between God's consciousness and human consciousness. There is no such distinction in monistic idealism, we are that.

It is as if there were three Einsteins. The material realist Einstein is creative because he possesses a great computer power of reasoning, maybe even hidden algorithms; this is the Einstein of imagination who feverishly scribbles mathematical equations on a blackboard. The idealist Einstein plays the violin under the inspiration and guidance of unconscious potentia. And the organismic Einstein, forever young, watches the other two and infuses them with creative purposiveness. How do we integrate the three pictures into one?

I have attended conferences at which the objective was for prominent theorists and researchers on creativity to meet and reach some consensus about how to instill creativity in education. But we were unable to reach such a consensus, primarily because the researchers did not share the same worldview. How we look at creativity depends crucially on our worldview, and it is difficult, if not impossible, to mitigate the differences without the aid of an integrative worldview. We could not even formulate a consensus definition of creativity at these conferences.

THE POINTS OF CONTROVERSY: AN IMAGINED DEBATE

To get a focus on the points of controversy, imagine a debate among the three classes of creativity theorists—a materialist, an organicist, and an idealist.

A material realist begins the debate. He says, "The body is a machine, the mind is a machine, the soul is a machine.[3] All of the human condition is only machine. Our free will is an illusion. Machines are causally determined objects; also their motions and changes are continuous. Discontinuous leaps of creativity are sheer whimsy!"

The idealist is not dismayed by this dogma. He merely smiles. "And I suppose you don't see any contradiction in how we can be creative—which needs freedom—and also be determined machines. How can we say we create anything new unless we are able to discontinuously, without cause, shift beyond the known? How can we jump creatively to the new if we are not free from the known? Haven't you seen the movie *Amadeus*? Mozart did not write his music bit by bit; he could see the whole thing all at once. He was able to take a discontinuous leap."

The organicist tries to mediate. "Perhaps we can find a middle ground. Obviously, human phenomena such as creativity must involve more than mechanistic, determined being. Let's not get caught in horizon-

---

[3]This is a direct quote from Jacques Monod (1972).

tal, strictly one-dimensional thinking. Human phenomena, nay, all phe- nomena related to living organisms, must involve a vertical dimension of becoming. Besides causal mechanisms, there must also be purpose."

The materialist is reluctant to give an inch. "But purpose, a final cause, is just initial cause in time reverse, don't you see?", he says sternly to the organicist. He then shifts his eyes to the idealist and says in a bantering tone, "And I wouldn't put too much credence in those reports of discontinuous shifts you are talking about, or haven't you heard? There was supposedly a letter that Mozart wrote in which he said things like, 'Whence or how they [his music] come I know not,' and 'Nor do I hear in my imagination the parts successively, but I hear them, as it were, all at once.' Idealists like you offer this as proof of disconti- nuity. But research has shown that this letter is almost certainly false. What do you say to that?"

The idealist responds evenly, "So Mozart's letter might not have been written by Mozart, so what? The past always takes on a mytholog- ical character. The question is not, did Mozart write that letter? Instead, the more relevant question is, why do these myths of discontinuous leaps persist? To find out, why don't you look at your own experience? Don't creative ideas always spring up suddenly when you least expect them, when you are not contemplating them? And if an idea is truly cre- ative, truly new, you cannot say that you found the idea in the space- time reality amid the objects of your experience or via reason and algo- rithms. We all use the word 'discovery' for such creative ideas, which means that intuitively we know that they are there, somewhere, not in the space-time reality, but transcending it."

The materialist looks a little subdued. "I still insist that creativi- ty is not what you organismic and idealist people think. I admit that occasionally there may be an appearance of discontinuity. But that's because the algorithms of the relevant programs of the brain-mind are hidden from what appears as our subjective experience. And I don't believe there is any creative act that is truly a discovery; instead, all are inventions of the programs of the brain-mind. What you propose is not scientific—those vain ideas of purpose and transcendence. If creativity involved those things, it would be impossible, unpredictable, uncontrol- lable. We know that creativity—the ability to find novel solutions to problems—does exist; surely, then, it must have a scientific explanation and be subject to prediction and control. It cannot be discontinuous or transcendental. Okay?"

The organicist smiles, "Look who is being circular. But, of course! Undeniably, there are some creative acts that can be reduced to simple mechanisms for which a mechanistic theory is useful, and this type of creativity is subject to prediction and control. We maintain that the most exalted creative act must be holistic . . ."

She does not get to finish her sentence. "You holists!", interrupts the mechanist. Then he starts chanting. "The whole is not greater than the parts. The whole is not greater than the parts. The whole is not . . ."

The man from the idealist camp tries to play peacemaker. "Folks, folks. It is true that holism has never been shown to be correct or useful, but don't throw the baby out with the bathwater. The holists are making a very good point by injecting concepts such as purpose in the study of creativity. You know why? Because a creative act requires consciousness. Purpose is a phenomenon of consciousness. Purpose is not teleology, to which my mechanist friend justly objects. The organizing principle behind creativity is a purposive, transcendent consciousness."

But now pandemonium breaks loose, and suddenly the organicist and the materialist join forces against the idealist. "We don't believe in transcendence," they shout in unison.

After order is restored, the organicist continues. "Consciousness, yes. Consciousness as organizing principle, maybe. But transcendence, no. There is no need to be mystical and go back to the dark ages. You idealists remind me of the Freudian who saw a sexual motif everywhere; similarly, you drag in transcendence everywhere. Why can't you see that consciousness must be an emergent phenomenon of the brain?"

"Because that doesn't work," the idealist maintains. "As the Sufis say, 'You cannot get yogurt out of water.' Consciousness cannot be an emergent phenomenon of matter and still be causally potent. Also, how are you going to get a subjective experience beginning with ingredients that are objective by definition?"

The mechanist is impatient. "The idea of a causally potent consciousness, emergent or otherwise, is meaningless anyway. Only matter and its laws are causally potent. Didn't somebody say, 'A physicist is an atom's way of knowing about atoms.' But I want to go back to the claim that creativity is the gift of the transcendent realm. Coleridge made a big point of going to heaven in a dream and finding his poem *Kubla Khan*. But subsequent research has shown that Coleridge exaggerated. Maybe he developed the idea gradually, taking help from here and there, putting together bits and pieces."

"Write a poem putting together bits and pieces, and see if you like it, your own creation or your computer's," challenges the idealist. "It's not that simple! Poets need inspiration. And they do go to the transcendent realm of consciousness even though the process is unconscious. 'Heaven' is our collective unconscious, and there is good evidence for it.

And as for the quip about physicists being epiphenomena of atoms, I think it is the other way around. A physicist is consciousness's way of knowing about consciousness, which includes atoms."

"Consciousness, unconscious, discontinuity, transcendence, purpose. What a needless proliferation of ideas to explain a behavior which we will soon find our computers emulating," muses the mechanist.

"Promissory materialism," declare the organicist and the idealist in unison.

"I don't understand why you hold on to the material realist worldview that rejects discontinuity, transcendence, and consciousness," continues the idealist. "Our own experiences speak for the truth of these aspects of creativity."

The organicist interjects to the materialist, "By relying too much on the computer, you are leaving out development. A major issue of creativity is, why isn't creativity, which is practically universal among children, not so among adults? You can't answer such questions with computer modeling. Computers have once-and-for-all fixed representations. But both the world and the organism change. You have to deal with the nature of self-development of individuals."

"But you have no mechanism, no concrete theory, to deal with the organism or self-development," the material realist objects. "Your theories are vague and wishy-washy. Can you give a demonstration of the whole being greater than the parts? And vagueness applies to your theories, too, my idealist friend. Show me how a causally potent consciousness intervenes in the affairs of the material world and I will show you dualism—that you assume separate worlds of matter and consciousness. And then I will ask you: what mediates the interaction of these worlds?"

Both the organicist and the idealist look dumb-founded with this latest attack.

Is there any way to make sense of all these disparate ways of thinking about creativity? There is. As mentioned in Chapter 1, quantum physics has created a window of opportunity for escaping the theoretical impasse with an interpretive and integrative framework built on two foundations—quantum physics and the monistic idealist philosophy of the primacy of consciousness. Such a paradigm resolves the age-old idealist quandary as to how consciousness can intervene in the affairs of matter while neatly avoiding dualism (Goswami, 1993a). This is further elaborated in the next section.

PHYSICS AND YOUR WORLDVIEW

The success of Newtonian classical physics during the last three centuries in explaining natural phenomena and in providing us with wide-ranging technology has entrenched our worldview in material realism. According to Newton's second law of motion, if we know a material object's initial position and velocity (the so-called initial conditions), then an *assumption* of continuity (that motion is continuous in space and time) and a knowledge of the forces acting on the object enable us to calculate all the future (as well as the past) movements of the object. Thus, if the world consists of material objects alone, then the initial conditions of the objects of the world determine its future: All is causally determined from the past. In this way an underlying assumption of materialism (that all things are made of matter) and Newton's laws guarantees determinism (the future is fully determined by the past), and together they guarantee objectivity (the motions of objects are independent of us, the observers). Supplement this with the principle of locality, Einstein's discovery that all signals in space-time must travel within the speed limit of 300,000 km/s (the speed of light), and you have the basic tenets of material realism. Sprinkle on it the idea of epiphenomenalism for aspects of the world that do not show any obvious connection with matter and mechanism (such as, consciousness is an epiphenomenon of matter), and you will begin to think that material realism has omnipotent explanatory powers.

But 20th-century studies of the physics of submicroscopic objects have exposed the limits of classical physics. For submicroscopic objects, we find that fundamental tenets of material realism—continuity, determinism, and locality—are in direct conflict with experimental data. We cannot tell when a radioactive atom, a quantum system, will emit its radiation—its behavior violates strict causal continuity. We cannot simultaneously determine where an electron is and where it will go with utmost accuracy—this *uncertainty principle* rules out strict determinism. Two electrons at a distance exert influence on one another without any interchange of signals through space—somehow the bounds of Einsteinian locality are overcome by this *quantum nonlocality.*

Moreover, the mathematical theory of physics—quantum mechanics—that developed to explain the motion of submicroscopic objects throws grave doubt on the other tenets—objectivity, materialism, and epiphenomenalism. Paradoxes that have puzzled quantum physicists for the last 70 years arise if we hold on to objectivity, materialism, and epiphenomenalism.

Quantum mechanics is probabilistic: It predicts only the probabilities that a certain event will take place. For large conglomerates of objects this works fine as a predictive device. But quantum mechanics cannot lay out the motion of *single* objects in any unique way; instead, it depicts the objects developing as probability weighted, multifaceted structures called *possibility waves*—a superposition of possibilities, each of which is assigned a certain probability of manifesting. The question naturally arises: Who/what collapses (that is, converts) these multifaceted possibilities into one unique actuality in every event of observation? After all, it is a fact that we never observe a state of many facets for an object (e.g., we never find an electron simultaneously occupying two different positions on a photographic plate). Classical thinking has had no success with this quantum measurement paradox.

But the paradox dissipates if we posit an idealist interpretation of quantum mechanics—that quantum possibility waves exist in the transcendent domain of potentia postulated in monistic idealism, and that it is consciousness, us, that recognizes and chooses the one immanent facet out of the possible many in an observed event (Blood, 1993; Goswami, 1989; Von Neumann, 1955; Wigner, 1962). Quantum mechanics is fundamentally incompatible with material realism, which cannot deal with the existence of possibilities for a single object. Only consciousness can consider possibilities and choose among them.

Thus, a different way of seeing the world is needed to accommodate the behavior of quantum objects. And don't think that we can divide the world into a quantum/classical dichotomy, quantum mechanics for the submicroscopic world and classical for the macro. That does not work because submicroscopic objects make up macroobjects, so ultimately quantum mechanics governs the motion of all objects. Even macro-objects exist as possibility waves in an ocean of uncertainty—transcendent potentia—until consciousness chooses a particular actuality by looking (Figure 2.1). The success of Newton's laws in explaining the experimental data of the macroworld of our senses has to do with the correspondence principle—the idea that under certain situations, which prevail for most macroscopic objects, quantum mechanics very nearly gives the same predictions as classical Newtonian laws. But even for a TV set, quantum uncertainty prevails, and we cannot always find it exactly where Newtonian laws lead us to expect it.[4] And there are demonstrated exceptions to the correspondence principle—lasers, superconductors, and superfluids. I believe, as do many other researchers (Bass 1975; Eccles, 1986; Goswami, 1990, 1993a; Herbert, 1993;

---

[4]The deviations are minuscule but still detectable, thanks to recent laser technology.

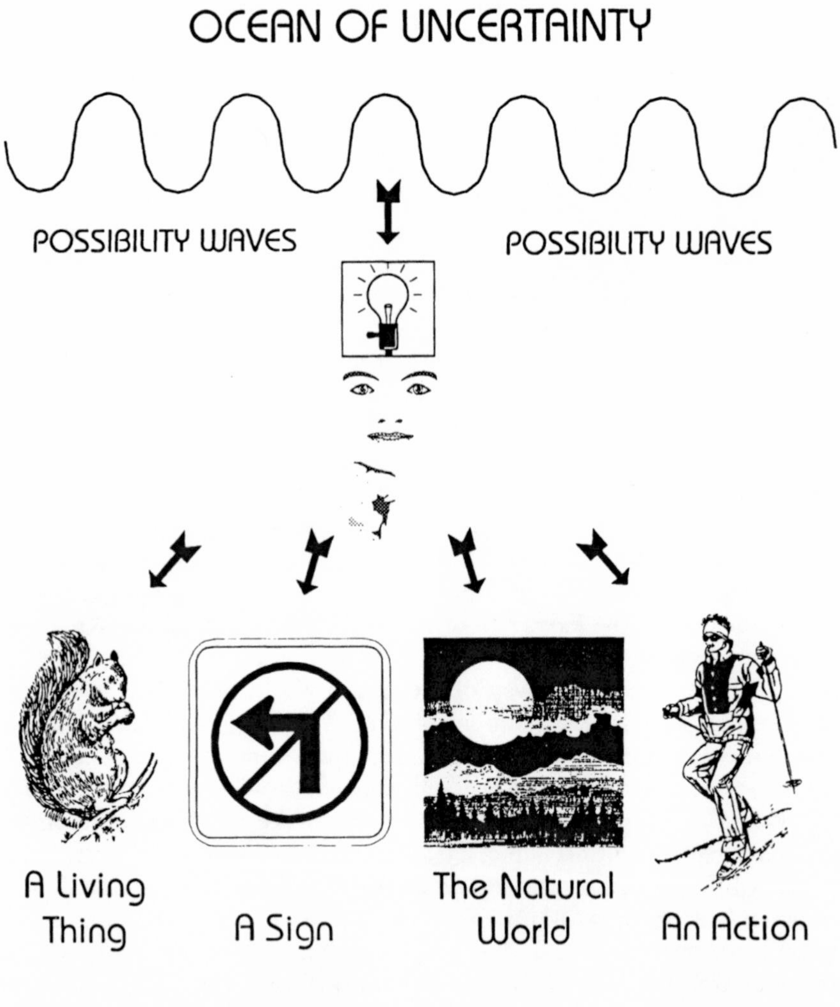

OCEAN OF UNCERTAINTY

POSSIBILITY WAVES   POSSIBILITY WAVES

A Living
Thing   A Sign   The Natural
World   An Action

Figure 2.1. Objects exist as possibility waves in the ocean of uncertainty (transcendent potentia). When we look, they appear in the world of manifestation.

Lockwood, 1989; Penrose, 1991; Stapp, 1982, 1993; Stuart, Takahashy, & Umezawa, 1978; Walker, 1970; Wolf, 1984), that the brain-is another one of these exceptions and that our creativity is a vibrant proof of it.

In summary, then, the worldview of material realism is based on classical physics, which has been supplanted by quantum physics. Material realism is incompatible with quantum physics; but monistic idealism provides a satisfactory, paradox-free metaphysics for quantum mechanics.

AN INTEGRATED WORLDVIEW AND AN INTEGRAL THEORY OF CREATIVITY

The worldview of quantum mechanics as interpreted by idealist metaphysics retains concreteness of mechanism without imposing the limits of determinism on the machines—quantum mechanics is fundamentally indeterministic. Now we can answer such questions of creativity as: Why is creativity—defined as something really new—possible at all, even though there is overwhelming evidence of determinism in the macroworld? If we ask a classical computer to come up with a solution to a problem, it will consult its old programs and furnish an answer on the basis of its programmed repertoire. Clearly, the answer would not be truly new. But a quantum mind will come up with, in addition to the old, a number of previously unexplored possibilities, among which may well be a never-before-manifested answer that is really new.

The integrated theory based on the new worldview exposited in this book also incorporates the question of becoming that is so compelling to organismic theorists. The theory is based on the application of quantum physics to the brain and the mind. Until recently, it was felt that quantum physics was important only in the realm of material phenomena. Now it seems that quantum physics gives us a revolutionary way of conceptualizing about ourselves, our minds, and thus about our creativity (Goswami, 1988, 1990, 1996a; see also McCarthy, 1993). In the present book, our exploration of creativity takes full advantage of this new idea of the quantum mind.

The value of the comprehensive, coherent perspective that quantum physics grounded in monistic idealism generates cannot be overstated. "A change in worldview can change the world viewed," said the author Joseph Chilton Pierce. Indeed so.

The theory of creativity that is formulated in this book preserves the mystery of creativity yet offers a scientific understanding for creative acts. It gives predictive power and influence to the phenomenon without denying what is truly miraculous, what cannot be explained—the particular insight and experience of an individual act of creation.

With this new theory as context, we see that we can fully deal with questions of definition and classification of creative phenomena. Now we can begin to appraise productively what are the basic properties of creative phenomena.

Why does creativity need both inspiration and perspiration? What does creative intuition specifically mean? How do the affects—the anxiety and the ecstacy—of creative experiences arise? What motivates us to be creative at all? All these questions will find satisfying answers in the new framework.

And there is more. Is creativity universal, or is it available only to an elite group? The new theory supports universality. But if creativity is universal, what prevents some of us from being creative? Can we do something about these barriers? Yes, says the new theory.

The main criticism that materialists raise against organismic and idealist theories of creativity is that the latter theories posit the ideas of transcendence, the self, and self-development but without having concrete models. The new theory dissolves this criticism with well-developed models of transcendence, the self, and self-development, as will be shown. Incorporating both creative and conditioned aspects of the self, the new view of the self even accommodates the materialist view.

Are children's and adults' creativity of the same nature? What about the manifestation of creativity in Eastern thinking? Is it the same as for Westerners? The new theory not only opens us to these questions but also gives strong hints as to how to implement greater creativity in our lives and in our society by integrating children's and adults' and the East's and the West's modes of creativity.

What does it mean to live a creative lifestyle? What does it entail to be creative in a business venture? What does it mean to love creatively? Answers emerge from the new theory that are far-reaching and satisfying.

How you see the world depends
on your worldview—your conceptual lens.
Be aware, my friend.
If your lens is not ground true,
your world may look mechanical. In such a world
creativity withers untended.
Polish your lens with consciousness
and gaze once more through the eyes of the creative.

3

THE EJJENCE OF CREATIVITY

What is creativity? It is the phenomenon connected with the act of creation. But what is an act of creation? Can we define an act of creation in a way that will satisfy everybody?

The dictionary defines creation as the "act of bringing the world into existence from nothing." Analogously, can we say that any creation, be it a poem or a theory of science, is the act of bringing something into the world from nothing? Many people who think about creativity today tend to shy away from such a definition. Nobody, it is said, makes something out of nothing.

We all try to define things in terms that fit our worldview. For example, the mathematician Jacques Hadamard (1939) defined creativity as follows: "It is obvious that invention or discovery, be it in mathematics or anywhere else, takes place by combining ideas." This way of looking at creativity fits the worldview that, I assume, Hadamard shares with most scientists: The world is causally deterministic. Past causes determine future events. A new idea must be seen as nothing but a new combination of already known ideas. Hadamard's limited worldview produced his limited definition of creativity.

Deterministic machines, computers for example, can solve problems by combining previously existing programs. If the solution is new and unexpected, and especially if it uses a novel, previously untried combination of programs, how can we deny it the label of creativity? Need our creativity be any different than the deterministic machine's?

But are we stuck with a machine view of ourselves? We are people with minds; we are also conscious. As conscious beings with minds, we are capable of true novelty, and so we can define creativity more in line with the dictionary—creation *ex nihilo*. The psychologist Rollo May, in his book *Courage to Create* (1976), says creativity "is the process of bringing something new into being." In this view of creativity, something genuinely novel comes into being in a creative act. And this genuine novelty is possible for us to manifest because we are not determined machines.

It is the old materialism versus idealism debate—are we made only of matter? Or is consciousness the ground of our being? If we are made only of matter, then it makes sense to say that we are determined machines and that even our supposedly novel, creative acts are not *really* new but only a rehash of old stuff. But if we are made of consciousness, what then?

Can creativity be both not new and new? I would argue that both of the earlier definitions have validity. Although I assume that the world is fundamentally idealist—that is, consciousness is the ground of its being—this idealist worldview encompasses the materialist view as a limiting case (the correspondence principle). As conscious beings, although we have the capacity to create something new from nothing, we also have the tendency to become conditioned and to manipulate our conditioned programs so as to create new and useful things.

Is it not a mistake to settle prematurely on one particular aspect or another of such a complex phenomenon as creativity? That would be like the expectant father in a hospital waiting room. When the nurse brings a trio of babies to him, declaring that he is the father of triplets, the man studies the babies and says, pointing, "I choose that one!" Most of us would agree that the man was being too hasty.

The quibble about definition is solved by recognizing that we have two basic kinds of creativity—situational and fundamental. Situational creativity pertains to solving new problems by combining old ideas in novel ways. Fundamental creativity pertains to true originality of which only consciousness in its unconditioned freedom is capable.

Because most people today subscribe to a materialist view of the world, situational creativity has dominated the discussion of creative acts in the recent past, even that while neglecting their subjective aspects. But thanks to advances in quantum physics, the case for a causally potent consciousness is strong and getting stronger. Thus the time is right to focus on all of creativity's aspects, on both fundamental and situational creativity.

WHAT IS NEW?

What is the "new" that is so unique to creativity? That should be simple: New means something that has never before been manifested. But then suppose I construct a sentence with absurd words that in all likelihood has never before appeared in the English language or even write a whole poem made of such sentences. Would that be creative just because it's new? We suspect that, although such a poem may not have appeared before, it could have—anyone could have done something similar. The poem is not *really new*.

On the other hand, Jackson Pollock did some great paintings seemingly by just pouring paint over a canvass in a way very similar to writing a poem with arbitrary combinations of words. What's the difference?

The point is that Rollo May's definition for creativity is not about newness in a trivial material sense. The definition of new is more subtle. This is what the materialists miss when they flatly declare, "There is nothing new under the sun." There may not be anything new, materially speaking, in a poem of arbitrarily juxtaposed words or in a poured-on painting, but if new meaning in consciousness emerges from those acts, then there is creativity. It is this new meaning—whether from situational or fundamental creativity—that the idealist focuses on. And it is this aspect of creativity—meaning—that distinguishes creativity from problem solving. Even situational creativity is not just problem solving.

FROM A BRICK TO A RED DRESS: THE CONTEXT OF CREATIVITY

Can one make a red dress out of bricks? If you could get an adult to take this question seriously, she might scratch her head and comment on the atomic commonality between a brick and a dress or make some equally erudite response. But a child, asked this question, may answer more imaginatively that, if we make a brick building, the red brick will be like a red dress for the building. This shift from the usual meaning of brick exemplifies a contextual change.

Etymologically, the word *context* comes from two Latin words—*com*, meaning together, and *texere,* meaning to weave. Context refers to the relationship of a system to its environment, of a figure to the ground on which the figure appears.

Perhaps the most familiar experience one has with contexts is the way the meaning of a word changes in different backgrounds of other words. Consider the two sentences:

The ass is a useful domestic animal.
Anybody who does not appreciate context is an ass.

The word *ass* has a different meaning in the second sentence because it is used in a new context.

Einstein gave another example of the difference context makes. If you sit on a hot stove for one minute, it will seem like an hour; but one hour with your sweetheart will seem like a minute.

Remember, the problem of defining creativity is the problem of defining what is new. Using this idea of contextual change, we can define what is new in both fundamental and situational creativity.

First, in fundamental creativity something is really new when it is new in a brand new context, a context *ex nihilo*. Now an unambiguous definition of fundamental creativity can be given: Fundamental creativity is bringing into manifestation something new in a new context.

Two important ingredients of the definition are still implicit. First, the new context must have enduring values such as truth or beauty. Second, the shift to a new context is a discontinuous shift in consciousness. The previously known contexts do not prepare us for it, nor do they cause it. So, finally: *Fundamental creativity is the manifestation of something new in a new context of value through a process that involves discontinuity.*[1]

Consciousness manifests reality through a matrix of contexts, which Easterners call the *Vijanamaya Kosha* which I translate as *theme body* and Plato called the *archetypes* that transcends space and time. For science, these are the eternal laws that set the context for movement of matter and mind. For the arts, these are timeless themes such as love and justice. These great themes are so vast that the artist discovers "new truth" in them by building a bridge between them and the specific context of a particular time and place.

What is the new in situational creativity? Situational creativity is based on old contexts, but have we extracted all their meaning and value? Furthermore, when we combine old contexts, there is the additional possibility of new meaning and value. Thus, situational creativity consists of *creating a new product or solving a problem in a way that reflects new meaning and value in an old context or a combination of old contexts.*

And, of course, the perception of new meaning and value in old context(s) is also a discontinuous change in consciousness. No algorithm can be given for it, although it is not as revolutionary as the shift

---

[1]The importance of value in creativity has been emphasized by Haefel (1962).

to a new context. Thus *discontinuity is paramount in creativity.* It is this discontinuity that separates situational creativity from mundane problem solving. It is in their search for meaning and value that situational creatives succeed in finding novel solutions to problems whereas ordinary problem solvers get nowhere.

There is some data that strongly suggest the validity of what I am proposing, namely, that problem solving is not creativity—not even situational creativity. There are supposed "tests" of creativity that measure a person's ability to think about a subject using as many contexts as possible; they ask such questions as, How many ways can you use a fan? How many titles can you come up with for a given story? If [known] context hunting is what we do in creativity, then certainly this kind of "divergent thinking" test is relevant. The tests are reliable, no doubt; if a person takes a test over, he or she tends to get a similar score. But there seems to be no correlation between the test scores and the *actual* creativity of the person tested, so the tests' validity is doubtful. The transition from trivial contexts of problem solving to meaningful contexts of creativity is itself not trivial.

To summarize, the essence of creativity, both fundamental and situational—and I shortly present data to support this view—involves discontinuity, consciousness, and meaning. Mechanistic theories of creativity, because they model us as Newtonian machines, cannot make room for any of these aspects. Idealist theories (and, in part, even organismic theories) have room for them, but until now, they have lacked concrete models. The integration achieved in this book is to show that by invoking quantum mechanics within an overall monistic idealist framework, all these essential aspects of creativity can be incorporated and yet a scientific model can be given. This is the subject of Part 2.

EXAMPLE: THE NINE-POINTS PROBLEM

Consider the following problem, called the nine points problem:

Connect a 3 X 3 rectangular nine-point array (Figure 3.1a) using the smallest possible number of straight lines without taking the pencil off the paper.

It seems that you need five lines, doesn't it? Suppose I tell you that that's too many. Can you see right away how to get a smaller number of straight lines to do the job?

Perhaps not. Perhaps, like many people, you think you have to connect the points while staying within the boundary defined by the outer points of the rectangular array. If so, you have defined a context for solving the problem, and this is not the right context.

So you have to find a new context in which a smaller number of straight lines will do the job. If you permit yourself to extend your lines beyond the rectangle (note that nowhere in the problem as stated are you forbidden to do that), you need only four straight lines to connect the points (Figure 3.1b). This is a simple example of discovering a new context. Keep in mind, this is not creativity in the way we have defined

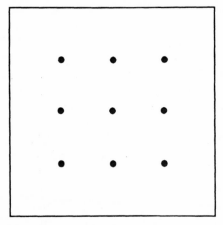

Figure 3.1(a). The nine-points problem. Connect the points using as few lines as you can without raising your pencil.

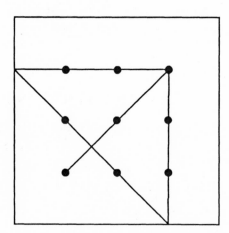

Figure 3.1(b). The solution of the nine-points problem. Extend your context.

it (you haven't done anything of new meaning or value), but this idea of extending the boundary beyond the existing context is crucially important in creativity. In fact, the first rule for a creative is, if the old context is not working, find a new one. And sometimes, creativity is that simple: just recognize that what is not forbidden is allowed.

It always starts with asking a question. Consider the following episode from *Alice in Wonderland:*

> "It's always six o'clock now," the hatter said mournfully.
> A bright idea came into Alice's head. "Is that the reason so many tea-things are put out here?" she asked.
> "Yes, that's it," said the Hatter with a sigh: "it's always tea-time, and we have no time to wash the things between whiles."
> "Then you keep moving around, I suppose?" said Alice.
> "Exactly so," said the Hatter: "as the things get used up."
> "But what happens when you come to the beginning again?" Alice ventured to ask.[2]

Alice asked the right question, intuiting that the conceptual context of the Mad-Hatter's perpetual tea party was limited and a change needed to happen. But in *Wonderland* her question was not followed up. The March Hare changed the subject. This is another thing about being creative: you must follow up your questions when the intuition strikes exposing the limits of the present context.

So now you have a good idea of what context means and what a shift of context is. In real-life creativity, similar things are involved with very important additions: value and significance.

EXAMPLES OF FUNDAMENTAL CREATIVITY: PICASSO'S GUERNICA AND THE BOHR ATOM

Now comes the crucial question: Is the definition just given of fundamental creativity—the discovery of something new with a discontinuous shift to a new context of value—consistent with the data? It is. As an example, consider the art of Picasso. (Chapters 12 and 13 include more examples.)

In the 1920s, Picasso was painting bathers by the ocean in a context that reflected the escapism of the roaring 20s," which swept the

---

[2]Quoted in Boden (1994); see also the discussion afterward.

United States and Europe. But look at Picasso's work in the 1930s. The bathers are still there, but now they are mechanical; often made of metal, they have an inhuman, machine-like quality. Picasso had discovered a new context within which to portray the human condition—a future when human beings would limit themselves as sparkless, mechanical machines. Then in 1937, with *Guernica,* came another sweeping change of context. The figures in Guernica are not only mechanical but also torn apart; they prophesy the fractionation of the condition of humanity in the middle-to-late 20th century: fractionation between subjective experience and objective reasoning, between science and ethical/moral values, between dogma and spirituality, between creativity and conformity (May, 1976).

In their discovery of new contexts, artists often jump way ahead of their time. Looking at his paintings, a contemporary, Gertrude Stein, complained to Picasso, "Your figures don't look much like human beings." But Picasso replied, "Don't worry, they will."

In contrast, if we compare Hollywood film fare from year to year, what do we find? The names of the films, the stars, and the technologies change, but do the contexts really change? Only infrequently. (A Hollywood producer once told me that there are only seven basic story lines used in Hollywood films.)

The work of the Danish physicist Niels Bohr with quantum leaps is another example of fundamental creativity. The British physicist Ernest Rutherford combined the old context of the solar system with that of the atom. He could see that electrons revolving around the nucleus under the latter's electrical attraction, in analogy with planets going around the sun under the sun's gravitational attraction, might work as a model of the atom. This is an example of the transference of an idea from one context to another via analogy—a good example of situational creativity, but there is no fundamental creativity yet. The model has a problem: Rutherford's atom cannot be stable. Just as artificial satellites of the earth spiral into the earth as they lose energy in collision with the atmosphere, the electrons (according to the laws of classical physics) must crash into the nucleus as they lose energy by continuously emitting radiation. Bohr found an unconventional answer to this dilemma outside the established context of the old, Newtonian physics, and he paved the way for the discovery of a new physics.

For Bohr, the orbits of the electrons in an atom are discrete and stationary—frozen stations in space that are said to be "quantized." The electrons emit radiation only when changing orbits but emit none while in these orbits (violating the rules of then-known physics). Furthermore, the electron's motion is not continuous when it changes orbits but is a discontinuous leap, a quantum jump (see Figure 1.1, upper). When the electron is in the lowest such orbit, it has no lower orbit to jump to, so the atom is stable in this configuration.

When Bohr finished his paper on his radical new discovery, he sent it to Rutherford in England forward on for publication. But Rutherford had difficulty in appreciating Bohr's novel shift of context. Bohr had to travel to England and convince Rutherford in person. Subsequently, another physicist brought Bohr's work to Einstein's attention. It is said that Einstein's eyes sparkled with excitement as he said something to the effect that Bohr's discovery will go down in history as one of the greatest.

How radical is the idea of the quantum leap! A quantum leap is literally like a jump from one rung of a ladder to another without going through the intervening space, something that nobody has ever seen (Figure 1.1, lower). In order to "see" the truth of such quantum leaps in the atom, Bohr had to have a discontinuous shift of context in his understanding of physics, a turning about from blind reliance on Newton's laws to new quantum laws that had not yet been discovered.

Similarly, in the tragedy of the Nazi bombing of the Spanish town of Guernica, in the images of torn-up bodies in a torn-up town, Picasso experienced a discontinuous shift of the context of the mural he was working on at the time. He "saw" the fragmentation of entire humankind which he then immortalized in the painting.

EXAMPLES OF SITUATIONAL CREATIVITY

As an example of situational creativity, consider the case of the perception of a direct analogy that enabled Alexander Graham Bell to invent the telephone. Bell wrote the following about his invention:

> It struck me that the bones of the human ear were very massive, as compared with the delicate thin membranes that operated them, and the thought occurred that if a membrane so delicate could move bones relatively so massive, why should not a thicker and stouter piece of membrane move my piece of steel . . . and the telephone was conceived. (quoted in Barron, 1969)

Another example is James Watt's invention of the steam engine. One day Watt noticed the steam in a tea kettle forcefully lifting the lid of the kettle. If steam can do that, can it run a locomotive? was the thought that James eventually translated into the steam engine. Both Bell and Watt saw new meaning, new possibility, in the juxtaposition of two analogical contexts in their mind.

Why did Bell and Watt succeed whereas many other researchers failed to arrive at the invention of the telephone and the steam engine? What makes such people so special? Is it their computational abilities of searching the proper "problem spaces" (containing various known contexts) of their minds or their subjective ability to anticipate and see meaning and value?

The point is that the particular mix of contexts or the particular analogy leading to situational creativity most often cannot easily be anticipated from existing contexts. When there is novelty and surprise even in reasoning, we should not miss the fact that the novelty and surprise occur precisely because consciousness is seeing new meaning and value in the act, and thus fundamental new understanding is involved.

It is conceivable that, given both contexts, a computer might also be able to come up with the analogy by searching its problem spaces, and it would have done it algorithmically. Computer programs can be good at problem solving by fitting the problem to a previously known context that works. There is a program called *Soar* which has in its memory various problem spaces for dealing with problems. When given a new problem, the program searches first for an appropriate problem space. It then looks for a solution within the context(s) in that problem space. If it reaches an impasse, it shifts to a new problem space, and so forth, until it finds the solution. There is nothing discontinuous here; all is algorithmic. Is this creativity?

The engineer John Arnold once argued that, at least in engineering, all the preparation work for an inventive project can be done by a computer. But at the end, when the computer delivers a number of alternatives, then the question of decision making arises. Granted, a decision also consists of mechanical aspects; the probabilistic evaluation of the outcome of each of the alternatives may well be carried out by a computer. But the computer cannot assign values or meaning to the predictions, develop criteria for desirability, or judge the aesthetics. "There is still ample opportunity and necessity for creative human work . . . very definitely in the stage of decision making" (Arnold, 1959).

James Watt's invention of the steam engine and Alexander Graham Bell's invention of the telephone were, no doubt, problem solving, but they took the ingenuity of patient men precisely because the inventions required a novel "seeing" of hidden meaning, not obvious from a cursory inspection of the problem, and risky decision making. And yet, certainly an appropriately programmed computer *could have* invented these products, and somebody else (the programmer) could have seen their new meaning and value. There is no need to elevate the novelty of a steam engine to the novelty of Newton's theory of universal gravitation. The clarification of new meaning in situational creativity applies to a limited arena of that particular situation; fundamental creativity is called fundamental because its applicability encompasses many, many situations.

PROCESS IN CREATIVITY

The sudden and discontinuous nature of the creative insight is by far the most spectacular aspect of an act of creativity. But all is not discontinuity and insight; the sudden and discontinuous creative insight is but a part of a protracted process.

In dealing with the wholeness of the act of creativity, we must note not only what is discontinuous and extraordinary but also what is continuous and mundane. The creativity researcher Howard Gruber, who has written one of the most definitive studies of scientific creativity on the work of Charles Darwin (Gruber 1981), makes this point strongly. Darwin's own autobiography describes a creative moment of insight when, while reading Malthus's *Essay on Population*, he came to recognize the crucial role of fecundity in the theory of natural selection in biological evolution. But according to Gruber, a study of Darwin's notebooks shows that, although this was the final moment of insight, there was also a gradual process interspersed with many smaller insights.

Of what does the entire creative process consist, then? The creativity researcher Graham Wallas (1926) was one of the first to suggest that creative acts involve four stages that are now quite commonly accepted. These four stages are: *preparation, incubation, illumination,* and *verification*. What do these stages entail? In simple terms:

Stage 1 (preparation): gather facts and existing ideas about your problem and think, think, think. Churn the ideas around in your mind-field, looking at them in every way that comes to mind.

Stage 2 (incubation): relax. The problem is not going to go away. Meanwhile, you can play, sleep, and do all the things that relax you. (Include especially, bath, bus, and bed—they have demonstrated relevance. Archimedes made his "Eureka" discovery while taking a bath; the mathematician Henry Poincare had an insight while boarding a bus; and the chemist Frederick von Kekule discovered the molecular structure of benzine while dreaming in bed.)

Stage 3 (illumination or insight): eureka, ah-ha, right when you least expect it, maybe when you see a frog jump while on a fishing trip.

Stage 4 (verification or manifestation): the fun is over, or is it just beginning? Manifest, evaluate, and verify what you have.

Preparation begins with an intuition, a vague feeling about a possible problem. It then involves doing the relevant groundwork: gathering information, asking questions about the existing structure, and so forth. It consists of getting acquainted with the field, obtaining real mastery.

But mastery alone won't do. As the psychologist Carl Rogers (1959) emphasized, preparation also means developing an open mind, a destructuring of the existing belief-system(s) that sets the stage for the acceptance of the new. An excellent illustration of the importance of an open mind is the case of the 17th-century physicist Johannes Kepler who discovered the revolutionary idea that the solar planets move in ellipses around the sun. But long before Kepler's final insight, he actually had pondered logically the possibility of the ellipse as an option for planetary orbits but had discarded it as a "cartload of dung." He was not yet prepared.

Incubation, for Wallas and many researchers, involves preconscious or unconscious mental activities. When Bohr was working on his model of the atom, he saw the solar-system atom in a dream, suggesting unconscious incubation going on in his psyche. Outwardly, we can equate incubation with relaxation—"sitting quietly, doing nothing"—as opposed to preparation, which is active work.

Illumination, of course, refers to the sudden ah-ha insight, the stage at which discontinuity and acausality enter creativity. The existence of such a stage is widely agreed on, and we have centered our attention on it prior to this section.

But it is in the transition from unconscious to conscious, from stage two to stage three, that creativity expresses its discontinuity. The composer Richard Wagner discovered the overture to *Das Reingold* in a reverie, a state intermediate between sleep and wakefulness. This is Wagner's account:

> Returning [from a walk] in the afternoon, I stretched myself, dead tired, on a hard couch, awaiting the long-desired hour of sleep. It did not come; but I fell into a kind of somnolent state, in which I suddenly felt as though I was sinking in swiftly flowing water. The rushing sound formed itself in my brain into a musical sound, the chord of E-flat major, which continually re-echoed in broken

forms; these broken forms seemed to be melodic passages of increasing motion, yet the pure triad of E-flat major never changed, but seemed by its continuance to impart infinite significance to the element in which I was sinking. I awoke in sudden terror from my doze, feeling as though the waves were rushing above my head. I at once recognized that the orchestral overture to the Reingold, which must have lain latent within me, though it had been unable to find definite form, had at last been revealed to me. (1911)

For an example in science, consider Kekule's dream insight about the structure of the benzene molecule. The problem was how carbon atoms bond with one another and with hydrogen atoms. The prevalent notions of such bonding all involved linear bonding. Kekule's discontinuous leap to the idea of circular bonding came to him in a dream in which he saw a snake biting its own tail. The dream does not leave any doubt that unconscious processing was involved in the discovery.[3]

Finally, verification involves manifesting the idea of the insight, checking the solution, and ending up with a product—the manifest novelty. With verification, there is also a restructuring of the belief system, the repertoire of learned contexts.

There have been other schemas of the stages of creative acts involving a greater or fewer number of stages. For example, D. Fabun (1968) has suggested that the desire to find a solution to a "burning question" begins the creative process, an idea that I heartily endorse. Some authors have emphasized the role that intuition plays. Other researchers of creativity have emphasized the importance of problem finding as part of the search for the solution. Sometimes problem finding *is* an important insight in fundamental creativity.

Importantly, as Gruber has pointed out, Wallas's picture is an idealized one. Real creative acts most often consist of many episodes of work, relaxation, and mini-discontinuous insights—little bangs—until

---

[3]More recently, however, science historians J. H. Wotiz and S. Rudofsky (1984) have challenged the authenticity of Kekule's dream experience; according to these researchers, this is a case of blatant scientific fraud—Kekule just made up the story. If this is true, the interesting issue is not fraud, because the story does not affect the authenticity of Kekule's great idea. The really interesting question is, why would Kekule make up such a story? Simply to amuse his listeners at the after-dinner speech when he first recounted the dream? Or is there more to it? I think that if Kekule did indeed make up this, he was trying to convey a deeper truth through his invented story—the importance of unconscious processing in his creativity.

the final illumination occurs when everything falls into place, as in the perception of the whole gestalt of fragmentary images.

Howard Gardner reminds us of something else that is important. According to Gardner (1993), there are different types of "intelligences," and for each, the creative process must be different. For example, a creative novelist like Gertrude Stein would work in the linguistic mode, a mathematical physicist like Einstein would do most of his processing in the mathematical mode, an artist like Picasso would employ the visual-spatial mode, a musician such as Mozart would employ the musical mode, and a dancer like Mikhael Barashnikov would be kinesthetic in his processing. I agree with Gardner; I also feel that although the details of the creative process for these different types of intelligence are different, Wallas's stages do apply.

If we accept Wallas' stages, the need for an integrated theory of creativity that incorporates the discontinuity of a creative insight and the importance of unconscious processing becomes self-evident (see Part 2).

CREATIVE PROCESS IN A LONG TIME SCALE

We must also recognize that creativity manifests in several different time scales, and each of these time scales is important. In the short time scale, Wallas's stages play out more or less linearly.

In the intermediate time scale, different stages of the creative process are simultaneously engaged in different creative pursuits within what Howard Gruber calls a *network of enterprises*.

Finally, at the long end of the time scale, there is the entire creative life of the individual to consider. In this time scale the creatives—the fundamental creatives, anyway—try to influence their field and often succeed. Picasso made cubism the dominant paradigm in art for many years. Einstein did not himself succeed in finding a unified force field for elementary particles, but his quest is still the guiding motif for many elementary particle physicists.

Gardner and his collaborators, especially Csikszentmihaly (see Gardner, 1993), think that it is the interaction among the individual person, his or her domain of influence, and the judges in the surrounding field that determine what is creative and what is not (Gardner, 1993). In my opinion, in the short and intermediate time scales, creativity is personal; personal judgment is the primary determinant of creativity and social judgment is secondary. However, in the long time scale, Gardner et al may have a point.

WHAT ABOUT THE SCIENTIFIC METHOD?: A DIALOG WITH AN AFFICIONADO OF THE SCIENTIFIC METHOD

Afficionado: Isn't it true that in science, at least, researchers use what is called the *scientific method,* as laid down in many textbooks, to discover or invent their product?

1. Find a problem.
2. Make a hypothesis or a series of hypotheses—a theory that may solve the problem.
3. Analyze the predictive consequences of your theory.
4. Do experiments to test the predictions. Repeat steps 2 through 4, as necessary (trial and error).
5. Make a synthesis of theory, predictions, and verifications.

I rather like the scientific method. No mystery, no unconscious processing, no discontinuous insight or illumination. Also missing are intuition, a burning question, an open mind—in short, all the subjective aspects. Why can't objective science, at least, be done in this objective way?

Author: You are not alone in this preference. Many pedagogues of science still believe that science is a strict, logical, reason-based, completely objective affair—although a mountain of evidence suggests the contrary. If the practitioners of science, great or small, limited themselves to this so-called scientific method, we would never have great leaps of thought and understanding in science. But scientists in the main feel embarrassed that their objective science should depend on subjective creativity for its development. So they hang on to the myth of the scientific method.

Af: I see. You are saying that the scientific method is a step-by-step model for doing science as problem solving, not as a creative enterprise.

Au: Exactly. How do you make a hypothesis except on the basis of what you know? If you are not looking for new meaning, let alone new contexts, how are you going to solve a problem that requires a novel solution?

Af: But can you deny that most scientists use the scientific method to do their work? Then it follows that scientists as a group engage in creativity far less than artists, writers, and musicians.

Au: I don't deny that many scientists look on science as a professional enterprise and do career science, using the scientific method for problem solving. These are the scientists who clutter up the scientific journals, and they do occasionally produce something novel (by chance) without ever investing their subjectivity in it. But don't assume that people in the arts invariably engage in creativity whereas scientists wallow in the scientific method. The truth is, one can use the scientific method to write a poem or draw a painting. If one is interested only in the objective and mechanical aspects of situational creativity (let somebody else discover the new meaning, if any!), in art as professional problem solving, or in computer style (well, maybe not completely), then the answer is yes. More explicitly, here are the steps to "scientifically" write a poem:

1. Find a worthwhile subject (the problem).
2. Produce a few ideas to proceed; they don't have to be original. Unabashedly draw on some of your favorite poems for starters. And by all means, be subtle.
3. Do it! Produce a poem following each of your ideas.
4. Decide which one works best.
5. Integrate the best of the other versions into your best choice. Of course, you don't do experiments, trial and error, to verify a poem, but you do test it out in the public arena. If people like it (it sells), you have succeeded.

Af: Interesting. I have to try that some time. But are you sure people actually use such reasoned steps to write a poem or draw a painting?

Au: Thousands of poems (and especially lyrics—just listen to some of today's pop music) seem to be written this way every year. And the same method should work in other arts with little modification. However, be aware. The poet Robert Graves spoke of shivers in the spine when writing a poem; others speak about palpitations in the heart and feelings of intoxication. If you opt for the scientific method to write a poem, you will never experience such sensations in your body.

Af: There you go again. You are determined to inject mystery into creativity. Why engage in a quantum theory or idealist science of creativity then?

Au: The writer Jack Kerouac saw writing as sacramental, as did Allen Ginsberg and other "beatniks," and they created an entirely new trend in American poetry. "We were writing for our own amusement and the amusement of our friends, rather than for money or for publication," said Ginsberg in an interview. To be sure, poetry written via the scientific method may be easier to sell, but such writing does not bring the joy of creativity.

And what gave you the idea that our new science should demystify creativity? The quantum leap is a helpful concept, but it retains the mystery because the mystery is fundamental.

Af: I like that. So you are saying that both scientists and artists use creativity to do their wonderful work, mystery and all. Whereas the less wonderful stuff is done by the reason-based scientific method in both trades. But aren't there any differences between creativity in science and in the arts?

Au: There are some real differences between the sciences and the arts. Science has a large objective component. Moreover, because of progressivity—science builds on earlier work—and also from the nature of experimental science, problem solving often does play an important role. For most science, then, at least in principle, it may *seem* that an objective approach is enough. Art, however, is fundamentally subjective, created to connect with the subjective experiences of real people. An artist, then, has no excuse to stay within the bounds of the problem-solving approach. Such a limit compromises creative integrity and, most importantly, the artist misses out on the creative joy that drew him or her to art in the first place.

What is creativity?
The making of something new, we all agree.
If what you originate
newly combines already known elements,
then, oh creator, call your creativity situational.

Only if the flower of your creation
blooms in a new context, as well,
is your creativity fundamental.

Be patient and persistent. Stoke the creative process
with your burning question.
When a flaming leap of context bursts forth,
the radiant answer
takes you to Einstein's ecstacy.

4

INNER CREATIVITY

According to the definition in the last chapter, an act of creativity is the discontinuous exploration of new meaning in new and old context(s) of value. For example, Einstein's discovery of the theory of relativity revolutionized how we look at time. Before Einstein, we looked at time as absolute, as independent of everything else. After Einstein, the context for thinking about time became relativity: Time is relative, it depends on motion.

Suppose, as a student, I want to learn Einstein's theory. It seems very difficult and obscure at first, but at some point, with tenacity, understanding dawns. I have broken free from my old conception of time, and from this new perspective I can understand Einstein. Is this a creative act? Although there is no discovery of a new context, there is understanding of new meaning. But there is no product in the outer arena. And certainly, far less creativity is needed to understand something like relativity than to discover it or to apply it meaningfully. And yet I have discovered a new context for myself, and that surely has value.

My own first ah-ha experience in the pursuit of physics came with my first glimmer of understanding relativity. With a thumping heart, I wrote the following lines (never mind the naivete, I was only a teenager):

Suddenly I understand relativity.
My eyes shine.
For a moment I think
I am Einstein.

More importantly, when we read about people like Mahatma Gandhi, Martin Luther King, or Eleanor Roosevelt, we recognize that such people discovered ways to serve humanity that escape many of us. Yet the change of context that they discover is personal. Does that qualify as creativity?

Yeshe Tsogyel, who was the consort of the 8th-century mystic Madmasambhava, played a crucial role in the founding of Buddhism in Tibet. At one point in her life, she was raped by a gang of bandits, who later became her disciples. What enables one to so radically transform cruelty?

The world's civilizations are greatly indebted to people such as Tsogyel, Buddha, Lao Tzu, Moses, Jesus, Mohammed, Shankara, and the like, who found and communicated spiritual truth to all humanity. Are their discoveries creative acts?

And what about the people who follow the spiritual paths laid out by these masters? The transformation of those who rediscover the universal truths of their masters enables them to serve humanity better. Do their acts count as creativity?

Finally, what about people in ordinary life who discover unselfish love in relationships with other people and the world? Do their discoveries amount to creativity?

The answer lies in realizing that creative acts fall into two broad categories that I call *outer and inner creativity* (Goswami, 1993a). *Outer creativity* refers to creativity that yields objective products in the outer arena. *Inner creativity* involves creative transformation of the self and yields a subjective yet discernible product. Abraham Maslow (1968) recognized the importance of inner creativity, which was called *self-actualizing creativity* (outer creativity he called *talent-driven creativity*).[1]

Acts of outer creativity—new discoveries in the public arena—are usually judged in the context of what already exists. A new context is added to an existing multitude of old contexts in the public domain (as in Einstein's discovery of relativity). Although deep analysis (see part 4) shows that outer creativity is not restricted to geniuses, the arena of outer creativity is certainly dominated by people we call great men and women.

Inner creativity, in contrast, is about a transformation of the individual self that yields new personal contexts. It is evaluated in comparison not with others but with one's own old self. Here there are also great exemplars (like the Buddhas). But ordinary people also display

---

[1]Maslow also collected definitive data on self-actualized people—people who had progressed to a new identity of the self beyond ego.

inner creativity in their learning, understanding, and in the new and expanded contexts of their personal lives; the contributions to inner creativity of such unsung heroes form the backbone of human communities.

In our present culture the commercialization of such natural expressions of inner creativity as singing, dancing, and art creates much confusion about creativity. Exalting the competitive expression of these fundamental human activities in the outer arena (because only outer creativity is valued) leads to an unfortunate inhibition of spontaneous acts of joy. But in Bali, where inner creativity is highly valued, people naturally express themselves in music, art, and dance; objective criteria are not seen as relevant or appropriate (although this is changing somewhat under external pressure).

CREATIVITY IN CHILDREN

How should we classify the creativity of children? Everybody "knows" that children are creative. "We are all infant prodigies," said the novelist Thomas Mann. But children rarely discover or invent anything new (except to them!) in the objective arena.

At a conference that I attended on creativity theory in 1990, a major debate centered around whether creativity in children is the same as creativity in adults, which to a large extent is genius creativity. It should be clear that the concept of inner creativity enables us to resolve this issue.

Children's creativity is mostly directed toward ego development. Their creativity is inner creativity expressed through the stages of ego development, which follow a series of transformations of the context of the child's learning and living (see Chapter 8).

INNER CREATIVITY IN ADULTS: CREATIVE SPIRITUALITY

Inner creativity in adults is directed toward transcending the ego to arrive at a more holistic identity for the self. What is ego? In Freud's theory, the ego is shaped by the instincts and the impulses of the unconscious id. In behaviorist social-learning theory, the ego is shaped by the stimulus-response-reinforcement mechanisms of our environment. In Piagetian theory, ego development follows social learning and creative internalization of the contexts of social learning. Giving validity to all these views, it is important to recognize that our past creative and conditioned learning, both environmental and genetic, both conscious and unconscious, shapes the ego (see Chapter 7).

I look at myself in a certain way; I have a self image, a character, a way of doing things out of a repertoire of learned contexts. In addition, I may have one or more personas, masks that I wear in my social interactions. Is this all there is to my self? Does our self-development terminate with the ego identity? Perhaps the ego is only a utility station for our self-identity!

Conventionally, the search for a holistic identity beyond ego is carried out under the aegis of religion and spirituality. But not every aspect of religion is creative, and spirituality means many things to many people. Only spirituality recognized as the creative discovery of our inherent identity with the transcendent spirit within us is inner creativity. Then spirituality is seen clearly as the journey of discovery of the adult human potential.

That spirituality ultimately involves a creative change of context in our lives is most clearly stated in the story of young Nachiketa in one of the Upanishads. Nachiketa wants to know the spiritual truth, but who can teach it to him? Nobody but the God of death, Yama. So Nachiketa goes to Yama and finds the truth about his spiritual nature.

This story suggests that the discovery of the spirit, true spirituality, involves the death of our identity as a conditioned ego; that's why only the death-God can teach it. Only when the identity with the old is dead can the new infuse our lives and we can be (inner-) creative. Only when our identity with the conditioned adult ego is surrendered can we move on to expanded horizons of self-development. (Note that I am speaking not of ego-death, but only of the death of our identity with the ego.)

The Sufi poet Rumi (1988) wrote:

Journeys bring power and love back into you. If you can't go somewhere, move in the passageways of the self. They are like shafts of light, always changing, and you change when you explore them. (p. 2)

Adult inner creativity is about these journeys beyond ego. It is the pursuit of creative development of the full human potential.

INNER CREATIVITY IN ACTING

Is there creativity in acting? Actors and actresses perform in the outer arena, but they do not create anything new in the sense of outer creativity. However, they do participate in inner creativity (and perhaps even in outer creativity to the extent that their performances precipitate in the audience an encounter with meaning).

In Shakespeare's time, enacting a tragedy was the actor's way to practice transcending the ego level to the self beyond ego. The noble hero of a Shakespeare tragedy suffers from inner conflict. There is no resolution except, just as the earlier Nachiketa story indicates, transcendence of the ego, which is portrayed as death.

Consider the case of Hamlet. He was torn between the ethos of the time—the ego's ethos—of avenging his father's murder and a higher ethos—thou shalt not kill. The only resolution was tragedy, the death of the ego-identity, which in his case occurred through actual physical death.

In primitive cultures, acting involves wearing masks, by which process the wearer becomes the god or animal that he or she is portraying. But anthropologists have noted that masks are worn to stimulate transcendental experiences: They are vehicles for inner creativity, transformation. "In these masks you continually find beings transforming into other beings. A man is a bear, bear is a killer whale. The artist is showing a shared spirit—that all beings are in some way the same."

Today, instead of Shakespearian tragedies, we are back to a more primitive form of acting, except that the actors and actresses wear more subtle masks; the characters are usually ordinary people, not gods and animals. But the purpose of acting remains the same—to discover for oneself the unity behind the diversity of different characters and their different melodramas. In acting, there is a wonderful opportunity to transcend the human melodrama and discover the core of our being. "At one point," muses the actor Louis Gossett about a role that he successfully played, "I don't even know who I am anymore. By the story's end he's (the character) grown into his truest self, and I didn't quite realize what a deep thing that would be to me. When you start to implement yourself and use your soul, you discover more."

Unfortunately, many actors and actresses get caught up in living the life of many egos and the mind of many masks. Instead of exploring deep into their psyches, they investigate horizontally, keeping to the same level as their own ego. Thus their performances are no longer ones of the creative discovery of transcendent unity but mere technique in the craft of acting.

INNER CREATIVITY IN RELATIONSHIP

In acting, we wear masks and assume someone else's identity to escape our ego-centeredness. In a relationship, we also have the opportunity to be in somebody else's shoes, but more subtly.

The problem is, our ego thrives in homeostasis. This includes not only our own situation, our own patterns, but also the tendency to manipulate our relationships into the mold of our own homeostasis. And if we allow movement in a relationship, it is often a horizontal movement within the contexts defined by our ego. Breaking through these tendencies is a creative challenge, and the kind of creative acts that penetrate such an impasse and restore fluidity to frozen or static relationships may catapult us beyond ego. In other words, relationship growth is inner creativity.[2]

Traditionally women's spirituality has always emphasized relationship (Anderson & Hopkins, 1991). And thanks to the women's liberation movement and, more recently, the men's movement and the work of such people as the poet Robert Bly (1992), the demanding "R" word is no longer anathema to men, even in the West.

RELIGION AND MORALITY: INNER CREATIVITY AT THE SITUATIONAL LEVEL

So far we have been discussing inner creativity at the fundamental level. Although true transformation of the individual context of living occurs only with fundamental creativity, for which spiritual insight is an essential component, there is a very important role for situational creativity as well—the popularization and explication of meaning of the paths that the great exemplars of inner creativity have traveled. This is how the great religions and ethical and moral systems of the world have gained influence.

But the dominance of people of situational creativity in the areas of religion and morality produces much consternation and confusion. Situational creatives cannot always live by the contexts they preach; their beings are not always transformed. Although they may display unusual clarity and wisdom, they also may create confusion in the minds of their followers when their inability to practice what they preach is obvious. There is no substitute for fundamental creativity.

---

[2]For a review of some traditional methods of inner creativity (called *bhakti* yoga) using relationship, see Goswami (1993a, Ch. 17).

THE FOUR-FOLD SPLENDOR OF CREATIVITY

Let's summarize the typology of creativity. I am recognizing two broad categories of creativity—inner and outer. Outer creativity refers to creative acts in the sociocultural or knowledge arena. Inner creativity involves acts in the arena of the self.

What is creativity? To see the potency of creativity, we must realize that creativity is a discontinuous jump out of the existing system. When this discontinuous jump out of the system involves a new context of value that manifests a new product, it is an act of fundamental creativity.

Then there is situational creativity. Although it largely involves reason-based and algorithmic procedures, it also involves the subjective exploration of new meaning in old contexts that discontinuously culminates in a surprise, a product that could not be anticipated.

Within each of the categories of outer and inner creativity are these two types of creative acts, fundamental and situational; the phenomenon of creativity seems to manifest in a four-fold polarity (Figure 4.1). All great art and all great scientific discoveries fall into the category of fundamental outer creativity. Technological invention belongs in the category of situational outer creativity. Fundamental inner creativity involves a change in the context of living. Situational inner creativity consists largely of products involving reason-based clarification of the contexts of living discovered via fundamental inner creativity. The world's great religions and systems of ethics and morality mostly grew out of the situational creativity of people. Buddha and Jesus were fundamental inner creatives, but the people who founded and developed Buddhism and Christianity were mostly situational creatives.

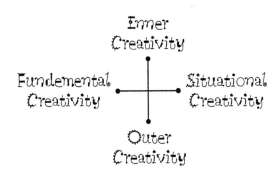

Figure 4.1. The four-fold polarity of creativity.

POLARITY AND INTEGRATION

One problem in developing an integrated theory of creativity has always been the many-faceted nature of this leprechaun—it is not a single phenomenon but consists of several phenomena. We can invoke materialist/mechanist theories to explain the mere mechanical, problem-solving aspects of creativity. But to understand the value and meaning that are involved in creative acts, organismic theories seem more appropriate because of the emphasis on purpose. And to understand inner creativity, we need an explicitly idealist theory that poses consciousness as the ground of being. The quantum idealist-science approach explicated in this book encompasses all the different phenomena of creativity because it involves an integration of all these different worldviews.

In idealist science, we emphasize both outer and inner creativity because the purposiveness of the universe expresses itself in both inner and outer directions—and not as independent developments, either.

The manifest universe is the result of consciousness dichotomizing itself into separate subject and object for the sake of experience (see Chapter 7). The separateness, however, is a "pretend" one and is, in the final philosophical reckoning, an illusion. The outer objects thus projected are employed by consciousness to manifest its fundamental themes—this is the project of outer creativity. Science, then, is the attempt by consciousness to explicate the laws of creation that are part of its theme-collective, the context-bank.

And there is also an evolution of inner movement, inner creativity, because the outer development depends on the growth of the inner. In return, the outer contributes new contexts for inner growth. They are mutually dependent developments.

How do we account for the two levels, fundamental and situational creativity? Why two levels? In idealist philosophy, which grew out of the experiences of real people's inner creativity, consciousness partakes of two levels of self-identity (idealist science confirms this, see Chapter 7). The first is the ego, which is personal; the second "inner" self, variously called the *atman* (in Hinduism), the Holy Spirit (in Christianity), and so forth, is universal, transpersonal. (In idealist science, it is called the quantum self.) The two levels of creativity reflect the two-level identity of our self. In our ego identity, in which we live most of our adult lives, we are capable only of manipulating the old and interested primarily in prediction and control. Naturally, inventive arts and sciences suit us because they need only little forays into the universal inner self, involving less risk to the ego. But ultimately, of course, inventions depend on the discovery of new contexts. So we also engage in fundamental creativity in which we more substantially engage with our inner self-identity. It is rarer because it is riskier to the ego. It fits: two different self-identities, two different types of creativity.

In your pursuit of creativity, how close do you want to be to the One? Einstein wanted to be close to the mind of the "old one." He never looked back; he was hooked on fundamental creativity. But others of us are perfectly happy exploring and elucidating the discovered contexts of fundamental creatives and only occasionally glimpsing the One.

You can display the product
of your outer creativity
like a sun-lumined blossom on the bush.
Its perfume you share with others.

But you are the blossom
that opens from inner creativity.

Have you meditated,
accepted the inner invitation?
Follow the trail of transformation.
Then only, oh creative, you share your being.

PART TWO

QUANTUM CREATIVITY

Reader: I like some of what you are saying, but I wish you had some other way to say it. Frankly, I don't like physics. It scares me, and that applies to quantum physics, too. Understanding creativity should be simpler.

Author: I sympathize. Einstein said something to the effect that we should make our theories simple, but not simpler than they really are. I hope the definitions and classifications of creative phenomena in the last two chapters have amply demonstrated that understanding creativity requires the introduction of discontinuity, consciousness, and meaning into the theory. And these attributes necessitate a quantum physics framework.

R: Let's take discontinuity. I'm not sure what discontinuity is. Things or thoughts, they always seem continuous to me. Truly, I don't remember a clear-cut case of having an experience of discontinuity.

A: On the contrary, I think intuitively you do realize that creative acts are discontinuous leaps, and therefore, you know what discontinuity is. In a delightful Sidney Harris cartoon, Einstein, baggy pants and all, stands before a blackboard with chalk in hand, ready to discover a new law. On the board, the equation $E = ma^2$ is written and crossed out; under it $E = mb^2$ is also crossed out. The caption reads, *"The Creative Moment."* Why do you laugh at it? It is a marvelous caricature of a creative moment precisely because we all intuitively recognize that a creative insight involves a discontinuous shift of context and does not follow such "reasoned" steps.

R: You make a good point. But is quantum physics the only vehicle to explain the discontinuity of creativity?

A: I'm afraid so. All Newtonian mechanisms are continuous.

R: Alright, I'll accept that. Now, let's turn to consciousness. You say it takes consciousness to consider quantum possibilities and to choose an actual event from among these possibilities. Why?

A: Remember, quantum objects are possibility waves because of the play of the uncertainty principle. Quantum objects expand as waves of possible events (involving such attributes as position and momentum) in the cloud of ignorance that the uncertainty principle creates. Only consciousness contains the knowledge that can remove ignorance.

R: Are you asking me to believe that this room I am in, this desk I work at, this earth under the gravity force of the sun, all disappear from existence as soon as nobody is looking?

A: I didn't say all these things disappear from existence. They exist, but only as potentia, as possibility, when no one is looking. Sometimes, for example, for massive objects like a desk, the possibility is pretty compulsory, so whenever you look, you find the desk at the same place. This is the correspondence principle. And as for gravity, it and all other natural laws continue as parameters that determine the possibilities according to the quantum laws of motion, that determine how matter will manifest when we look.

R: I see. I have another concern. I know about manifest choices. When I come to a crossroads, I decide whether to turn or to go straight. But I don't understand choosing from waves of possibility. Where are they? Why don't I see them before I choose?

A: Possibility waves themselves cannot be manifest in their simultaneous multiple forms. They reside in a transcendent domain of reality. But who says you don't "see" them? You don't see them as objects separate from you in space-time, to be sure. But creatives claim to process possibilities, and it is in the processing that one never-before-considered possibility pops out. Then they bring these gems from transcendent heaven to earth. You do, too, in your creative acts. We all do it routinely in childhood. Only our conditioning, our entrenched habits—the functional fixedness of our minds—keep us from doing it more frequently as adults.

R: That's worth thinking about. But I have an objection to your idea that consciousness makes actuality out of possibility. Suppose you and I both consider the same possibilities? Who gets to choose?

A (laughing): Me, of course, I am the physicist. But seriously, this is a very paradoxical issue that stymied any real consideration of a consciousness-based interpretation of quantum mechanics for a long time. In the literature it is called the paradox of Wigner's friend. Wigner arrives at a street light at the same time that his friend drives up from the crossroad. They both want a green light. The light is operated by a radioactive atom whose quantum probabilistic decay shifts the light. So whose choice counts? If Wigner says it is his choice that counts, he is thinking in terms of what philosophers call solipsism, that is, only Wigner's consciousness is real and everybody else is just Wigner's imagination. But if Wigner's friend has a choice as potent as Wigner's, then pandemonium will erupt all over the world when such clashes of choice take place.

R: You have articulated the paradox very well. Thank you.

A: Thank Wigner. But do you see where the difficulty comes from? It is thinking that we *have* consciousness, that we possess individual consciousness as we do individual brains. You have to radically shift your idea of what consciousness is. The consciousness that chooses actuality from quantum possibility is one. In that consciousness where choice happens, we are all one; there is no separate you or me who chooses.

R: But I don't feel that you and I are one. I see myself as quite separate from you.

A: This is not a creative perception but a very conditioned one. The one becomes many because of conditioning. At the moment, your ego is asserting itself (as is mine) as we engage in rational, intellectual discourse. Creativity is one of the rare instances when we glimpse the oneness of consciousness.

R: That seems clear enough. But if it is one consciousness that creates, what's the brain for? What's the individual for?

A: The brain contains the mystery behind manifestation. Somebody once said, if the brain were so simple that we could understand it, we would be so simple that we couldn't. One of the not-so-simple-to-understand things about the brain is why self-reference—the subject-object split of the world—occurs in its presence. This part of the book deals with that question.

R: One last question. What is the role of the mind in all this?

A: The mind gives meaning to the interaction of consciousness and matter. Think of yourself watching television. All those pictures are simple electronic movements on the screen. Who puts into those electronic patterns the picture of Jenny becoming angry with her boyfriend for paying too much attention to Violet? You do, with the help of your mind. It's routine when we watch television. But when our minds are imagining something new that brings new meaning, we are creative.

5

CONTINUITY AND DISCONTINUITY

At Carnegie Mellon University, the artificial intelligence researcher Pat Langley, then a doctoral candidate in computer science, wrote a program, *Bacon,* that, seemingly true to its namesake, was able to discover a scientific law (Langley et al., 1987). When he punched in some numbers representing the distances of the solar planets from the sun and some other numbers representing the orbital periods of the planets (the length of their "years"), *Bacon* figured out after some computing that the square of a planet's orbital time period varies in direct proportion to the cube of its distance from the sun. This relationship is Kepler's third law of planetary motion, discovered by that eccentric, 17th-century genius only after years of patient research. Is the program *Bacon* as or more creative than a creative human like Kepler? Significantly, the program uses a set of algorithms—systematic, reason-based procedures— for solving problems by putting given contexts together that the programmer gave it. Could it be that Kepler was using similar algorithms, although hidden from his awareness?

The answer is no. The context of *Bacon*'s "research" *was* given by its programmer simply by telling *Bacon* to consider the relationship of the numerical values of the distances of the planets from the sun and their time periods of revolution. Kepler's genius, on the other hand, lay precisely in discovering this context for looking at the astronomical data of his mentor, Tycho Brahe, a context that was then programmed into Bacon in the form of a particular set of data. *Bacon*'s skill is admirable,

65

but it is nevertheless simply technological artfulness; it is mechanical problem solving.[1]

Why is the classical computer not able to shift to a new context or to see new meaning? Computer programs process symbols, not the meaning or context of symbols. The context is given by the programmer. You may wonder if we can reserve some of the symbols to act as the meaning of other symbols. But then we will need other symbols for the meaning of these "meaning" symbols. The problem goes on *ad infinitum* (Banerji, 1994; see also Penrose, 1991, 1994).

To summarize, computers act on the basis of algorithms that are based on continuity. Creative discoveries like Kepler's involve discontinuity and are fundamentally nonalgorithmic. Norbert Wiener, a pioneer of computer science, said, "Render unto computers the things that belong to computers, and unto man the things that belong to man." Wiener was right in recognizing the limits of a classical computer.

A prisoner's legs were injured in a machine shop accident. He was sent to the prison hospital where he was closely guarded as an incorrigible. Unfortunately for the prisoner, his left leg developed gangrene and had to be amputated. Being religious, the man insisted that he be given the leg so that he could give it to a friend for proper disposal. When his friend visited, the prisoner gave him his leg while the guard watched silently.

But the prisoner's condition worsened and his right leg too became gangrenous and was amputated. Again when his friend came to visit, the prisoner delivered this leg for proper disposal. Now the guard became suspicious. After the friend left, the guard confronted the prisoner. "What is all this, giving your legs to your friend? Are you trying to escape?"

Well, no prisoner ever has escaped piece by piece—it's all or nothing. Similarly, nobody has ever discovered a new context for a creative act bit by bit. Bit-by-bit activity, reasoning, comes into play only after the creative change of context occurs; then a structure based on the new context is built. Reason lets us explore and extend as far as possible within the known context, but it does not enable us to jump levels. It is not adequate for a creative act of novelty in context or meaning because, ultimately, reason is based on continuity.

In this outlook, we view computer programs for what they realistically can represent, a great potential for helping us to combine learned contexts or to search the problem space for a learned context that will fit a new situation. But the exploration of new meaning and context will always belong to us, conscious beings.

---

[1]Essentially the same point is made by Gardner (1993).

DISCONTINUITY IN CREATIVITY

Creative ideas come to us, in physicist Nicola Tesla's phrase, "like a bolt of lightning." Creative thoughts that shift our contexts or reveal new meaning are discontinuous leaps from our ordinary stream-of-consciousness thoughts, as the following example clearly shows.

Henry Poincare pondered a mathematical problem for days, but nothing happened in his stream of consciousness, in his step-by-step thinking. But later, on a trip, the creative idea—a new context for mathematical functions—came unexpectedly, discontinuously, as he was boarding a bus. The idea had no connection to his thoughts at the time or to the content and contexts of his previous, bit-by-bit, continuous thinking on the subject, he later reported (Poincare, 1924).

Similarly, it is said about certain great composers such as Mozart and Brahms that their music came to them as a whole theme, not with bit-by-bit continuity. And the romantic poet Samuel Coleridge was said to be inspired with the entire poem of *Kubla Khan*.

One of the most spectacular original discoveries in science is Heisenberg's co-discovery of the fundamental mathematical equation of quantum mechanics. Niels Bohr's idea of quantum jumps had been experimentally verified so that, by 1925, everybody knew that Newton's equation of motion did not hold in atomic physics. But that was practically all they knew; nobody had any idea about how to proceed to create the new mechanics.

In this context, Werner Heisenberg, a young man in his 20s, discovered that if he took the possible quantum jumps in an atom and arranged them in an array, these quantities obeyed an equation that no classical physicist had ever seen but that had all the new properties expected from the new mechanics. These arrays were known in mathematics; they are called *matrices*. But Heisenberg had never heard of them and seldom had anybody used such quantities in physics. They are very different from ordinary numbers. If you multiply 3 by 4, you get 12; if you multiply 4 by 3, you still get 12. For ordinary numbers, the order of multiplication makes no difference—a property called *commutativity*. Heisenberg's new quantum quantities, the matrices, do not commute; for them the order in which you perform their multiplication does make a difference.

When I naively entered the dating scene many years ago, I quickly discovered that for daters the order of the two questions, "Do you like me?" and "Do you love me?", mattered very much. I had to learn to discriminate. Heisenberg taught the world of physics to discriminate the order for multiplying quantum quantities, and quantum mechanics was born. Quantum mechanics is so great a new context that we still are deciphering its meaning, as this book exemplifies.

From the objective standpoint of materialism, subjective analyses of discontinuous shifts in consciousness, such as Bohr's discovery of quantum leaps and Heisenberg's discovery of quantum mechanics, are suspect as evidence for the discontinuity in creativity, so we continue to debate this important issue. But there is another source of suggestive support: Mythology, said the philosopher William Irwin Thompson, is the history of the soul (consciousness). The importance of discontinuity in creative acts is immortalized by the story of Newton's apple—the falling of an apple is said to have triggered a discontinuous shift in Newton's thinking on gravity.

DISCONTINUITY IN NEWTON'S DISCOVERY OF GRAVITY

It was 1665, and a plague had broken out in Cambridge, England. The University of Cambridge closed, and Isaac Newton, who was teaching at the university, moved to his mother's farm in Lincolnshire. There one day in the garden, Newton saw an apple fall to earth. This triggered in his consciousness the insight of universal gravity: Every object attracts every other with the force of gravity.

What does the apple story mean to you? Apples fall every day; hardly anyone notices. This was just as true in Newton's time as it is in ours. Yet the apple story tells us of Newton's enlightenment by this trivial event. How can this happen?

According to many historians, the apple story is not fact but fancy, perhaps started my Newton's niece. But why does the apple story survive? I think that the suddenness of creativity is such a common experience among scientists that it has been mythologized in the apple story. Indeed, I think Newton's apple story portrays how a creative act *has to be.*

Unfortunately, Newton left no hint about the discovery process that led him to the law of gravity. But it is not difficult to reconstruct Newton's discovery in a way that shows how the sudden insight came about.

The planets revolve around the sun in nearly circular orbits. Before Newton, Johannes Kepler analyzed the planetary motions and formulated some laws. One of Newton's beginning questions was to find an explanation for Kepler's laws.

Newton himself formulated the laws of motion that tie the motion of objects to the external forces acting on them. Newton must have recognized that planetary motion should be the result of an attractive force exerted by the sun on a planet (or in the case of the moon's motion around the earth, an attractive force from the earth to the moon). The problem was there was no such known force.

Another of Newton's curiosities involved Galileo's work on bodies falling toward earth. Seeing the apple fall triggered in Newton's consciousness the creative idea that the two movements, the apple's and the moon's, owe their origin to a universal "gravity" force that the earth exerted on each of them.

In psychology there is a word, a very revealing word—gestalt. Basically, it means the whole, the perception of an integrated pattern instead of a collection of separate fragments. Suddenly, discontinuously, the pattern clicks in the mind of the beholder, as when the gestalt of the young and the old woman in the same lines of Figure 5.1 appears.

The perception of the gestalt is in the realization of the harmony of a musical composer's pattern of notes. It is in the sudden burst of pleasure one gets by looking at some of M. C. Escher's drawings and recognizing the "wholeness" of the artist's pattern. For a student of science, the perception of Newton's gestalt in his discovery of gravity brings similar satisfaction; I hope you've gotten a glimpse of it here. In the throes of creativity, the scientist is not different from a musician or an artist.

I want to make one more point. On a bathroom wall at a freeway gas station, I once saw this riddle: What do Captain Kirk (of Star Trek) and toilet tissue have in common? I spent a few seconds thinking but could not figure out the answer. It was written upside down below the question: They both get rid of Klingons. There is no doubt in my mind that if I searched my memory long enough, I could have solved the riddle. Nor do I doubt that if a computer is equipped with the right problem space, it can solve this riddle.

How are Newton's puzzle and its solution different from this? Newton must have asked, what do the moon and the apple have in common? Well, they both fall toward the earth, although to see that the moon falls, too, is more complicated (Figure 5.2). So earth must be exerting a force on both, the gravity force. Strictly logical, right?

But we are forgetting something. There was a great prejudice (the prevailing context) at the time—the earth was not supposed to exert a force on a heavenly object, the moon. Earthly and heavenly laws were considered to be different; the Greeks told us so. Moreover, no force had ever been known to act at a distance without the intermediary of a rope or a medium or something.

Figure 5.1. A gestalt picture, *My wife and my mother-in-law*, originally by W. E. Hill.

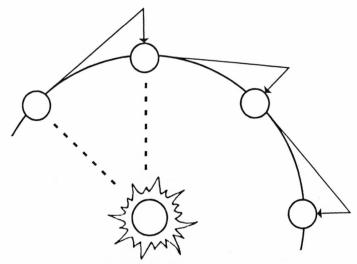

Figure 5.2. The moon remains in orbit around the earth by both traveling tangentially to the orbit and falling toward the earth.

In suggesting that the earth exerted a gravity force on the apple as well as on the moon, Newton was suggesting gravity as a universal force—any two objects interact this way—even though his idea was against the prevailing common sense that there can be no action at a distance. (It took another 250 years before Einstein resolved this difficulty by proving that gravity is curved space and there is no action at a distance after all.)

Thus, the new context for physics that Newton's research unveiled was one no computer could ever find in its problem space made out of known contexts and prevailing prejudices. As the physicist Paul Dirac said, great ideas overcome great prejudices.

UNDERSTANDING DISCONTINUITY

One problem with understanding discontinuity is that we routinely see continuity operating in the macroscopic world around us (in other words, Newtonian physics works there). Fortunately, mathematics has easy-to-understand examples of discontinuity. For example, consider the mathematical concept of infinity. Try to think of an infinitely large number. As soon as you have thought it, say 10^{100} (that's 1 followed by 100 zeroes), it is not infinity, it is a large finite number. You cannot think *continuously* a number that is truly infinite. Infinity is a discontinuity! We can conceptualize it as a number that is large beyond comprehension, but we cannot experience it by bit-by-bit continuous approximation.

Unfortunately, our usual thought patterns are dominated by our seemingly continuous stream of consciousness. So it is easy to rationalize away the discontinuity of a creative act claimed by another person or even one of our own: There must have been a stream, we just don't remember it. But as children, we don't have such inhibitions or rationalizations. To truly appreciate that some of our experiences are indeed discontinuous, it is good to ponder our childhood experiences.

As a child, when I first memorized numbers and learned to count up to 100, I did it because my mother drilled me. She fixed the context, and I did rote learning; the numbers themselves had no meaning for me. Next I was told to consider sets of two—two pencils, two cows—or sets of three—three bananas, three pennies. Then one day, all of a sudden, the difference between two and three (and all other numbers) became clear to me because I had learned to look at numbers within a new context, the concept of the set. And nobody taught this to me. Although the people in my environment facilitated my "getting" it, in the ultimate reckoning it was I who discovered the meaning. And it was like a bolt of lightning! From then on whenever anyone said three, I knew what she meant.

Gregory Bateson, with his definition of levels of learning, offers further insight into the idea of a discontinuous shift of context in learning. According to Bateson (1980), lower level learning, which he called learning I, is learning within a given, fixed context, for example, conditioned or rote learning. And learning II, a higher level learning, is the capacity to shift the context of learning I.

Let's acknowledge the obvious: Level II learning is creative learning, it contributes to inner creativity. It may be re-creation in the historical or objective sense and is much facilitated by good teachers, but nobody can teach it to us.

EXPERIMENTS WITH DOLPHINS

If you look back at your own childhood, you will find ample evidence of discontinuity in your experiences of learning II, as in my experience just cited. Try an exercise. Close your eyes and remember when you had your first experience of (a) comprehending what you were reading, (b) understanding math, (c) executing a spontaneous dance step or bursting out in song, or (d) conceptualizing the context of a number of contents. You will see what I mean. Creative experiences have an interesting signature: the anxiety of seeking without knowing what is sought and the ecstasy of finding, of experiencing the successful leap to uncharted territory. You will remember the agony and the ecstasy, too.

But from an objective-science view, such personal experiences are "subjective," and therefore unreliable. Fortunately, the following work with dolphins offers compelling "objective" evidence of the discontinuity in learning.

A dolphin at the Oceanic Institute in Hawaii had been trained to expect food at the sound of the trainer's whistle. Later, if she repeated whatever she had been doing when the whistle blew, she again would hear the whistle and be given food. This dolphin was employed to demonstrate training techniques to the public, who were told, "When she enters the exhibition tank, I shall watch her and when she does something I want her to repeat, I will blow the whistle and she will be fed." But in order to demonstrate the training technique in repeated public performances, the trainer had to reward a different (new) behavior with the whistle and food at each new performance. Bateson (1980) recognized the significance of the dolphin's behavior in terms of levels of learning:

> All this had happened in the free natural history of the relationship between dolphin and trainer and audience, before I arrived in Hawaii. I saw that what was happening required learning of a higher logical type than usual, and at my suggestion, the sequence was repeated experimentally with a new animal and carefully planned: the animal would experience a series of learning sessions, each lasting from 10 to 20 minutes. The animal would never be

rewarded for behavior which had been rewarded in the previous session. Two points from the experimental sequence must be added: First, it was necessary (in the trainer's judgement) to break the rules of the experiment many times. The experience of being in the wrong was so disturbing to the dolphin that in order to preserve the relationship between her and her trainer (i.e., the context of context of context), it was necessary to give many reinforcements to which the porpoise was not entitled. Unearned fish. Second, each of the first fourteen sessions was characterized by many futile repetitions of whatever behavior had been reinforced in the immediately preceding session. Seemingly only by accident did the animal provide a piece of different behavior.

In the time out between the fourteenth and the fifteenth session, the dolphin appeared to be much excited; and when she came onstage for the fifteenth session, she put on an elaborate performance that included eight conspicuous pieces of behavior of which four were new and never before observed in this species of animal. From the animal's point of view, there is a jump, a discontinuity. (pp. 336-337)

The discontinuity in the dolphin's learning was dramatically evident; there was no gradual improvement until the correct response was learned. Instead, all of a sudden, between the 14th and 15th tries, the dolphin "got it"—from nothing to everything—in a single jump. And we can feel rapport with the way the dolphin acted; her excited behavior indicates the same kind of ecstasy, of ah-ha! insight into new meaning, that we experience in creative moments. (Interestingly, behavioral researchers who have replicated this experiment emphasize the fact that it was important that the dolphins occasionally be offered "unearned" fish, plenty of them, to keep them going [Prior, Haag, & O'Reilly, 1969].) The dolphin experiments provide important empirical evidence that acts of creative learning (and, by implication, all acts of creativity) are acts of discontinuity.

The discontinuity of creativity comes with another telling characteristic—certain knowledge. Remember an occasion when sudden insight revealed the solution to a problem or helped you understand a relationship. Now compare the quality of your certainty on that occasion with one when you relied only on reason. You will see what I mean.

TAKING THE QUANTUM LEAP

Can we see discontinuities in the physical world? We must look at quantum physics for fascinating examples of discontinuity. For instance, when an electron jumps orbits, it does not travel through the intervening space between the discrete orbits. The electron is first here, and then it's there. It disappears in the old orbit and reappears in the new without passing through the space between orbits. And we cannot assign a cause to an individual jump of an individual electron, we can only predict on the average how long it takes a lot of electrons to jump between two orbits of a lot of atoms. The electron's quantum jump is a little like how we imagine real magic to be (not the magic that magicians perform!)—a pumpkin becoming a carriage before Cinderella's eyes with all-of-a-sudden discontinuity.

Can we do quantum mechanics without this magic, without these quantum jumps? Erwin Schrödinger, the co-discoverer of quantum mechanics, was himself biased in favor of continuity. When he visited Bohr in Copenhagen, he protested for days against quantum jumps. Eventually, however, he conceded the point with this emotional outburst, "If I had known that one has to accept this damned quantum jump, I'd never have gotten involved with quantum mechanics." To this Bohr replied, "But we are all glad that you did." The discontinuity of creativity ceases to be puzzling once we realize that it is akin to the electron's quantum leap. An old pattern of thought dies as a new thought pattern replaces it, but there is no causal or local connection between the two events.

Quantum objects develop in time as waves of possibility. If we follow an electron's behavior with the mathematics of quantum mechanics, we find that between measurements the electron spreads as a wave of possibility; but when we measure, it is revealed as a particle localized at one place (Figure 5.3). How can a wave with possibilities to appear in many places collapse at one place on our observation, at once, faster than the speed of light? It is because the event of quantum collapse from possibility to actual event is a discontinuous process.

Similarly, our thoughts are quantum objects. They, too, expand in possibility (becoming superpositions of many possible thoughts) when we are not paying attention to them. If, by chance or perseverance or both, a new possibility arises, and we collapse it by looking, we have a hit, a quantum hit, a discontinuous collapse of a creative event that reveals a new context or a new meaning (see chapter 8).

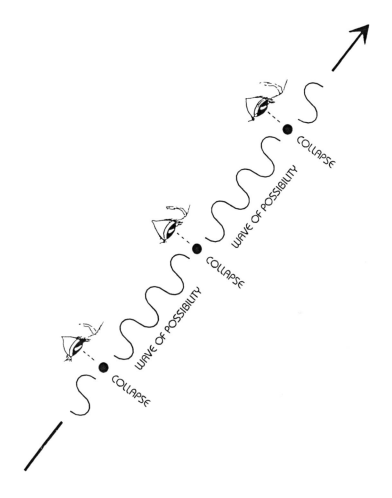

Figure 5.3. When we look, we find the electron localized at one place. But in between observations, an electron spreads out as a wave of possibility in transcendent potentia.

A creative thought is a quantum hit,
no less,
a quantum leap to new context or meaning.
Babies do it, dolphins do it.
Artists, poets, musicians, scientists—
quantum leapers all.
They are not scared by discontinuity.
Are you?

6

WHERE DO CREATIVE IDEAS COME FROM?

The creative act is discontinuous. Here you are, stuck in old, known contexts, and suddenly—bingo, eureka, ah-ha!—a new context appears in your mind's arena. You've discovered a transcendent truth of great beauty. But where was your mind in between the old and new contexts? Let's first look at some old metaphors for the creative journey.

The English romantic poet Samuel Coleridge was quite graphic in describing his own creative journey and its symbols upon waking from a dream. "What if you slept," wrote Coleridge, "and what if in your sleep you dreamed? And what if in your dream you went to heaven and there plucked a strange and beautiful flower? And what if, when you awoke, you had the flower in your hand?" And Coleridge did! His flower was his famous poem, *Kubla Khan.*

What is Coleridge talking about? It sounds so fiction! In fact, science fiction has a concept similar to Coleridge's "heaven." It's called *hyperspace.* I still remember the first time (in the 1960s) I encountered the science fiction concept of hyperspace—it was in Isaac Asimov's *Foundation,* I think, and it just swept me away in imagination. Asimov did not give his reader any picture of what this hyperspace might be except that it enables one to make big jumps through entire galaxies.

Later, I read other science fiction writers who pictured hyperspace as connected with a "quantum jump." Such a jump happens when an electron jumps from one orbit to another in the solar-system configuration within an atom. In this strange jump, the electron never passes through the intervening space between orbits. Instead, it disappears in one orbit and reappears in the other. Where is it between orbits? In hyperspace, according to science fiction writers. When you watch *Star Trek* on television and the captain of the *Enterprise* says "Energize," where do the energized bodies go? To hyperspace, assumes science fiction.

But truth, in fact, is stranger than fiction. In the imagination of *Star Trek* writers, nothing new happens when objects materialize back into ordinary space—but they are missing something really wonderful. In quantum physics, the electrons between jumps are possibility waves in transcendent potentia where probability and uncertainty reign. In this picture, what happens on a quantum leap is uncertain, making room for creativity to enter the picture. Thus the transcendent potentia, the realm of quantum possibilities, serves as a better metaphor for the source of creativity than hyperspace or Coleridge's heaven.

The metaphor of the transcendent domain of possibilities to characterize the quantum jump is similar to that used by people of many cultures to describe an act of creation, as in this myth of a Native American tribe of California:

> Everything was water except a very small piece of ground. On this were the eagle and coyote. Then the turtle swam to them. They sent it to dive for the earth at the bottom of the water. The turtle barely succeeded in reaching the bottom and touching it with its foot. When it came up again, all the earth seemed washed out. Coyote looked closely at its nails. At last he found a grain of earth. Then he and the eagle took this and laid it down. From it they made the earth as large as it is. (quoted in Malville, 1975, pp. 92-93)

An act of creation is seen here as diving deep into another world (the domain of potentia)—the ocean, for these people—to find a grain of new "earth" (possibilities) from which to build.

When the electron jumps from a higher energy level to a lower level in an atom, light is emitted. Thus, when the electron dives into the unknown ocean of uncertainty that we call potentia, it brings back something; because the electron plunges into another world, it brings something new to our world—a brilliant photon (the quantum of light). It is the same with us. As in the just cited creation myth, our creative acts come from a transcendent domain of potentia to which we dive to mine the hidden treasure of the quantum mind. As we plunge into that unknown world, taking a quantum leap from the ordinary mind, we encounter precious jewels of formless entities. These are the archetypal themes—the contexts—that form the essence of creative work. As we bring them back through quantum measurements in our brain-mind system, forms take shape around the formless archetype—bells ring, joy reverberates, and a creative act is born.

CREATIVITY AND MATHEMATICS

Several years ago I was complaining to the dolphinologist John Lilly about the difficulty of explaining transcendence; that many researchers don't understand the radicalness of creative discoveries because they don't understand transcendence. Lilly said, "I have a simple proof of transcendence. I simply ask, Where does mathematics come from?"

The mathematician Roger Penrose expresses a similar view in his book, *The Emperor's New Mind* (1991). Penrose invites us to explore the famous Goedel's theorem to see clearly the nonalgorithmic nature of discoveries in mathematics.

Speaking simply, the purport of Goedel's theorem is this: Whatever mathematical system of algorithms is used to ascertain mathematical truth, if the system is sufficiently elaborate, there is always a proposition within the system that the system cannot prove. Although the mathematician can see the validity of the proposition without a doubt, the algorithmic system of logic is unable to prove it (Penrose, 1991). In other words, mathematicians, when they discover mathematics, *jump out of the system.* They bring mathematical truth from a transcendent world.

In the same vein, if mathematical scientific laws guide the behavior of material objects, they must exist a priori to matter, transcending the material world.

ABSOLUTE AND RELATIVE TRUTH

Acts of creativity are acts of value, eternal absolute values. One of these values is truth. All acts of fundamental creativity are in some way attempts to express some absolute transcendent truth—this truth is a common aspect of the archetypal themes. "My country is truth," intuited the poet Emily Dickinson.

Confusion arises because often what a poet or artist portrays looks nothing like what we ordinarily call truth—the whole truth. The face of the artist's truth shifts from context to context; it is, as the

Russian painter Wassily Kandinsky said, "constantly moving in slow motion." This is because absolute truth is transcendent,. No perfect description of it in immanence is possible, as Herman Hesse reminds us in these lines from *Siddhartha:*

> Everything that is thought and expressed in words is one-sided, only half truth; it all lacks totality, completeness, unity. When the illustrious Buddha taught about the world, he had to divide it into Sansara and Nirvana, into illusion and truth, into suffering and salvation. One cannot do otherwise, there is no other method for those who teach. But the world itself, being in and around us, is never one-sided. Never is a man or deed wholly Sansara or Nirvana. (1973, p. 112)

Reality consists of both Nirvana and Sansara, both the transcendent (potentia) and the immanent (manifestation); our creativity attempts to express the transcendent absolute in the relativity of the immanent; it tries to encapsulate the infinite within finitude. It never quite succeeds and thus never meets its goal. A television character, trying to explain his garbled statement, said, "You should have heard it before I said it." Strangely, he had a point. Expression compromises truth-value.

Even our scientific laws do not express absolute truth, the whole truth. Science progresses when old laws yield to new ones as interpretations of the data change or theory and new data emerge, ever extending the domains of science.

Realizing that creativity is goal directed—one of the goals being to bring transcendent truth into immanence—we can understand the emphasis on product for a creative act. The product enables the creator to share the discovered truth with the immanent world; this sharing is part and parcel of creative purposiveness.

With the idea of truth-value for an act of creativity, we begin to understand how we judge a particular act but not another to be creative. Creative are those acts in which we sense a truth-value. The archetypal themes are well represented, although in some cases (as in the case of Copernicus' heliocentric system or Van Gogh's great impressionist art), this recognition of truth-value may take a long time.

Sometimes a particular creative artist is so successful in depicting an archetypal theme, the truth-value of his or her art is so authentic, that the art becomes immortal. Shakespeare's plays touch us even today (as they will millennia hence) because he was a master in his exploration of archetypal themes, especially emotional themes. "Truth is that which touches the heart," said the novelist William Faulkner. Was he thinking of Shakespeare? Othello's jealousy, Shylock's greed, MacBeth's lust for power come alive on stage even today because *we* feel alive and one with the truth of the emotions they generate. Compare this to the best-selling entertainment put out by the publishing, movie, and music industries every year; they don't lack in the archetypes, but they lack in truth-value, and very few of them sell well beyond a season.

BEAUTY

Creative truth may not come with perfection, but it comes with beauty. The poet John Keats said, "Truth is beauty, beauty truth." Another poet, Rabindranath Tagore, wrote, "Beauty is truth's smile when she beholds her own face in a perfect mirror." If the authenticity of a creative insight cannot quite be judged on its truth-value, which is bound to be relative, at least it can be judged by its beauty.

Physicist Paul Dirac, one of the early architects of quantum mechanics, discovered a mathematical equation that predicts the existence of antimatter, material stuff that annihilates regular matter on contact. At the time, there was no reason to believe that such a thing existed, but Dirac was guided by a keen sense of beauty. "It seems that if one is working from the point of view of getting beauty in one's equations, and if one has really a sound insight, one is on a sure line of progress." Indeed, Dirac's prediction came true a few years later.

Similarly, Einstein, in his quest for a theory to connect gravity to the curvature of space, was guided by the great beauty of nature's symmetry. After he discovered his theory and it was verified, a newswoman asked Einstein how he would have felt if the experiment had not confirmed his theory. To that Einstein said, "I'd feel sorry for the dear Lord. My theory is right."

A legend about the medieval Bengali poet Jaidev makes a similar point. Jaidev was in the middle of a scene in his masterpiece, *Gita Govinda*, in which Krishna is trying to appease his angry consort Radha. An inspired line of great beauty came to the poet's mind, and he wrote it down. But then he had second thoughts. Krishna is God incarnate, how could Krishna say such a human thing. So he crossed the line out and went for a walk. The legend is that while the poet was gone, Krishna himself came and resurrected the line. So great is the power of beauty in creative acts.

But what is beauty? Who judges it? Some authors try to find intellectual, emotional, or sociocultural causes for aesthetic experience;

some say beauty is experienced intellectually by seeing order and harmony where ordinary people see chaos. Yet it is a truism that beauty is in the eyes of the beholder, the creative person. Dirac put it well when he said, "Well—you feel it. Just like beauty in a picture or beauty in music. You can't describe it, it's something—and if you don't feel it, you just have to accept you are not susceptible to it. No one can explain it to you." When Pythagoras defined beauty as "the reduction of many to one," he was speaking of a very personal, transcendent experience. The poet Khalil Gibran said the same thing:

> And beauty is not a need but an ecstasy
> It is not a mouth thirsting nor an empty
> hand stretched forth,
> But rather a heart enflamed and a soul enchanted.
> It is not the image you would see nor the
> song you would hear,
> But rather an image you see though you
> close your eyes and a song you hear though
> you shut your ears.
> It is not the sap within the furrowed bark,
> nor a wing attached to a claw,
> But rather a garden for ever in bloom and
> a flock of angels for ever in flight. (1971, pp. 75-76)

TRANSCENDENCE AND QUANTUM NONLOCALITY

The dictionary definition of creation—to bring something into being or form out of nothing—is an enigma until you recognize that *nothing* also means no thing. Creation is bringing form out of transcendent possibilities that are not things. All quantum objects evolve as possibilities in transcendent potentia until brought to immanence—thingness—by collapse via conscious observation. However, can we experimentally verify the transcendence of "objects in potentia"—no things? We can.

In quantum mechanics, we can correlate objects so that they remain interconnected even while they travel (in potentia) vast distances. When we observe, then the correlated quantum objects collapse into actualities, into separateness, but the nature of their collapse shows without doubt that they were correlated. How was the correlation preserved over a long distance and without an exchange of signals? Clearly, the correlation is nonlocal, existing in a domain of interconnectedness that transcends the immanent space-time domain of reality. It is in this way that transcendence is synonymous with quantum nonlocality.

Our understanding and acceptance of a transcendent realm has become widespread even among scientists as a result of an experiment in quantum physics conducted in 1982 by a group of French physicists led by Alain Aspect (Aspect, Dalibar, & Roger, 1982). This was an experiment in which two correlated quanta of light—photons—influence one another at a distance without exchanging signals. A description of this experiment will help to clarify further the nonlocality of the quantum measurement process.

Because quantum objects are waves of possibilities before we observe them, a photon has no attribute until a measurement is done on it. Aspect's experiment concentrated on a two-valued attribute of the photon called polarization, either along or perpendicular to some axis (an attribute that light acquires when it passes through a polaroid sunglass; the two-valuedness is clear when you realize that no light photon can pass through two crossed polaroids, one with axis vertical, the other horizontal). In Aspect's experiment, an atom emits a pair of photons so correlated that if one is polarized along a certain axis, the other should be polarized along the same axis. But quantum objects are only possibilities, so photons start as superpositions of both possible polarizations; only our observation can fix a polarization axis for them. And if we observe one correlated photon, thereby giving it a designated polarization, the other photon's polarization is also instantly designated, no matter how far it is from the first photon. If the two photons are so far apart when we measure one that not even light (which travels with the fastest speed in nature) can mediate its influence on the other, we must conclude that the influence is nonlocal, taking place without the intermediary of local signals. This is what Aspect and his collaborators found experimentally (Aspect et al., 1982).

Thus, the phase correlation of quantum waves, their dancing in step, is a nonlocal correlation existing in a nonlocal transcendent domain that connects one spatial location with another without going through the intervening space and without any time delay. Translated in terms of people, if two people are correlated (by interacting in some suitable way) and then move to the opposite ends of the earth, if one of them touches a cactus and feels the prick, the other one will feel the prick as well (Figure 6.1). Sound preposterous?

Physicist Leo Szilard once invited two other physicists, Murray Gell-Mann and Marvin Goldberger, to an international meeting on arms control. But Goldberger was busy and could come only for the second half of the conference. When Szilard looked at Gell-Mann, Gell-Mann said he could come only for the first half. Szilard thought for a moment and then said with his inimitable wit, "No, it is no good; your neurons are not interconnected." Gell-Mann who tells this anecdote, goes on to

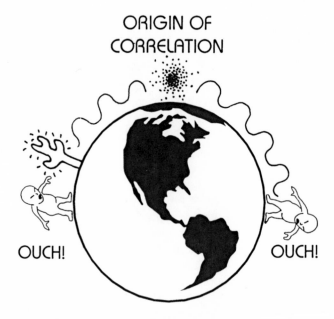

Figure 6.1. The miracle of nonlocal correlations. Once correlated at some origin, if one subject hits a cactus, the other feels a prick, too. Is this just a metaphor?

make some futuristic comments about how two brains might be wired up some day to the same computer, thereby sharing neurons.

Can two people share their neurons without a futuristic computer? Judge for yourself the meaning of the following experiment.

The recent experiment by the Mexican neurophysiologist Jacobo Grinberg-Zylberbaum and his collaborators (Grinberg-Zylberbaum, Delaflor, Attie, & Goswami, 1994) directly supports the idea of quantum nonlocality in human brains. This experiment is the equivalent for brains of the objective Aspect experiment. Two subjects are instructed to meditate together for a period of 20 minutes in order to establish a "direct communication"; they then enter separate Faraday chambers (metallic enclosures that block all electromagnetic signals) while maintaining their direct communication for the duration of the experiment. One of the subjects is then shown a light flash that produces an evoked potential (an electro-physiological response produced by a sensory stimulus that is measurable by an electroencephalogram, [EEG]) in the stimulated brain. But amazingly, in about one in four cases, the unstimulated brain also shows an electrical activity, a "transferred" potential quite similar in shape and strength to the evoked potential (Figure 6.2). (Control subjects who do not meditate together or are unable to establish direct communication never show any trans-

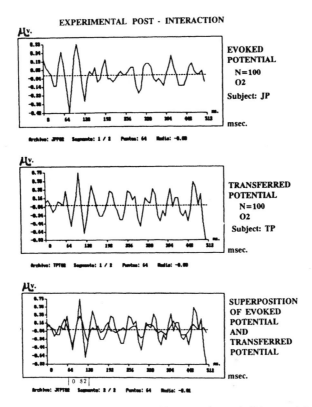

Figure 6.2. In Grinberg-Zylberbaum et al.'s experiment, if two subjects are correlated and one of them is shown a light flash that produces a distinct evoked potential in the EEG attached to his scalp, a transferred potential of comparable strength and phase appears in the nonstimulated partner's EEG. Note the difference of scale of the ordinate in the two figures. (Courtesy: Jacobo Grinberg-Zylberbaum)

ferred potential ([Figure 6.3].) The straightforward explanation is quantum nonlocality—the two brain-minds act as a nonlocally correlated quantum system. In response to a stimulus to only one of the correlated brains, consciousness collapses identical states in the two brains; hence, the similarity of the brain potentials.[1]

Clearly, there is a striking similarity between correlated brains and correlated photons, but there is also a striking difference. The similarity is that in both cases the initial correlation is produced by some "interaction." The difference is that in the former case, as soon as the possibility wave is collapsed by measurement, the objects become

[1]A technical note. The nonlocality of collapse by consciousness is crucial in understanding how different brain areas can be involved, as they usually are, in mental events, including creative thoughts.

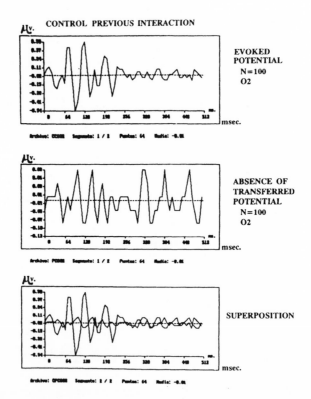

Figure 6.3. A control subject without correlation, even when there is a distinct evoked potential in the stimulated subject's EEG, shows no transferred potential. Note scale. (Courtesy: Jacobo Grinberg-Zylberbaum)

uncorrelated; but in the case of the correlated brains, consciousness maintains the correlation over the 100 light flashes that are needed to get the average evoked potential. This difference is highly significant. The nonlocality of correlated photons, although striking in terms of demonstrating the radicalness of quantum physics, cannot be used to transfer information, according to a theorem attributed to the physicist Philippe Eberhard (1978). But in the case of the correlated brains, because consciousness mediates the correlation, Eberhard's theorem does not apply, and message transfer is not forbidden.

     If we apply this situation to the creative act, it follows that there may be instances in which two people may have the same creative idea across space and time but without any local contact between them. Evidence for this kind of correlated creativity may lie in the many instances of multiple discoveries—discovery of the same theme, be it in science or the arts, by two or more people separated in space and time (Lamb & Easton, 1984). The nearly simultaneous discovery of calculus by Isaac Newton and Gottfried Liebnitz and, earlier in this century, the co-discovery of quantum mechanics by Werner Heisenberg and Erwin Schrödinger are two examples of multiple creativity.

Some researchers, notably Dean Simonton (1988), argue that simultaneous discoveries are actually not the same discoveries: "The calculus of Newton was not identical to that of Leibniz." But they miss the point. The insight that Leibniz had was the same as Newton's, but it was manifested through different ego-structures. That explains the relatively trivial differences between their calculuses.

However, in view of the line of research by Grinberg-Zylberbaum et al. (1994), it may be possible to settle the issue of the mechanism of multiple discoveries via an objective experiment. To show quantum nonlocality directly in the creative process, perhaps we can hook up well-known pairs of scientific or artistic collaborators with EEG machines that measure their brain potentials and look for synchrony between the electrical activity of their brains when they are at the height of their creative collaboration and when they feel that they are in direct communication, albeit at a distance. Such experimental support of nonlocality has been found for subjects meditating together (Grinberg-Zylberbaum & Ramos, 1987).

BRAINSTORMING

Brainstorming is the name given to a process in which several people sit down together and discuss a problem with the idea of generating a large number of possible solutions. The idea is to create a permissionary atmosphere in which inhibiting criticisms are avoided and constructive combinations of ideas proliferate. Wild ideas are encouraged, as is quantity. Any judgment on the generated ideas is deferred.

There is controversy about the effectiveness of the process. For example, some studies claim that deferring judgment really may not help at all; subjects who self-criticize perform equally well or better in problem solving. I suspect that when we are dealing with problem solving, as in these studies, there may well be no particular advantage in brainstorming.

However, for projects that involve creativity—a subjective exploration of meaning and context—brainstorming may be effective because of nonlocal correlations among the participants. It might be illuminating to study people's EEGs for phase-coherent electrical activities as they brainstorm while working on a project requiring creativity. It is also imperative that the subjects chosen are true creatives and the question they ponder be a burning question (personally speaking) for all. Admittedly, such an experiment is difficult because people move when they brainstorm, but perhaps a suitable protocol can be worked out.

Another fruitful direction for research is dream sharing. Imagine having a relationship problem. After much discussion you and the other person go to sleep. The next morning, when you each relate your dream, it becomes clear that you shared nonlocal consciousness in your dreams which contained similar clues to the solution to your problem. Such dream sharing can yield truly astounding evidence of the nonlocality of consciousness (Magallon & Shor, 1990). If creatives, in the aftermath of working on a problem together, share the elements of the solution presented in their dreams, this would not only be a spectacular "proof" of the nonlocality of creativity but also open a new avenue for achieving creative breakthroughs in brainstorming.

Quantum nonlocality gives us a model for the transcendent origin of a creative idea, an event that paradoxically occurs in manifestation but simultaneously has its roots outside of the manifest world. The transcendent domain of potentia is both nowhere and everywhere— everywhere because nonlocal influences cover everything at every point of space, irrespective of the distance of separation, and nowhere because we cannot localize this influence anywhere in space-time.

Creativity dwells not
in analysis and comparison.
Its abode is the twilight zone
beyond locality.
There emperors and beggars,
creatives, critics, and ordinary people
bathe in the same shower of archetypal themes.

Consciousness moves,
and the quantum catapult of creativity
launches us from the known to the unknown
and back again. From unconscious darkness
comes the light of awareness.
Intuition transports us on quantum wings
into the stream of that movement.

We enter a painting
lose ourselves in music
feel the keen joy or pain of a poem
recognize ourselves in a story
see truth in a scientific law
because an archetype of truth and beauty
vibrates in our heart.
We have drunk from the same
archetypal nectar as the creative!

7

WHO CREATES?

Did you ever hear of Schrödinger's cat? He is the cat in a cage with a radioactive atom, a Geiger counter, a hammer, and a poison bottle. The atom in the cage has a 50-50 chance of decaying in an hour. If the atom decays, the Geiger counter ticks; the triggering of the counter breaks the poison bottle, and the poison kills the cat. If the atom does not decay, none of these things happen, and the cat remains alive at the hour. Quantum mechanics says that this cat is half dead and half alive after the hour (Figure 7.1). This is a paradox.

According to some physicists, quantum mathematics is incomplete; there must be unknown (hidden) variables that resolve the state of the cat to a unique one at all times (Figure 7.2, upper). Realists miss the importance of the paradox to our being. To most physicists, however, quantum mathematics is serious business: The cat really exists as a possibility wave of two contradictory states—dead and alive. Then it makes sense to say that only conscious observation—consciousness—brings about the unique dead-or-alive state of affairs that we see (Figure 7.2, lower).

A young aspiring Zenmaster was trying to discredit an older master in order to gain some of the master's students for himself. He caught a small bird, hid it in his hand, and challenged the master in front of a group of students: "If you are so great, tell us if the bird in my hand is dead or alive." His plan was simple. If the master said "dead," he would let the bird go free. And if the master said "alive," he would kill the bird before displaying it. In either case, the master would

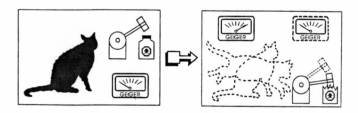

Figure 7.1. The paradox of Schrödinger's cat. On the left, a cat in a cage with radioactive atom (not shown), Geiger counter, hammer, and poison bottle. On the right, the cat, after the hour, is half-dead *and* half-alive. Does quantum mechanics makes sense?

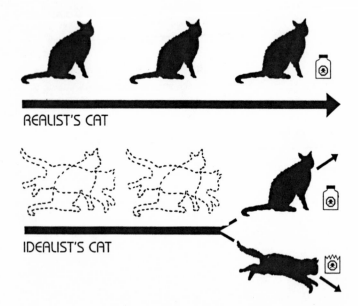

Figure 7.2. The difference between the realist's vision of the cat's progression during the hour (upper) and the idealist's vision (lower). The realist's cat develops in time, causally determined every point on the way. The idealist's cat becomes an evolving coherent superposition that becomes half-dead and half-alive on the hour. Only when *we* look, does the cat's state—dead or alive—actual manifest.

be embarrassingly discredited. "Is the bird dead or alive?", he challenged again. But the master answered him thus: "Really my friend, it is up to you." The old master knew that the bird had become a superposition of dead and alive in the mind of the young monk. For the quantum cat of Schrödinger, this superposition of two possibilities is the state of affairs even for its physical body. Is Schrödinger's cat dead or alive? It is up to consciousness to choose when one looks.

The paradox of Schrödinger's cat is not limited to the cat. The mathematician John von Neumann (1955) showed that if we successively send a whole hierarchy of insentient machines to observe the reading of each previous machine, starting with the one that first attempts to register the state of the cat, it is logical (because all the machines ultimately obey quantum mechanics) that all of them will acquire the quantum dichotomy of the cat's state, ad infinitum. In other words, the so-called "measurement apparatuses" cannot really "measure" a quantum system, that is, collapse its possibility wave. This is why I call them measuring-aid apparatuses.

When the cat catches the contagious quantum superposition of the radioactive atom, we are confronted with the possibility that all material objects in the universe are susceptible to contracting the quantum superposition if we involve them in the observation of the cat. The quantum superposition has taken on a universal contagiousness, a glaring disease of infinity. But the infinitely coupled chain of the system and its measurement-aid apparatuses—the von Neumann chain—does not collapse of itself. Even our brain, looked on as a material machine, cannot make up its mind (Figure 7.3).

If we were only the material brain, the paradox would be insurmountable. But we are not just a material machine. We are also conscious! The remedy for the infinity is to jump out of the system. The remedy is to posit that nonlocal consciousness outside the jurisdiction of quantum mechanics collapses the state of the brain from a domain transcending space-time, thus terminating the von Neumann chain. This is what von Neumann proposed.

Critics of von Neumann, especially material realists, raised objections of dualism: How can consciousness do anything to matter? We don't believe in mind over matter. The remedy of dualism is to invoke the metaphysics of monistic idealism: Consciousness is the ground of being and the material world is not separate from consciousness; it exists as possibilities within consciousness. The collapse consists in choosing and recognizing one facet from the multifaceted superpositions that represent the brain and all the multifaceted states (such as the dead-alive state of the cat) correlated with it.

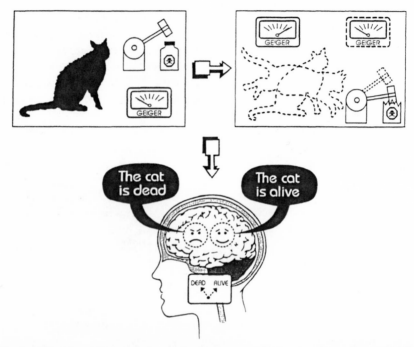

Figure 7.3. Von Neumann's chain. Even an infinite number of measuring apparatuses, including the brain-mind if it were insentient, cannot collapse the cat's dichotomy.

For an analogy, look at the picture in Figure 5.1. When we see the young woman (or the old), we are not doing something to the picture. The possibility of seeing the young woman (or the old) is already there among the lines. We are just recognizing and choosing one of the possibilities.

And the chooser is the one consciousness that we all are behind our diversities; this avoids the paradox of whose choice counts if there is more than one observer for a quantum measurement.

But the antagonist can point out another paradox. The transcendent consciousness of monistic idealism is the ground of being; it is omnipresent, so shouldn't collapse be continuously occurring? If this were true, we would be back to classical deterministic physics—everything always determined!

The resolution of the paradox is that collapse occurs when an observer with a brain looks with awareness. Awareness is the field or context of objects of our experience. When we don't look with awareness, we don't choose; and neither the possibility waves of external objects nor the quantum waves in our own brain collapse. This is the case when unconscious perception or processing is taking place. The difference between unconscious and conscious perception is choice[1] and, consequently, awareness. Consciousness is always present but not always awareness, without which the processing is unconscious.

There is one more paradox. There is no manifest awareness before collapse, before choice. What comes first, the subject-consciousness that chooses or the awareness? This is a chicken-or-the-egg question. The answer is neither; the choosing subject and the awareness of experience are co-created by a tangled hierarchy that is present in the operation of quantum measurement in the brain. The infinity of von Neumann's chain is realized in the brain in the form of a tangled hierarchy that gives us self-reference—our ability to refer to "I" as separate from the objects of our experience.

What is a tangled hierarchy? In a simple hierarchy the lower level affects the upper level, which does not react back (e.g., a space heater heats the room, not the other way around). With a simple feedback the upper level reacts back (e.g., if the space heater has a thermostat), but we still can tell what is upper level and what is lower in the hierarchy. In tangled hierarchies, the two levels are so intertwined (by a discontinuity in the causal chain) that we no longer can identify the different hierarchical levels.

To see how a tangled hierarchy arises in the brain, let us examine a crude model of the brain's response to an ambiguous stimulus (Goswami, 1993a). The stimulus is processed by the sensory apparatus and presented to the dual quantum system/measurement-aid apparatuses in the brain. The state of the quantum machinery expands as a superposition, and all the measurement-aid apparatuses that couple with it in their various roles of amplification and memory making also become superpositions. Of particular importance is the fact that some of the amplifying role is played by apparatuses that are basically of the same size as the quantum system,[2] and the distinction of which is quantum system and which is amplifying apparatus is blurred. In effect, these systems become intertwined in a tangled hierarchy. What happens when consciousness collapses the possibility waves of this tangled hierarchical system of the brain? Self-reference.

---

[1]See Goswami (1990) for a discussion of experimental evidence for this important point; see also chapter 9.

[2]This point has been emphasized by the physicist Henry Stapp (1993).

SELF-REFERENCE

To understand self-reference, consider the famous liar's paradox: Epimenides was a Cretan who said, "All Cretans are liars." This is an example of a tangled hierarchy because the secondary clause reacts back on the primary clause, and soon we lose track of which is primary (i.e., which gives truth value) and which is secondary. Is Epimenides telling the truth? If he is, he must be telling a lie. The answer every time reverberates; if true, then lie, then true, ad infinitum.

Compare the liar's paradox with an ordinary sentence, *the ball is blue*. An ordinary sentence refers to something outside itself, or at least an objective statement can be made of its content. But the complex sentence of the liar's paradox refers back to itself: It is autopoietic, making its own meaning. Tangled hierarchical systems are autonomous. That is how we get caught in their self-delusion—such a system closes within itself and is separate from all else. This is how the tangled hierarchy achieves self-reference (Hofstadter, 1980).

The self-reference arises because we are not able to see through the system causally and logically. It is the discontinuity—in the case of the liar's paradox, the infinite oscillation (infinity is a discontinuity)—that frustrates our logic once our consciousness identifies with the system. In the case of the brain, the discontinuity is that of quantum measurement in the brain, the infinite oscillation between the quantum system and its amplifying apparatuses (because their functions are ambiguous) forming the von Neumann infinite chain.

But there is one more characteristic of a tangled hierarchy that can best be seen by considering the self-referential sentence, *I am a liar*. In this compressed form of the liar's paradox, the self-reference of the sentence is not necessarily self-evident, as can be verified by showing the sentence to a child or a foreigner who is not very conversant with the English language. The response might be, "Why are you a liar?" A child may not easily see that the sentence is referring to itself. The self-reference of the sentence arises from the implicit, not explicit, knowledge of the English language that all native English-speaking adults have. The self-referential sentence is comparable to the tip of an iceberg; there is a vast level underneath that is invisible. This invisible level is an *inviolate* level—a level that is transcendent from a point of view restricted to the system (the sentence cannot go there). Yet it is the inviolate level (in the case of the self-referential sentence, the implicit conventions of our language and, ultimately, we) that is the "cause" of the self-reference of the system (Hofstadter, 1980).

We, our consciousness, are the inviolate level for the self-reference of the self-referential sentence. Similarly, we are also the inviolate level for our own self-reference. We, as transcendent consciousness acting from the inviolate level, collapse the possibility wave of the tangled hierarchical quantum system/measurement-aid apparatuses of the brain; in immanence, there is dependent co-arising of the subject that chooses and the object that is experienced in awareness. It is like the famous Escher picture of drawing hands (Figure 7.4)—the left hand and the right hand seem to draw each other, but behind the curtain of the inviolate level Escher is drawing them both. Similarly, in a quantum measurement in the brain, choice and awareness, subject and object, are apparently co-creating one another, albeit in the final reckoning consciousness is the only cause—even the cause behind self-reference. This self-creation is archetypically depicted as the auroboros—a snake biting its own tail.

Thus, the experiencing subject and the material world are epiphenomena. They are epiphenomena of consciousness, but they are epiphenomena with causal efficacy. The possibility waves of the material world are causally determined by material interactions among the elementary particles and the quantum laws (upward causation); and the subject chooses its experience from among these possibilities (downward causation). In contrast, materialists look upon the self as a causally impotent epiphenomenon of the material brain.

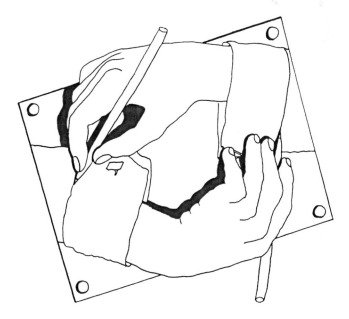

Figure 7.4. Adapted from *Drawing Hands* by M. C. Escher. From the "immanent" reality of the paper, the left and the right hands draw each other, but from the transcendent inviolate level, Escher draws them both.

Within the tangled hierarchy, consciousness forgets itself in its own creation, an action that the Indian philosopher Shankara appropriately called *maya,* illusion. Because of this veil of the tangled hierarchy, consciousness identifies itself with the manifest subject/self, the chooser of the experience. I choose, therefore, (tangled hierarchically) I am (Figure 7.5). This identity of consciousness with the self of the primary-subject experience (as opposed to secondary-self experience—see later) I call the *quantum self,* but it is known by many names in the spiritual traditions of the world. For example, Hindus refer to it by the Sanskrit word *atman,* and in Christianity it is called the Holy Spirit.

We are discovering some of the details of our brain processes in creativity. The measuring-aid apparatuses of the brain tangled hierarchically interact with the quantum machinery; as consciousness self-referentially collapses the brain's states of actuality, they are recorded in the brain. Occasionally, the record captures the music of creativity. (But where is the real action of the music taking place? The processing of meaning and context? The creative meaning is in the mind, not the brain. This is the subject of the next chapter.)

Who creates this music? In this song of creation, there is flow, there is ah-ha, there is spiritual joy, which the East Indians call *ananda,* the third aspect of the trinity, existence-consciousness-joy. It's not just the Indians who exhibit this knowledge of spontaneous quantum-self expression. Writers, artists, athletes, and musicians speak of "flow" experiences when they lose themselves, so thoroughly engaged are they with their acts (Csikszentmihayi, 1990). When the "apple" of insight hits the head, scientists, too, are spontaneous in their creative ah-ha experience, not constrained by the rational, logical stereotypes we have of them. In a certain definite sense, all creatives seem to access a mode of being in which creative spontaneity reigns rather than egoic deliberation. Who creates? Consciousness does (downward causation) in its quantum self-identity. This mode of being, the quantum self, is the real creator in all acts of creation, not our ego. Yet more often than not, past conditioning prevails in our behavior and actions. Why? What is the relationship of the quantum self with the ego?

HOW SCHRÖDINGER'S CAT BECOMES PAVLOV'S DOG

Experiences lead to learning, one aspect of which is developmental changes in the brain's recording substructure—the memories and representations of experience. Additionally, I believe that something profound also takes place in the quantum mechanics of the self-referential quantum system.

In response to a previously experienced stimulus, the quantum machinery of the brain not only interacts with the direct stimulus

Figure 7.5. I choose, therefore (tangled hierarchically as signified by the snake biting its own tail) I am.

(which gives rise to the primary awareness event) but also interacts repeatedly with the secondary stimuli of the memory replay; this gives rise to secondary awareness events on collapse. These reflections in the mirror of memory act as feedback of the past to the current situation; as a result, the probability of actualizing formerly experienced states gradually gains greater weight. The quantum brain gradually becomes conditioned (Mitchell & Goswami, 1992).

A well-known characteristic of learning is that learning a performance reinforces the probability of the same subsequent performance. Remember how Pavlov's dog was conditioned? Pavlov conditioned his dog by cleverly adminstering stimulus-response-reinforcement—reinforce the desired response to a stimulus by a reward (or punishment). This is the same process we see here, administered by nature. In essence, learning increases the likelihood that, after the completion of measurement, the quantum-mechanical states of the tangled hierarchical quantum system/measuring-aid apparatuses will correspond to a prior learned state. In other words, learning biases the quantum dynamics of the brain.

Especially interesting is that, in the limit of infinite conditioning of a task, the likelihood approaches 100% that a learned stimulus involving that task will trigger a conditioned response. In this limit, it seems that the behavior of the brain's dual quantum-system/measuring-aid apparatuses approaches classical determined behavior. Now Schrödinger's quantum cat becomes Pavlov's dog, so to speak. This is the brain analog of the correspondence principle.

Fairly early in our physical development, learning accumulates and conditioned response patterns begin to dominate the brain's behavior, despite the fact that the versatility of the quantum system is always available for new creative play. When the creative potency of the quantum system is not engaged, when the primary-awareness events are not attended, the secondary-awareness processes of memory-replay dominate; the tangled hierarchy of the brain, in effect, becomes a simple hierarchy of the learned classical programs—the representations of past experiences. Then we begin to identify with a separate, individual self, the ego, which perceives apparent continuity in the form of a stream of consciousness, thinks it chooses on the basis of its past experiences, and presumably has "free will." But in truth, this so-called free will of the ego-identity exists only to the extent that the conditioning can only approach 100% but never reach it.

Incidentally, the experiments of neurophysiologist Benjamin Libet and his collaborators (Libet, Wright, Freinsten, & Pearl, 1979) have demonstrated that there is almost half a second of time delay between the primary event of quantum collapse and our verbal awareness of the event. I think that this half-second is the time taken for secondary-awareness processing (see Chapter 11 for further details of Libet's experiment).

> For Pavlov's dog, conditioned certainty.
> But for Schrödinger's cat, ambiguous possibility
>   —there lies creativity.
> Capable in your fixed classical modality,
> you may rest on your laurels.
> But yours is a unique condition:
> Why fear ambiguity? It contains renewal.
>
> Have you a strong ego?
> Yes? Then take a risk, surrender
> to your quantum self. Go ahead
>   —see what happens.
> Pavlov's dog salivates, but gets the same old chow.
> For the truly delicious taste of creativity
>   —dine with Schrödinger's cat.

8

MEANING, MIND, AND CHAOS

Look at the picture shown in Figure 8.1a. Are you puzzling at what this might be other than a bunch of jagged lines? Could this be the picture of a broken fence with a couple of boards missing? Yes, you've begun to see the fun of the picture. What do those lines in the gap represent? Suppose we make up a story; a soldier is walking his dog behind the fence (Figure 8.1b), but of course, at this moment, from this angle, we can see only his bayonet and his dog's tail! You see it, too, don't you? (Kraft, 1996).

This is a typical psychology class exercise in imagination of how we make meaning. But with what? I've already argued that our much-glorified brain cannot make meaning; it is more of a symbol-processing computer. It is the mind that gives meaning to the brain's processing of symbols.

Think of the situation in another way. A sentence has a structure, the syntax, how the words are put together in an orderly fashion. But the grammar of syntax will not enlighten you about the meaning of the sentence, that is, its semantic content. Semantics is something extra.

So when computer scientists, those researchers of artificial intelligence, talk about the brain as computer hardware and the mind as software (Fodor, 1981), they discount a significant issue. Thinking of the mind as computer software is valid only up to the point where we raise the issue of meaning (Varela, Thomson, & Rosch, 1991).

How do we jump from symbol-processing software to meaning in connection with the computer? The meaning exists in the mind of the computer programmer who gives the meaning to the symbols of his or her pro-

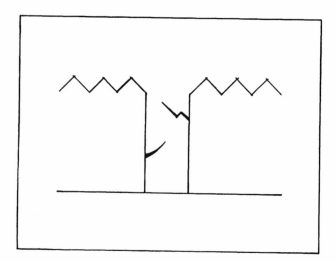

Figure 8.1a. Mind and meaning.

Figure 8.1b. Mind and meaning.

grams. Only then, does the computer software makes sense. So looking at the brain as a symbol-processing computer is useful because we can see clearly that we need a mind to give meaning to what the brain processes.

Ask yourself, also, how does your brain make sense of the world outside? Every computer is limited to processing its own symbols. Thus the brain as symbol-processor can know about the world only to the extent that the world affects its symbols as interpreted by the same internal logic used for the effect of symbols on symbols; it cannot know about the world as the world really is (Searle, 1987).

There are two problems here: One is that of meaning; the other is that of the knower. A computer lacks both. In previous chapters, we discussed: nonlocal consciousness as the knower. In our nonlocal consciousness, all the material world is within us. We can know the symbolic logic behind every part of the world because we originated it. The material world is bound by the laws of our theme body including the laws of physics, which we can discover creatively. But to give meaning to the world, we need another body, the mind, within consciousness.

It fits. When I see a flower, there are two objects in my awareness. There is the external rose in my external awareness. This external rose I can share with anyone else who may be looking at it. It is public. But concomitantly with the external rose, there is an internal rose of my thought. This internal awareness is private. Only I am aware of it.

So intuitively, we all *know,* we all directly experience our mind as different from the brain. My brain could be wired to EEG machines, opened up through surgery, or explored by positron tomography for all researchers to see what is happening inside my brain as I look at the rose. But no instruments or anything else would give the slightest hint to anyone about my internal awareness of the rose or what exactly I am experiencing privately.

This mind, whose objects are internal to our awareness, is what gives meaning to the physical objects of external awareness for which the brain acts as a sensing, self-referential measuring apparatus. The brain also makes a memory, a representation or map, so the next time it encounters the same object, the memory will evoke the same mental state that consciousness used the first time.

You have already, I hope, given up the prejudice that consciousness is brain. Now I am asking you to give up another prejudice—that mind is brain. Without giving up this prejudice, you will never truly appreciate creativity.

How do you draw a picture or sculpt a statue? You start with pencil and paper, to be sure, but something else is also important—your imagination. You imagine a mental picture of what you are going to draw or sculpt, and only then does something happen between the brain, hand, pencil, and paper (or brain, fingers, and clay).

Imagination helps us make new maps of the mind in our brain so that next time we can use these maps with ease. We can imagine within known contexts and their combinations how to solve a problem. While solving a problem, we may see new meaning in the old contexts that we are using—a case of situational creativity. Or else, the imagination makes a discontinuous leap to states of the mind that we never had before. When we are able to map this leap of imagination into our brain and into a manifest piece of art or science, we have delved into fundamental creativity.

SOLVING THE PROBLEM OF DUALISM

The scientist within us will shake his or her head. Aren't you forgetting the problems of dualism? If the mind is separate from the brain, if there is a mental world separate from the physical world, how do the two worlds interact? Don't you need a third substance besides mind and matter to act as a mediator? But then, of what is this third substance made? Do you want me to remind you of the law of conservation of energy in the physical world? The philosopher René Descartes proposed such a mind-brain dualism long ago that was properly discredited because of these very objections. What has changed so that we can overlook the objections?

A lot. We have discovered quantum physics, so matter has become less material—only possibilities in consciousness. Now think of the mind in those same quantum terms—as mental possibilities of meaning or as the locus of possible thoughts. Suppose consciousness collapses not only the possibilities of the brain but also of the mind to make the actualities of an experience (Goswami, 1996b).

Is there any evidence that consciousness collapses possibilities in two bodies that have no signal contact, no local interaction between them? The positive evidence has come from the Mexican neurophysiologist Jacobo Grinberg-Zylberbaum and his collaborators (Grinberg-Zylberbaum et al., 1994).

Grinberg-Zylberbaum's experiment has already been described (see Chapter 6). Two subjects are correlated by meditating together with the intention of direct communication between them. Then they are separated, put in electromagnetically insulated chambers, and wired up to separate EEG machines. When one of them is shown a light flash that produces an evoked potential in his brain's EEG, a transferred potential, similar in phase and strength to the evoked potential, is found in the other subject as well. The conclusion is that consciousness collapses similar states of actualities in both brains because they are correlated via conscious intention.

So although the direct interaction between the physical and the mental body is out (we must heed legitimate dualist objections), consciousness can mediate the interaction between them by collapsing correlated actualities, one in the brain, one in the mind—whenever it intends (Goswami, 1996b).

For this to be possible, we have to assume that the mind obeys quantum mechanics. Mental objects, thoughts, are quantum objects. Is there any evidence for that?

THE QUANTUM NATURE OF THOUGHT

You can experience the quantum nature of thought directly. The physicist David Bohm (1951) has pointed out that an uncertainty principle operates for thoughts. If we focus on the content of thought, we lose the direction the thought is following. On the other hand, focusing on the direction of thought leads to a loss of its content. Try it and see. The content of the thought is called its *feature;* the line of thought is the thought's *association.*

But only quantum objects are associated with conjugate, complementary variables! So Bohm's (1951) observation (and yours, if you have tried the little experiment) reveals only one thing: Behind a thought is a quantum meaning object that appears and moves in the field of our internal awareness just as physical objects appear and move in ordinary space.

But thoughts appear in awareness only when we are measuring them, when we are actually thinking (either in terms of feature or in terms of association). What does a meaning object behind thought do between our measurements, between thinking? It spreads as a wave of possibility. Although always manifested in awareness in a form described by complementary attributes such as feature and association, between manifestations thought exists in consciousness as a transcendent wave of meaning in possibility, exactly like quantum object of matter, with its transcendent multifaceted (wave/meaning) and manifest one-faceted (particle/thought) aspects.

The quantum picture also enables us to think about the physical and mental worlds differently from how we have been thinking of them. Normally, we think of both these worlds as made of substances. Of course, the mental meaning substance is more subtle—we cannot quantify it in the same way as we can the physical—but it is still a substance, or so we think. Change this view. Even the physical is not substance in the ordinary sense, let alone the mental. Both physical and mental worlds remain as possibilities until consciousness gives them substantiality by collapsing an actual experience.

COGNITION IS *RECOGNITION*

One difficulty in understanding perception with the brain alone (modeled as a computer) is that the representation of a sensory object in our brain after processing by the "higher" centers is not an exact replica of the object (when we see a pig, the brain does not make a three-dimensional pig within its neuronal substrata, there isn't room enough), and yet, somehow, we are able to translate the representation into the object and do it in such a way as to form a consensus with other observers. How does neuronal activity in the cerebral cortex evoke a perception of the object in external space-time?

The representational model is more suitable if perception is a matter of *re*cognition, not cognition. So who teaches the human biocomputer, the physical brain, its representations? Consciousness does—with the help of the states of the mental body. An unlearned stimulus produces an image in the physical brain in the form of possibilities of the quantum brain, but these possible images have no mental meaning. Consciousness ascribes mental meaning to the image with the help of mental states of the mental body. When consciousness recognizes and chooses a correlated pair of states, one in the physical brain (which becomes memory and forms the syntactical symbols of the representation) and the other in the mental body (which provides the semantics), a meaningful representation is made. The quantum measurement simultaneously collapses the physical object of the representation (which, according to quantum mechanics, is only "a pattern of disjoint tendencies" before collapse) in external space-time and the mental object in internal awareness. We see the external object and not the brain image, but the brain image contributes to our perception because it is correlated with the mental object that we experience. In this way, a color-blind person sees a tree in its fullness, not the brain image; yet, he does not see the tree as green because his brain-image does not have green-ness and, therefore, the correlated mental state does not call for green, either.

Once a representation is made and learned, subsequent action is a computer-style operation. A learned stimulus elicits memory, which is reconstructed every time the stimulus is presented and processed. It also elicits the learned brain response.

As consciousness recognizes and collapses a learned state in the quantum possibilities of the physical brain in response to a stimulus, it also recognizes and chooses the correlated mental state. Thus, in the process of perception, as representations of the physical world are made in the physical brain, there is a change in the mental body through modification of the probabilities of the experienced mental possibilities. In the reciprocal process of imagination, a physical brain representation is made from subtle mental states.

Perception produces not only physical representations or memory in the physical brain but also a tendency in the mental body for certain correlated states to collapse when a particular physical stimulus is presented. The same thing happens with imagination. Recall enhances the probability of further recall via nonlinear dynamics (see Chapter 7). In this way, the states of the mental body are individualized to fit a particular history. In other words, although potentially we all share the same mind structurally (the mind is an indivisible whole), a personal mind forms functionally as we acquire our individual patterns.

WHY THE MENTAL OBJECTS OF EXPERIENCE ARE PRIVATE

Perhaps most importantly, the awareness of mental aspects of perception—thoughts, concepts, and other mental objects—are *internal and private* in contrast to the awareness of the physical aspects of *external, public* objects, which we share with other people. There is an explanation in our new way of looking at the mind as a quantum mind.

What is the difference between physical and subtle mental substances? One big difference is the grossness of the macroworld of our shared perception of the physical domain.

Quantum objects obey the uncertainty principle—we cannot simultaneously measure both their position and momentum (mass times velocity) with utmost accuracy. In order to determine the trajectory of an object, we need to know not only where an object is now but also where it will be a little later; in other words, both its position and velocity, simultaneously. Therefore, we can never determine accurate trajectories of quantum objects.

Although the macrobodies in our environment are made of the micro quantum objects that obey the uncertainty principle, because of their grossness, the cloud of ignorance that the uncertainty principle imposes on the motion of macrobodies is so small that it can be discounted in most situations—this is the *correspondence principle*. Thus, macro bodies can be attributed both approximate position and approximate momentum and, therefore, approximate trajectories. In the physical world, we need the intermediary of the macrobodies, a macro measuring-aid apparatus, to amplify the possibilities of the micro quantum objects before we observe them and to make a record of the collapsed actuality after the collapse. Because of the approximate classical nature of the macro measuring-aid apparatus, we all can share the same collapsed actuality.

Mental substance is subtle and does not form gross conglomerates. In fact, as Descartes correctly intuited, mental substance is indivisible. For this substance, then, there is no reduction to smaller and smaller bits: There is no micro out of which the macro is made. So the mental world is a whole, what physicists sometimes call an *infinite medium*. There can be waves in such infinite media, modes of movement of meaning that must be described as quantum possibility waves obeying a probability calculus. And we directly observe these quantum modes without the intermediary of the macro measurement apparatus (there isn't any). But we pay a price. The observation and experience of the mental modes of movement are subject to the uncertainty principle. What this means is that any observation disturbs the mental object, so much so that repeated observations would not lead to the same experience of thought. If I have a thought and you try to think the same thought, your measurement of the thought will affect it so that it becomes a different beast. Therefore, thoughts (ordinarily) cannot be shared by two different observers; thoughts are private and experienced internally.

It also follows that because there is no macro measuring-aid apparatus in the mental world, it is impossible to create a tangled-hierarchcal measurement situation. Thus the mind cannot operate alone; consciousness needs the brain with its tangled-hierarchical dynamics to collapse the wave function of the correlated mind-brain duo.

Don't be puzzled that we are speaking of the mind in an objective fashion. The subjectivity of our experiences, both physical and mental, comes from consciousness. In the West, philosophers have made the traditional mistake of thinking of consciousness as an aspect of the mind; that's what is causing confusion. But now that we are correcting this mistake, look at the new possibility that opens up before science. We should now be able to study the mechanics of mind with mathematics. Some work has already begun in this direction (Sirag in Mishlove, 1993).

CHAOS IN CREATIVITY

A creative thought is a quantum hit from a superposition of possibilities. Simultaneously, consciousness collapses a macroscopic event in the brain that is recorded. This record can be thought of as the response of the brain to a creative thought, the new context for thinking about something. This record is also a map because triggering it from memory elicits the creative thought from the mental body in consciousness. The collapsing of an event in the brain from its quantum possibilities requires suitable measuring-aid apparatuses for amplification and recording. For all our discovered contexts that constitute the existing mental maps for our brain, there already are measuring-aid apparatuses right for the occasion. To make a map of a new context is to set up a suitable new measurement apparatus for a new correlated response of the quantum system of the brain.

When we investigate a new meaning of an old context or transfer an old context to a new problem (situational creativity), there is no ambiguity about what measuring-aid apparatuses in the brain to use in collapsing a new possibility into actuality. The context determines the measuring-aid apparatus to be used.

But a problem arises in the case of fundamental creativity, in which a new context is to be discovered in thought and mapped in the brain. Consciousness will be able to map the new context in the brain only if there are new measuring-aid apparatuses with which to map it. But the tendency of the brain is to do the habitual thing. Somehow these habits have to be destructured and new responses structured in the brain before a creative quantum leap of the mind can be collapsed. It seems that the brain has this special ability to destructure an old order in the presence of new conditions and, subsequently, to bifurcate into a new structure or order because part of it obeys *chaos dynamics.*

CHAOS DYNAMICS

Recently there has been a lot of talk, at least in the popular press, about chaos theory as the solution to all our problems, from the big bang creation of the universe to the movement of dirty water in the kitchen sink. A chaotic system, although deterministic, is highly sensitive to the initial conditions, so much so that its future behavior cannot be predicted for long. The errors in the knowledge of the initial conditions keep multiplying exponentially, making predictions of the future increasingly less accurate.

Metaphorically, the fluttering of a butterfly wing can change the weather—because the weather is a chaotic system. This is the reason for the essential long-term unpredictability of our weather system, regardless of how well we collect the initial data or how big a computer we use to make our calculations. The unpredictability of chaotic systems follows from their nonlinear dynamics. For linear dynamics, a sum of causes produces a corresponding sum of effects. For nonlinear dynamics, the cause-effect relationship is not so neat and predictable; the previous value of a variable effects the current value in a complicated way, giving rise to new possibilities for the development of the system. In effect, this means that for nonlinear chaotic oscillations, only a slight change in the initial conditions will produce quite new behavior that cannot be predicted a priori. Even though the system obeys Newtonian physics and is determined, in the presence of a suitable stimulus (the metaphorical butterfly) a nonlinear system behaves unpredictably. The onset of turbulence in a liquid is a practical example. You may be enjoying a water fountain from a prudent distance when, all of a sudden, the water douses you in a splash.

But the important thing about systems of nonlinear chaos dynamics is that the end product is not necessarily random; a bifurcation of paths may occur that leads to new order in the system.

A marble placed in a bowl always settles to the bottom after a few oscillations. The force that restores the body toward the center of oscillation is proportional to the displacement; such oscillation is linear. The oscillation is damped by friction, hence the settling down. Let's be a little technical and make a plot of the system's motion. This is a plot of the system's velocity as a function of its position—in this plot the periodic damped oscillation of the pendulum is represented by a series of curves gradually converging to a point (Figure 8.2). Thus, the designation of motion under a "simple point attractor" is given to such a system. For a simple pendulum with a force driving it, the driving force battles friction (as in a wrist watch). Now the motion converges to a closed curve. Hence, we say that the attractor for the motion is a limit cycle (Figure 8.3). In both situations, the motion of the system is completely predictable after a time.

But when the restoring force is nonlinear and has a cubic dependence on the displacement in addition to the usual linear dependence, the phase portrait of the system is no longer a closed curve. For example, it can be complicated as shown in Figure 8.4. This case the motion of the system, although in a qualitatively similar pattern, has a fundamental quantitatively unpredictable nature about it (we cannot say on which of the many similar curves the system will settle at a given time). The motion now is said to be under the spell of a "strange" attractor. This is chaos dynamics (Gleick, 1987).

What is interesting in a chaotic system is that in the presence of nonlinearity when the conditions are right, there can be new order—order within chaos, new "basins" of attractor behavior. A bifurcation is nothing but a change from one strange attractor to another. Change the conditions, and the system may jump out of the basin of an old attractor and settle into the new basin of a new attractor.

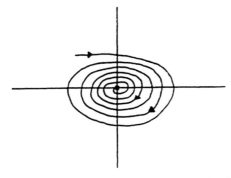

Figure 8.2. The motion of a pendulum with friction included. It is a spiral converging to a point attractor signifying the decay of the pendulum's motion to rest.

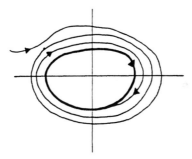

Figure 8.3. A friction-damped pendulum driven by a periodic force. In this case the spiral converges to a limiting one (the bold curve), called the *limit cycle attractor,* signifying that the pendulum's motion is completely determined by the external force when the limit cycle is reached.

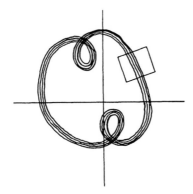

Figure 8.4. A typical motion for a strange attractor. Quantitatively speaking, the motion never repeats.

The neurophysiologist Walter Freeman and his collaborators Freeman, 1991) deciphered the chaos dynamics—the change from one attractor to another—in the brain that are involved in learning a new olfactory stimulus. The chaos dynamics of the measuring-aid apparatus in the brain in creativity, namely, in learning a new discovered context, should be similar.

SHIVA'S DANCE

Suppose we have measuring-aid apparatuses that are really chaotic systems that are in a quiescent phase corresponding to an equilibrium basin of an attractor. The response of the system to a noncreative thought is now quite predictable. The brain system is able to respond even to an imaginative thought that brings new meaning to an old context, as in situational creativity, because chaos dynamics permits small deviations in the trajectory. But such imagination does not require the brain system to move out of its attractor basin. I propose that a quantum creative thought of fundamental creativity in the mind acts as a kick in the pants for change in the brain, that is, a trigger that drives the chaotic system out of the attractor that holds the old order—the old response pattern for the problem at issue—out of its equilibrium basin.

At the end of the preparation stage in creativity, we have to empty our mind and also break up the old connections in the brain in anticipation of the new. To map the creative idea that eventually comes to an open mind requires an open brain. We must not let our secondary responses be cluttered by old, conditioned, learned contexts; this is the precondition for the next stage—insight—but how do we satisfy it? This involves a *destructuring* of the conditioned memory stores of the brain, and this is where chaos dynamics plays the first of its crucial roles. In order to map the primary-process thought in response to our intuition to create, the brain's chaotic system destructures its conditioned pattern of connections (among the neural assembly forming the appropriate attractor basin). The intensity of our burning question and the quantum response to it are in the mind; how does the brain respond so that consciousness can collapse a new brain state using new measuring-aid apparatuses? Enter the quantum uncertainty principle a trivial act (such as shaving and cutting your face) can trigger the brain to action. These quantum uncertainties may be enough to change the initial conditions sufficiently to affect the chaos dynamics, enabling the system to come out of the old attractor basin. The chaotic system of the brain now "vegetates" under the spell of a new attractor—call it the empty attractor. This is the stage where we have crossed a threshold from wanting to create to having to create. We have the necessary empty mind, empty of previous prejudice, and the brain is empty also, in keeping with the emptiness of mind. The destructuring is completed. As Picasso said, "Every act of creation is first of all an act of destruction."

The third illumination stage of a creative process consists of the tangled encounter of perspiration, the will to hold the burning question within an empty mind, and the inspiration of the quantum primary insight. When the insight comes, it culminates in the ah-ha experience that all creators covet.

The creative quantum thought, the primary experience of the creative ah-ha, provides the change of context that rebinds the pieces of the gestalt together in a new coherent whole, a new context. The mapping of this in the brain involves, mechanically speaking, another drastic change of the measuring-aid apparatus.

I am proposing that when a quantum creative thought or insight is ready to see the light of consciousness in the mind, another trivial stimulus, say, a frog jumping into a pond, may act as a trigger for the uncertainty principle to come into play in the brain once again, enabling the classical chaotic memory of the brain to change, to jump attractors once more. In correlation with a creative thought, the chaotic system of the brain makes a jump out of the vegetating state under the empty attractor into the basin of a new attractor, which now forms the locus for new mappings. The new attractor leads to new connections of the neuronal assembly as the new investigations around the new context are made.

Even after the brain has successfully made a map of a novel mental idea, a new attractor basin, the idea has to be given form using the ego's learned repertoire. If the necessary form is unavailable in the ego's repertoire, the creative may have to go idea hunting once again. Thus, the fourth and final stage of the creative process, the manifestation stage, consists of repeated encounters between the quantum novel idea and the classical known form until the requirements of both idea and form have been met. In the aftermath of a creative ah-ha insight, the measurement system of the brain may have to undergo a series of restructuring transitions to an eventual new dynamical order that satisfactorily manifests the map of the creative insight. Only a chaotic system can handle such oscillations.

In this way, the creative process is much like Shiva's dance in Indian mythology (Figure 8.5). Shiva, *Nataraja,* the king of the dancers, dances under a halo of cosmic flame. In one hand he holds fire to destroy the known world, to bring chaos, to destructure the old order,

Figure 8.5. Shiva's dance. In one hand he holds the drum to announce creation; in the other he holds the fire of destruction. The dwarf under his feet represents ignorance. It is a wonderful metaphor for the creative act.

whereas in the other hand he holds a drum with which to welcome the new creation, the new order. In this integrated description of creation dynamics, the crucial features of the underlying mechanism are chaotic destructuring of the brain, unconscious proliferation of coherent super-positions of thought, quantum leaps of insight in thought, and chaotic restructuring of the brain.

Is there any evidence for the brain's chaos dynamics in creativity? First, there is reason to expect chaos dynamics to be significant in the present context. A creative response to an original idea has an unquestionable individuality. Two scientists may creatively discover the same theory, but they will rarely put exactly the same flesh on the idea. The individuality of a creative act may arise from how the individual brain processes the idea beginning with the quantitative dissimilarity of one trajectory under a basin attractor from another (although all trajectories under the same attractor are qualitatively similar).

The primary event of a quantum creative insight, the immediate perception of a new context that establishes a new connection among previously held pieces of information, is given flesh in the subsequent brain dynamics. The other indelible mark of chaos dynamics in the creative process is that often the end product is not reached in one step but involves large oscillations (as in turbulence). There is plenty of evidence for such oscillations in the creative process (Piechowsky, 1993). For example, there are many stories in the revered East Indian mystic Ramakrishna's life that suggest chaotic oscillation in the manifestation stage of his spiritual fulfillment. Such oscillations have also been documented in the life of the American mystic known as Peace Pilgrim (1982).

PIAGET'S FINDINGS ON CHILD DEVELOPMENT

How does the ego develop according to the theory presented here? The acquisition by the child of each new context must be identified as a quantum leap of thought that is also preceded by destructuring and followed by restructuring of the brain. For young children, there must be an enormous number of these quantum leaps, with accompanying development of the brain maps via chaos dynamics. (This undoubtedly accounts for the continual joy and delight we see and envy in young children.) Between events of quantum leaps and the chaotic development of the brain's substructure, there is a kind of homeostasis in which the child learns continuously via situational problem solving—learning I in Gregory Bateson's (1980) terminology (see Chapter 5)—or even investigates the learned contexts for new meaning. As discussed earlier, the quantum leaps involved in events of situational creativity do not require the chaotic upheaval needed by fundamental creativity.

As the child grows older, the duration of the homeostatic stages increases and the quantum leaps requiring chaotic upheavals become less and less frequent. The more conventional learning during the homeostatic stages of child development now leads to richer and richer self-identity with the learned contexts and how they are used. When a sufficiently rich repertoire of contexts has been built, which enables the growing person to act in most life situations, the person can be said to have acquired an ego. Before learning, the possibility pool of the mind from which consciousness chooses its states spans the mental states common to all people at all places at all times. With learning, certain responses gradually gain greater weight over others. This is the development of an individual mind that defines our ego-character. This character supplements the ego identity garnered from content memory in the brain in connection with a personal history. The development of the ego thus consists of a series of periods of rapid quantum growth from one homeostasis to another and of slow continuous growth within a homeostasis.

Children's creativity is thus directed toward ego-development, which follows a series of transformations of the context of the child's learning and living. The empirical verification of this developmental schema was the psychologist Jean Piaget's great contribution. Piaget's work is also the basis of much later thinking on creativity.

The developmental process in the child has two aspects that must be balanced: environmental events and the changes these events produce in the organizational structure of the child. The child adapts to environmental changes through a process of assimilation and accommodation. *Assimilation* is the processing of information that fits the child's organizational structure, or, alternatively, if the information does not fit, assimilation consists of changing the information to fit the internal structure of the organization. *Accommodation,* on the other hand, is the process by which a child changes its structures to fit discordant environmental data. Together they constitute what Piaget called *equilibration,* the process of adaptive cognitive structural change brought about in the child.

Piaget (1977) found three kinds of equilibration. Give an infant a finger and he or she starts sucking. This is a child who has accomplished a process of simple equilibration. *Simple equilibration* consists of developing a one-to-one fit between object and action, for example, finger and sucking. *Reciprocal equilibration* consists of equilibrating two simply equilibrated schemes and objects into one whole. For example, a baby who has learned to grasp an object and to suck his or her fingers will put the two skills together to bring a pacifier to his or her mouth. The third type of equilibration is called *hierarchical equilibration*—a process in which equilibrated systems and schemes are integrated contexually.

It is the third type of equilibration that is most significant and requires creativity—creative learning. The first two types of equilibration need nothing but level I learning—learning within fixed contexts or juxtaposing two learned contexts to solve a problem (Bateson, 1980). A movie of conditioning produced by Skinnerian psychologists shows that even a pigeon is able to equilibrate two schemes and objects. The pigeon was first taught to peck an object and then to move an object. When the pigeon was left with a moveable tool and a peckable object too high to reach, it moved the tool within reach of the pecking target, jumped on the tool, and began pecking. But integration of the elements of level I learning of contexts requires level II learning—learning to learn—an ability to take apart and put together the contexts (remember the dolphin experiment in Chapter 5). This needs the ability to understand and abstract the conceptual rules that govern the schemes—a creative leap that Piaget called *reflective abstraction* and we recognize as a quantum leap of the mind. This no one can teach the child, and no pigeon can do. It truly requires an act of discovering something new in a new context or of seeing new meaning—creative learning. Yet every child accomplishes this many times on the journey to its adult-ego, and as a result of each of these events of creative learning, the child reaches a new stage of development, a new and richer self-identity.

Thus, according to Piaget, and in complete agreement with the theory developed here, child development consists of alternative stages of acquiring and exploring contexts and meanings (homeostasis) and integrating them (the quantum leap of hierarchical equilibration). When enough contexts are learned and their meanings are explored and integrated, the child acquires a character and a persona to supplement the content identity with the personal history, all this together is the ego.

QUANTUM/CREATIVE AND CLASSICAL/ DETERMINED SELVES

An adult person is capable of operating in both modes—the ego and the quantum self (Figure 8.6). The quantum primary mode is where probability, uncertainty, and acausality reign supreme and where creative responses, not just the learned ones, remain available through the possibility pools of the quantum mind. It is the fountain of our intuitive insights into contexts and meanings, the flashes of imagination that cannot be abstracted from prior learning and that are the source of our creativity. All our creativity is quantum creativity and involves our quantum self.

The classical-ego mode, associated with our continuous, conditioned, and predictable behavior, augments our creative ideas and meanings with reason, enables us to develop and manipulate these ideas and meanings into full-blown forms, and enjoys the fruits of our accomplishments.

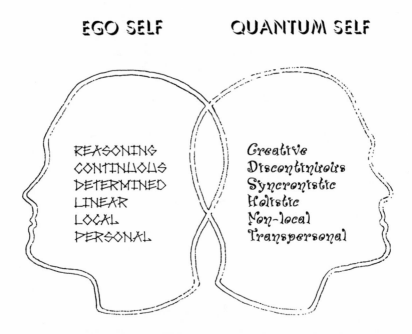

Figure 8.6. The classical and quantum modalities of our self-identity.

The idea of the two self-identities, ego and the atman, was discovered in Eastern psychology millennia ago. For example, in one of the Upanishads, is this exquisite metaphor: Two birds, united always, and known by the same name, closely cling to the same tree. One of them eats the sweet fruit; the other looks on without eating" (Nikhilananda, 1964). The one that eats the sweet fruit of the world is, of course, the personal ego. The witness is the universal atman, the quantum self in our terminology.

Finally, I offer a caution. The quantum and classical self-identities of consciousness do not constitute a dualism. We must remember that these are simply modalities of consciousness, and neither has any self-nature apart from consciousness. The mechanism of manifestation, including the structure of the mind and the brain, imposes these identities on consciousness. However, whereas the quantum self-identity is compulsory for experience, the ego-identity is not (all we have to do is "just say no" to a conditioned habit of response—no amount of conditioning is infinite; unfortunately, as most of us know, conditioning can be powerful, so saying no is not as easy as it sounds!)—and creativity is our greatest reminder of that.

IS MIND BRAIN? EMPIRICAL DATA

I was talking to a scientist, a psychiatrist, at a conference on yoga. This psychiatrist is sympathetic to yoga but has difficulties with some of the ideas that the traditional yoga literature holds—such as the idea of a mental body apart from the physical one (Nagendra, 1993). He conceded the power of some of my theoretical arguments but shrugged in defiance. "It's just theory." Then it occurred to me. "No, it's not just theory," I said. "There is empirical data that an aspect of the mind, the memory of propensities, survives the death of the physical body." My friend said, "If there is empirical data, I have to reconsider my whole position." He sounded genuinely subdued.

I was talking about reincarnational data. There has always been much anecdotal evidence for reincarnation, which is believed by half the population of the world, including 25% of people in the West (Gallup, 1982). But more recently, thanks to the work of such luminaries as psychiatrist Ian Stevenson of the University of Virginia and psychiatrist Satwant Pasricha, reincarnational research has achieved clear scientific reliability (Pasricha, 1990; Stevenson, 1974).

One important conclusion of this research is that, indeed, after we die, our mental bodies with their propensities, habit patterns, and the learned contexts that give them individuality continue on until they are "reborn"; that is, a child is born with the same propensities, habit patterns, and learned contexts that it held in its previous life.

That a genius like Mozart is not made in one life but many lifetimes of work to achieve such precocious musical mastery is an old idea. The inventor Thomas Edison intuited the situation correctly when he said, "Genius is experience. Some seem to think that it is a gift or talent, but it is the fruit of long experience in many lives. Some are older souls than others, and so they know more." What reincarnation researchers have done is to verify with public data these age-old educated guesses.

One comment in passing. The computer model of creativity claims that creativity is problem solving, that there is no mystery in it. The more we look at it, the more we find it to be otherwise. Not only does creativity involve a conscious self beyond the familiar ego, but its meaning comes from a subtle world, the world of the mind. To paraphrase Alexander Pope,

> The laws of creativity lay hid in night.
> God said, "Let computers be," and there was light.
> It did not last, the devil shouted, "Ho!
> Here's quantum mind. Restore the status quo."

9

THE IMPORTANCE OF
UNCONSCIOUS PROCESSING

The creative process, according to Wallas (1926), consists of the four stages of preparation, incubation, insight, and manifestation. Of these four, preparation and manifestation belong to the "classical" stages of the creative process; you could understand them, at least to some extent, with Newtonian models of us. But the other two stages, incubation and insight, are strictly quantum. So far, I have emphasized the quantum leap of sudden insight. In this chapter, the importance of incubation—unconscious processing—in creativity is explored.

Next to illumination or insight, incubation or unconscious processing is the most mysterious part of the creative process. For Freud, who pioneered the idea of the unconscious, it was the repository of repressed instincts; thus, ideas that come from the unconscious are not necessarily socially desirable. They consist mostly of libido, that is, they are primarily sexual. According to Freud, creative people have an unusual capacity to sublimate the sexual drive and process unconscious undesirable images into socially acceptable forms that may appear novel and creative. However, these unconscious images originate in conflict; for example, Leonardo da Vinci's particular style of portraying women (e.g., the *Mona Lisa*) originates, according to Freud, in the repressed feelings of what his mother's smile meant to him in his childhood. I do not find this explanation very credible.

Carl Jung's (1971a) more viable way to conceptualize unconscious processing views the unconscious as a collective unconscious—a universal unconscious for all humanity that transcends the boundaries of time, space, and culture. Jung found that creative ideas often emerge in the garb of universal symbols that he called *archetypes*.[1]

But what is the unconscious? How can there be processing going on when we are unconscious? It seems confusing at first. In a previous chapter, I discussed the concept of transcendent potentia of quantum possibilities from which creative insights come. I think what Jung calls the *collective unconscious* and what the quantum physicist calls *transcendent potentia* are similar things. The unconscious is the transcendent domain where our thoughts exist in potentia as uncollapsed quantum possibilities, not as actualities. Collapse requires awareness. The unconscious is the absence of awareness.

So the unconscious is a misnomer because consciousness—the ground of being—is always present. What we normally call *conscious* are those processes for which awareness is also present. But there are situations in which our awareness is not present. The unconscious pertains to these situations. The unconscious is comprised of those processes for which consciousness is present but awareness is not. Is this still confusing? Some examples of the plentiful data on the occurrence and importance of such processes in our psyche will clear up the matter.

First, there is the phenomenon of blindsight. The psychologist Nick Humphrey (1972) found a human subject with defects in his cortex that had caused him to become blind in the left visual field of both eyes. But the man could point to a light on his blind side with accuracy and distinguish crosses from circles and horizontal lines from vertical ones in the blind side of his visual field. But when asked how he "saw" these things, the man insisted that he just guessed, in spite of the fact that his "hit" rate was far beyond chance. Cognitive scientists now agree that blindsight represents unconscious perception—perception without awareness, or an example of unconscious processing.

Research done both in the United States and in Russia provides further physiological and cognitive evidence for unconscious perception (Shevrin, 1980). Researchers in both countries have measured the brain's electrical responses in different subjects to a variety of subliminal messages. Stronger responses were usually found when a meaningful picture (e.g., a bee) was flashed on a screen for 1000th of a second than when a more neutral picture (such as an abstract geometrical figure) was shown. Furthermore, when subjects were asked to free associate after these subliminal exposures, the picture of the bee elicited such words as *sting* and *honey*. In contrast, the geometrical figure of a trian-

---

[1] Note the difference between Jungian archetypes and Platonic archetypes.

gle elicited hardly anything related to the object. Clearly, there was perception and processing of the picture of the bee (because the picture of the triangle was ignored), but without awareness!

Third, still more evidence for unconscious processes comes from the research on split-brain patients whose cortical connections between the two hemispheres of the brain are severed, but whose hindbrain (associated with feelings and emotions) connections are intact. In one experiment, a woman was shown the picture of a nude male model in her left visual field (which connects to the right brain hemisphere). The woman blushed but could not explain why (Sperry, 1983). Clearly, the unconscious perception process affected her conscious behavior without her being aware of a cause.

THE IMPORTANCE OF UNCONSCIOUS PROCESSING

Mulla Nasruddin was looking for something under a street light. A passerby began to help him look. But after a while, when he did not find anything, he asked Nasruddin, "Mulla, what have you lost? What is it that we are looking for?"

"My key, I lost my key."

"But where did you lose it?" The helper was impatient.

"In my house," the Mulla answered.

"Then why are you looking here?", shouted the helper in disbelief.

"There is light here," said the Mulla complacently.

The problem solvers among us always look where the light is. They look with conscious processing. But if the problem requires a new context or a new meaning from the transcendent domain of possibilities, the light does not help. The key is in the house, in the dark caverns of the unconscious. That is where one has to go.

Most of us consciously react to associations; while reading a book, we get ideas and may write them down for later reference. But such conscious associations make only fragmentary contributions to a truly creative breakthrough.

Arthur Koestler (1964) noted that a different kind of association—an association of opposites that he called *bisociation*—may be more helpful to the creative process. "The basic bisociative pattern of the creative synthesis [is due to] the sudden interlocking of two previously unrelated skills, or matrices of thought," he declared. The more startling the bisociation, the more striking and novel is the creativity of the act.

As an example, consider the minotaur of Picasso (Figure 9.1). The collage of conflicting symbols—the violent minotaur, the dagger,

Figure 9.1. A minotaur showing the essence of bisociation.

and the leaf as the symbol of life—creates a bisociation (or should we say polyassociation?). Could the painting have originated from the processing of such a bisociation in Picasso's unconscious?

A similar idea comes from the psychologist Albert Rothenberg (1976)—he calls it *Janusian thinking* (Janus is the Roman god with two faces who can simultaneously see the front and back of things). Rothenberg thinks that the idea of the Eugene O'Neill play, *The Iceman Cometh,* may have been the result of Janusian dichotomous thinking. Iceman means death, as the play overtly indicates. But covertly, a joke that O'Neill knew may have had an impact on his thinking. A household refrigerator needed attention. When the husband came home, he called up to his wife, "Has the iceman come yet?" The wife called down, "No, but he is breathing hard." Sex, Rothenberg notes, is a signifier of life, the opposite of death.

Are Koestler and Rothenberg right in saying that we are creative because bisociations and Janusian thinking are going on in our unconscious? I think so because it is impossible to resolve the dichotomy of a bisociation or of Janusian thinking on the basis of conscious analysis from the vantage point of known contexts. When confronted with such a dichotomy, our mind's quantum state becomes a superposition, a wave of contradicting possibilities, that it cannot resolve.

CREATIVITY AND THE DOUBLE-SLIT EXPERIMENT

A thought experiment with electrons illustrates how unconscious processing works as opposed to conscious processing. Consider the double-slit experiment, ideally suited to study the possibility-wave nature of an electron. In this setup (Figure 9.2), a beam of electrons passes through a two-slitted screen before hitting a second fluorescent screen.

After passing through the two slits of the first screen, the possibility wave of each electron divides into two waves that "interfere" with one another; the result is displayed as spots on the fluorescent screen. If the crests of the two waves arrive together at a place on the screen, we get constructive interference—reinforcement of possibility (Figure 9.3a)—the probability for an electron to arrive is maximum and shows as bright spots on the screen. Crest and trough arriving together at a place make destructive interference—no possibility of any electron landing there at all (Figure 9.3b)—and show as dark regions on the fluorescent screen. The total pattern, called an interference pattern, consists of these alternate bright and dark regions (Figure 9.3c).

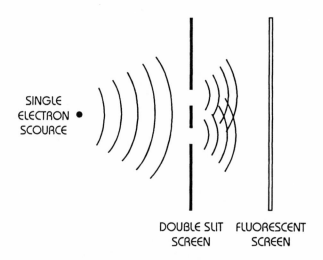

SINGLE
ELECTRON •
SCOURCE

DOUBLE SLIT   FLUORESCENT
SCREEN   SCREEN

Figure 9.2. The double-slit experiment with electrons.

But now suppose we make the electron source very weak, so weak that at any one time only one electron passes through the slits. Will we still see the interference pattern? Yes. Each electron interferes with itself to make the pattern. But now we ask a wicked question: How can a single electron split into two? On one hand, without such a split, how can the electron interfere with itself? On the other hand, it may be hard to imagine that an electron, an object that, like a particle, gives a clear localized tick at a Geiger counter, can pass through two slits at the same time.

Does the electron really pass through both slits? Let's look and see. We can imagine a light beam strong enough to illuminate the electron, so we can see at any given time which hole it passes through. So we turn the light on, and as we see an electron pass through a slit, we also look to see where the flash appears on the fluorescent screen. Every time an electron goes through a slit, we find that the flash appears behind the slit it just passed through. After a time the electrons make a fringe pattern like that in Figure 9.4; the interference pattern has disappeared. The electrons are now behaving like little baseballs.

So when we watch the slits with a light, the electrons do not split. By our looking, we encourage the electrons to behave as localized particles, localized at one slit. But when we do not watch the slits, the electrons behave as waves and pass through both slits. Of course, you already know that looking affects the electrons.

What does all this have to do with creativity? A creative insight is always preceded by unconscious processing. What we call unconscious processing is nothing but the generation in the mind of transcendent quantum waves of many possibilities many possible meanings.

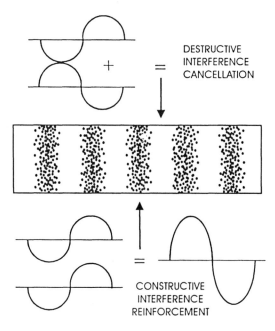

Figure 9.3. (a). Waves arriving at the fluorescent screen in phase reinforce each other (constructive interference). (b). Waves arriving at a point out of phase cancel each other out. (c). The resulting interference pattern of alternate bright and dark fringes.

The double-slit experiment clearly tells us about the occasional advantage of not knowing over knowing. If you try to know which slit the electron passes through, the electron becomes limited as to where it can arrive on the fluorescent screen. But if you do not insist on knowing, the electron has access to many more places it has many more possibilities. This is how creativity works. When encountering an ambiguity, if you do not demand immediate knowledge of the answer, possibilities open up. Your thoughts can go where they have never gone before in possibility. The unresolved superposition of meaning continues to grow in potentia in response to further ambiguous stimuli and gives rise to many more associations in potentia than if the ambiguities were consciously resolved.[2]

[2]A technical note. Material realists assume that coherent superpositions at the macroscopic level collapse by themselves very quickly or, at least, lose their phase relationships (technically this is called *decoherence*) so that they no longer can produce interference phenomena. However, in idealist science, there is no collapse unless and until consciousness so chooses. And for a confined system like the the quantum system of the brain, there is no reason to believe that any decoherence takes place.

Figure 9.4. In an arrangement where a flashlight is aimed at the slits so we can see which one an electron passes through, the interference pattern disappears and electrons behave like classical tiny baseballs.

Howard Gruber (1981; see also Cohen, 1985) points out that Darwin made extensive use of metaphors in developing his theory of evolution. What is a metaphor? A metaphor involves the mixing up of lexical and contextual meanings of words in such a way that a clear situation of context becomes an unclear situation in which the ambiguity creates extra possibilities. A metaphor allows us to think in an ambiguous pattern. It helps trigger the development of a thought into a superposition involving the unknown.

Artists seem to seek out ambiguous situations; they seem to like to play with the boundaries of things to see what happens. Max Ernst wrote:

> I was struck by the way the floor, its grain accentuated by many scrubbings, obsessed my nervously excited gaze. So I decided to explore the symbolism of the obsession, and to encourage my powers of meditation and hallucination I took a series of drawings from the floorboards by dropping pieces of paper on them at random and then rubbing the paper with blacklead. As I looked at the drawings that I got in this way—some dark, some smudgily dim— I was surprised by the sudden heightening of my visionary powers, and by the dreamlike succession of contradictory images that came one on top of another with the persistence and rapidity peculiar to memories of love. (1960, p. 67)

So Albert Rothenberg (1976) was very intuitive to call this ambiguous thinking that builds uncollapsed superpositions in our brain Janusian thinking. Janus simultaneously sees the front door and back door of a building, the two sides of a coin, and if you will, the many-splendored facets of a quantum superposition like the dead cat and live cat of Schrödinger's paradox. In their unconscious processing, all creatives are highly Janusian.

There is considerable evidence that many creatives engage in what Howard Gruber (1981) has called a *network of enterprises*. Having a network of enterprises enables one to unconsciously process one problem while consciously working on another.

Incubation is not just time away from the active pursuit of a problem; it is also a hotbed of unconscious proliferation of ideas and associations. For unconscious processing, ambiguous stimuli are crucial. Art and metaphor can contribute to ambiguity. A doubt about the old— Is this right? or Is this wrong?—can give rise to ambiguity (Orlov, 1981; Oshins, 1983). Any previously unlearned stimulus can contribute to producing these unresolved superpositions, which expand to create a multiple-branched tree of ideas in possibility.

But all of this is in the unconscious; we do not choose until we see the whole pattern. Is it really true that possibilities wait uncollapsed in the mind before consciousness is ready to collapse them into one gestalt? In experiments by Helmuth Schmidt (1993), radioactive decay events, which are random, are recorded by counters and computers, and even printed out, except that nobody looks at the data for a time. After perhaps a few months, an independent observer who has the sealed printout chooses a direction of deviation from the randomness that he or she wants to see, and psychics, looking at the computer output, try psychokinetically to influence the randomness of the radioactive decay in the chosen direction. They succeed, even though months have elapsed since the original decay process. Concurrently, it is verified that if an observer thoroughly examines the print-out beforehand, the data cannot be influenced by any psychic maneuver. The conclusion is simple, straightforward, and astounding: Quantum events remain in possibility until consciousness looks at and actualizes them.

We process unconsciously and do not choose until we see the gestalt. And, of course, we do not see until we choose; the tangled hierarchy of a primary-awareness event remains ever present. From the transcendent side it is *God*—the unmanifest creative principle in us—processing; from the manifest side of the tangled hierarchy, it is the quantum self choosing on recognizing the gestalt.

UNCONSCIOUS PROCESSING AND THE QUANTUM: DATA

To recap, in conscious processing, the collapse of a possibility wave by consciousness (via choice and recognition) takes place in the presence of awareness. But in unconscious (or subliminal) perception, in which consciousness is present but not awareness, there is no collapse of the possibility wave. Cognitive experiments using polysemous words bear out this distinction.

In a representative experiment, Tony Marcel (1980) used strings of three words in which the middle word was ambiguous in its associations with the other two words. His subjects watched a screen as the three words were flashed one at a time at intervals of either 600 milliseconds or 1.5 seconds between flashings. The subjects were asked to push a button when they consciously recognized the last word of the series. The original purpose of the experiment was to use the subject's reaction time as a measure of the relationship between congruence (or lack of it) among the words and the meanings assigned to the words in such series as *hand-palm-wrist* (congruent) and *tree-palm-wrist* (incongruent). For example, the bias of the word *hand* followed by the flashing of *palm* may be expected to produce the hand-related meaning of *palm,* which then should improve the reaction time of the subject for recognizing the third word, *wrist* (congruence). But if the biasing word is tree, then the lexical meaning of *palm* as a tree would be assigned and the meaning-recognition of the third word, *wrist* should take a longer reaction time (incongruous). Indeed, this was the result.

However, when the middle word was masked by a pattern that made it impossible to see with awareness though unconscious perception continued, there was no longer any appreciable difference in reaction time between the congruent and the incongruent cases. This is surprising because presumably both meanings of the ambiguous word were available, regardless of the biasing context, yet neither meaning was chosen over the other. Apparently, then, choice, and therefore quantum collapse, is a concomitant of conscious experience but not of unconscious perception. It is our consciousness that chooses—we choose, therefore we are—but we choose only when awareness is present.

The Marcel experiment also demonstrates the existence of superpositions of possibilities of thought-maps in the brain. Before choice, in the quantum description, the ambiguous state of the brain subject to a pattern-masked, ambiguous-word stimulus is a superposition of two possible thought-maps.[3]

---

[3]Modifications of the Marcel experiment using strings containing two ambiguous words have been suggested that may produce double-slit-like interference phenomena; see McCarthy and Goswami (1993).

Preparation: Gandhi spinning cotton
on his wheel, preparing for satyagraha.[4]

Incubation: Picasso at a sidewalk cafe in Paris
sitting quietly, doing nothing.

Insight: Amadeus, feverishly recording the notes
of the *Requiem,* its music filling his mind space.

Manifestation: Madam Curie, extracting a grain
of radium from a mountain of uranium.

When infinity plays my finite
instrument—creation! I tune my instrument and listen
for the invitation to creativity. Opto ergo sum.

---

[4]*Satyagraha* is a Sanskrit word meaning aspiring to truth.

10

PURPOSE AND FREEDOM
IN CREATIVITY

There was a famous king in ancient India named Vikrama. He had two poets in his court, but he favored one, Kalidasa, over the other. Many members of the court could see no difference in quality between the poetry of the two poets—a poem is a poem is a poem. So one day they asked the king why he favored Kalidasa over the other as they both seemed to write poetry equally well. The king promised a demonstration.

The court assembled in the king's garden in the still dormant springtime. Many trees were leafless, but one tree looked particularly dead. The other poet was summoned first. Pointing to the "dead" tree, the king asked him to compose a verse on what he saw ahead. The poet complied in a matter of seconds, and his verse can be translated thus: There is dead wood ahead of us. When Kalidasa was given the same task, his verse was: A great tree, void of juice, shines ahead.

The court never again complained. Whereas the lesser poet saw the verse-making as a problem and solved it adequately, Kalidasa jumped contexts. He was able to see a shining future behind the leafless tree because he himself was alive and spontaneous. Whereas the other poet was acting from his ego—*he* composed his poem, Kalidasa was acting from the quantum self—the poem created itself. In the quantum self, the actor and action tend to become one with the field where the action takes place. In this oneness, there is a purposiveness that enables the creative to see the extramundane where others see only the mundane, and there is freedom that enables him or her to choose and express the extramundane.

THE PURPOSIVENESS OF CREATIVITY

Only a little thought is necessary to realize that a common concomitant of all creative acts, fundamental or situational, inner or outer, is purposiveness. Purpose is a future goal that directs present behavior. Creative acts are not the result of random forays; instead, they are goal-directed. A creative act happens when somebody does something (contextually or meaningfully) new of value with some sort of a future vision in mind, however vague it may be.

Two kinds of purpose guide human acts. The first kind, the common kind, relates to what we may call relative purpose—it is a purpose of social origin relative to space, time, and culture. Our industry, technology, government—all serve some relative purpose. We solve problems that our societies face or invent things to satisfy a particular need or desire of the society, all to serve relative purpose.

This applies not only to industry, technology, and government. A musician may see a certain demand in the society and invent music that fills that demand. Then there is fashion; most new designs also serve relative purpose.

But there is another kind of purposive act that is guided not only by space, time, and cultural values but also by a component that transcends them and derives from a source that reflects a different vision altogether. Vincent Van Gogh, no doubt, was a product of his culture; yet he had a sense of this kind of universal purpose when he wrote to his brother Theo:

> Yes, lad, if one perseveres and works on without minding the rest, if *one tries honestly and freely to fathom nature, and does not lose hold of what one has in mind,* whatever people may say, one feels calm and firm, and faces the future quietly. Yes, one may make mistakes, one may exaggerate here and there, but the thing one makes will be original. (1937, p. 210; emphasis added)

Do you know what he is talking about? This kind of fundamental purpose plays a driving role in all creative acts—fundamental or situational, inner or outer.

However, confusion is common in evaluating the role of purpose in creativity. It is not teleology—purpose as a final cause. The teleological view may lead to thinking about creativity in terms of continuity, as in material realism, but instead of past causes continuously guiding our acts and thus determining them, future purpose does so. If continuity prevails, then, although the causal arrow is reversed, determinism returns through a back door. And creativity is antithetical to determinism.

The purposiveness of creative acts is not teleological but is itself creative. There is a general pattern of purposiveness and design in creative acts, however, the final goal is not fixed but opportunistic, contingent on the situation. The theater director Peter Brook (1968) expresses this idea perfectly:

> What is necessary is an incomplete design; a design that has clarity without rigidity; one that can be called "open" as against "shut." . . . A true theater designer will think of his designs as being all the time in motion, in action, in relation to what the actor brings to the scene as it unfolds. The later he makes his decision, the better. (p. 114)

DISCONTINUITY, PURPOSE, AND FREEDOM

Cause, everybody knows, is the relationship of the past to what is happening in the present. Purpose, on the other hand, is the relationship of the future to what is happening now. One problem in understanding the nature of creativity—and the reason that both classical physics and pure teleology are inadequate explanations for it—is that it seems to involve both cause and purpose.

It is the quantum mechanism in the brain and the mind that allows our creativity to be driven by both cause and purpose. It allows us, in a sense, to have our cake and eat it too. A quantum system evolves in time in two ways. The first is causally continuous and deterministic, strictly according to the dictates of the mathematics of quantum mechanics—the Schrödinger equation (which you can think of as an algorithm). It is true that we get evolving possibility waves, but these waves are completely determined from the algorithm. No indeterminacy here. But then in the second part of the time development of the quantum system, the possibility wave is collapsed discontinuously to a unique actuality. This part of the evolution of the quantum wave is indeterminate and nonalgorithmic (there is no way to predict which possibility will be realized) and appears random when we examine many events.

But beyond the randomness of collapse for a large statistical ensemble of events is conscious choice for the collapse of an individual event. This choice, when made in the quantum-self modality, is completely free.[1] Consciousness can and does use this freedom of choice to inject purpose in a creative act.

---

[1]Subject only to the constraints of what is possible and of the total probability for the entire collection of possibilities, which must add up to one.

THE CREATIVE COSMOS AND THE COSMIC PURPOSE

Perhaps you have pondered the allegory of Plato's cave, where we are strapped in seats watching a shadow show on a cave wall that is the world of manifestation (Plato, 1980). But what is casting the shadows? The archetypal forms of a transcendent creative universe cast these shadows, but we cannot see these forms themselves, constrained as we are to look only in front of us, only at the shadows (Figure 10.1).

The philosophers of India have further elaborated the same notion. They have a concept called *Brahman,* which means undivided consciousness; in Brahman, nothing ever happen. but all exists as possibility including prakriti, nature.

So in the beginning, nature exists only in possibility, as does consciousness as subject, with its universal themes (akin to the Platonic archetypes) such as love, beauty, truth, and justice likewise remains unmanifest. An important part of the theme collective of consciousness are the laws of manifestation.

With the advent of idealist science, the laws of manifestation are becoming clear. Nature consists of matter and mind as possibility waves. The entire universe, according to physicist Steven Hawking (1990), is a quantum possibility wave; it evolves in possibility. But then the question arises as to who or what collapses the universe from the domain of possibilities to actuality? The answer lies in self-reference.

The material universe evolves in possibility until in one of the possible universes, the possibility of sentient beings and self-reference arises. Then the first quantum measurement of the universe occurs, and that particular pathway is manifested (Goswami, 1993a, ch. 9). We are here because of the universe, and the universe is here because of us. This essential circularity is part and parcel of our self-reference.

Manifestation of self-reference—the apparent division of consciousness into one part that sees and another that is seen—is necessary for consciousness to experience itself and its themes—love, beauty, justice, and so on. "We cannot escape the fact that the world we know is constructed in order (and thus in such a way as to be able) to see itself, but in order to do so, evidently it must first cut itself up into at least one state which sees, and at least one other state which is seen," according to mathematician G. Spencer Brown (1977).

The themes of consciousness exist as unmanifest archetypes until the matter with which to manifest them evolves to sufficient complexity. Once self-referential life originates, these themes begin to manifest. Initially, this involves only simple themes such as survival and maintenance. But themes continue to manifest with greater and greater

Figure 10.1. Plato's cave. The shadow show on the wall is due to the archetypes behind us that we do not see because we are strapped. Ultimately, light is the only reality.

glory as life evolves, bearing witness to the purposive creativity of consciousness (Goswami, 1994).

Then one day the ability to map the mind evolves, and on that day self-consciousness takes a giant leap—the ability appears to see oneself through manifest eyes as separate from the world and to be aware of that separate self. Self-conscious beings such as ourselves not only are able to manifest the purposive themes of consciousness but also are aware of their creativity because of the power of the mind.

We become most creative in our lives when we recognize that the cosmic purpose is trying to act through our lives and we become aligned with that cosmic purpose. As the novelist Nikos Kazantzakis noted, one has to open up a personal riverbed through which the universe may flow.

PERSONALIZING THE PURPOSE OF THE UNIVERSE

The poet Rabindranath Tagore (1931) describes an experience that he had as a boy that perfectly exemplifies what I am talking about:

> I still remember the day in my childhood when I was made to struggle across my lessons in a first primer, strewn with isolated words smothered under the burden of spelling. The morning hour appeared to me like a once-illumined page, grown dusty and faded, discolored into irrelevant marks, smudges and gaps, wearisome in its moth-eaten meaninglessness. Suddenly, I came to a rhymed sentence of combined words, which may be translated thus—"It rains, the leaves tremble." At once I came to a world wherein I recovered my full meaning. My mind touched the creative realm of expression, and at that moment I was no longer a mere student with his mind muffled by spelling lessons, enclosed by classroom. The rhythmic picture of tremulous leaves beaten by the rain opened before my mind the world which does not merely carry information, but a harmony with my being. The unmeaning fragments lost their individual isolation and my mind revelled in the unity of a vision. In a similar manner, on that morning in the village, the facts of my life suddenly appeared to me in a luminous unity of truth. All things that had seemed like vagrant waves were revealed to my mind in relation to a boundless sea. I felt sure that some Being who comprehended me and my world was seeking his best expression in all my experiences, uniting them into an ever-widening individuality which is a spiritual work of art. (p. 93)

It is clear that, in this experience, Tagore found a personal purpose for his art in harmony with the universal purpose of a "Being who comprehended me and my world."

When Einstein was 5-years-old and ill in bed, his father brought him a magnetic compass. The fact that the needle pointed to the north regardless of how he turned the case gave young Einstein quite a thrill. According to physicist Gerald Holton (1979), Einstein's childhood experience with the magnetic compass gave him one of his future themes of research—continuity. I think that it did much more. The fact that the needle pointed to the north regardless of how one turned the case gave young Einstein the sense of wonder about the nature of the universe that directed his scientific pursuit throughout life. He said later about his search, "[I have wanted to] experience the universe as a single significant whole."

The psychologist Howard Gruber (1978) discovered in Darwin's notebooks the recurrent image of the tree of life, an "image of wide scope" that seemed to have a profound influence on Darwin in his search. I think that the image of the tree of life in Darwin's notebooks is a reflection of Darwin's feeling of oneness with the universal purpose of evolution.

The French mathematician Evariste Galois was killed in a duel at the age of 21, but even so, he contributed to a new field of mathematics. What brought him to mathematics was a chance encounter with a geometry textbook written by a gifted mathematician. While in high school, young Evariste, who was schooled at home until age 11, studied the great masters of mathematics and began proving mathematical theorems on his own. Most of his work was published posthumously.

Reading that geometry textbook must have been an unusual experience for Galois, to say the least. The creativity researcher David Feldman (1980), and later Joseph Walters and Howard Gardner (1986), have called this kind of experience a *crystallizing* experience—it is a match between a developing person and a particular field of endeavor. And it is literally a match made in heaven because I think that the quantum self is involved in this matchmaking.

The crystallizing experience is also an experience of a profound intuition that "I have found my bliss, my particular way to contribute to the purposiveness of the universe." The mythologist Joseph Campbell coined the famous phrase, "follow your bliss." He had found his bliss early in seeking and finding the meaning of reality in the mythological history of the planet.

"It is the discovery of my relationship with the universe . . . that propels my translation," said the poet/artist Carolyn Mary Kleefield in an interview. At the age of 7, Kleefield saw dust particles dancing in the sunlight streaming through a window. This gave rise to her first creative expression, and it also led to a life devoted to creativity.

These experiences of great people are not unusual. Most of us have such experiences, but only some of us recognize their significance and follow their lead. Let such experiences show you that the creative spirit of the quantum self is attempting to guide you. Then you will resonate with these lines from William Wordsworth (Wordsworth, Abrams, & Gil, 1979):

> The mind of man is fashioned and built up
> Even as a strain of music, I believe
> That there are spirits which, when they would form
> A favored being, from his very dawn
> Of infancy do open out the clouds
> As at the touch of lightning, seeking him
> With gentle visitation—quiet powers,
> Retired, and seldom recognized, yet kind,
> And to the very meanest not unknown—
> With me, though rarely, in my boyish days
> They communed.

CREATIVITY IN FREEDOM AND FREEDOM IN CREATIVITY

Creativity and freedom are practically inseparable: Creativity expresses our freedom from the known. Conversely, if we are not free to choose an alternative meaning, a new context for action, how can we create? Thus freedom is a fundamental aspect of creativity.

There is plenty of evidence that free societies—democracies, for example—maintain the conditions for more creativity than coercive societies. Well-known examples of coercive societies that sowed fear, including wartime Germany and Soviet Russia, did not fare well at all in their creative output. In comparison, democratic societies do better because of the relative absence of the fear of punishment as a primary motivator.

There are psychological experiments that demonstrate that students think better when they are not under time pressure. Creativity is not efficient. Although deadlines are sometimes useful (Napoleon thought that mental excitement never failed to stimulate the creative planning of his battles), I think for most people freedom from external pressure is more conducive to their creativity.

As a young adult, the psychologist William James was depressed because he thought that the deterministic philosophy of reality was correct. He was ill for a couple of years, even suffering a breakdown. Then he discovered the philosophy of free will and decided that "my first act of free will shall be to believe in free will." That decision yielded not only good health but also lifelong creativity.

Just as there is creativity in freedom, there is also freedom in creativity. Great creatives clearly see that there is freedom in their creative pursuits. Einstein (1979) wrote about how he was attracted to physics:

> Out there was this huge world . . . which stands before us like a great eternal riddle, at least partly accessible to our introspection and thinking. The contemplation of this world beckoned as a liberation, and I soon noticed that many a man whom I had learned to esteem and admire had found inner freedom and security in its pursuit.

It is interesting that Einstein saw freedom and security as the twin fruits of the creative adventure. This is what many of us do not know: Freedom can bring security. Giving up ego-driven control can allow the greatest (albeit paradoxical) control of all—an inner surrender to the sense of universal purpose. To use baseball terminology, creative people who find security in universal purpose are no longer limited to sandlot ball (relative purpose, problem solving) but are free to play in the major league of universal purpose and creativity.

Einstein himself saw the purpose of his research as being able "to experience the universe as a single significant whole." Darwin similarly saw the grand scale of biological research: "The grand question which every naturalist ought to have before him when dissecting a whale, or classifying a mite, a fungus or an infusorian is, What are the laws of Life?" And the poet William Wordsworth felt that he was given the gift "to see into the life of things."[2]

People of relative purpose often think that they have freedom in their mundane problem-solving pursuits, that they freely choose those pursuits. But make no mistake about it; freedom is severely compromised when we are driven by our conditioned ego-agendas:

---

[2]All quotes in this paragraph are from Briggs (1990), pp. 76-77.

> Oh, weep, they say, for freedom and dignity!
> You're not free; it's your grandfather's itch you are
> scratching.
> You have no dignity: you're not a man,
> You are a rat in a vat of rewards and punishments,
> you think you've chosen the rewards, you haven't:
> the rewards have chosen you.[3]

Creativity reflects freedom only because in addition to relative purpose it is also driven by a deep search for meaning and a deep sense of universal purpose.

The scientists G. Nicolis and I. Prigogine (1990), in their study of the behavior of complex systems, tell an interesting story of two ant species, tapinoma and tetramorium. Both species use scouts to look for and find food sources, laying trails for others to follow. The ants of the tapinoma group are about 75% efficient in following the trails of the discovered food. However, the tetramoriums are not good followers; only about 9% of them succeed in following a clearly laid out trail, and others just wander around.

But if you think that the tetratorium is at a tremendous survival disadvantage, think again. When the food supply is stable, obviously there is an advantage in the tapinoma trait; it is more efficient. If the environment is unstable and the food supply is unreliable, however, the random wanderings of the tetramorium create an enhanced opportunity to discover scarce food, giving them the survival advantage.

Of course, we are not ants, and the behavior of the ant species is genetically programmed—there is no creative freedom. My purpose in telling the story is this: if ants had true creative freedom, they would be able to choose either kind of ant behavior, as appropriate. Ultimately, freedom is the capacity for appropriate action. This is the freedom that comes into play when one searches for meaning in fundamental or situational creativity.

The world does not exclusively operate deterministically, captive to its past conditioning; after every measurement, the quantum system in our brain regenerates and is open to possibilities. If one is free to act in the quantum self, one has access to new possibilities at every moment. The quantum world of idealist science is creative at the base level.

---

[3]This poem is attributed to Archibald MacLeish published in *Boston Globe* on October 9, 1971.

A Cossack saw a rabbi walking toward the town square every day at about the same time. One day he asked, "Where are you going, rabbi?"

The rabbi replied, "I am not sure."

"You pass this way every day at this time. Surely, you know where you're going." The Cossack was irritated.

When the rabbi maintained that he did not know, the Cossack became angry, then suspicious, and finally took the rabbi to jail. Just as he was locking the cell, the rabbi faced him and said gently, "You see, I didn't know."

Before the Cossack intercepted him, the rabbi knew where he was going, but after that, he no longer knew. The interception—we can see it as a quantum measurement—changed the future progression of events. This is the message of the worldview based on quantum mechanics. The immanent world is not determined by its initial conditions, once and for all. Every event of measurement is conscious intervention; it is potentially creative, continually baring new possibilities.

QUANTUM CREATIVITY SO FAR

Thus, the quantum model of creativity has a lot to contribute to one's understanding. It gives one a handle on all the usual questions:

- When is creativity? Creativity is when there is a discontinuity or a quantum leap in the act. Look for them and follow them up.
- Where is creativity? Creative ideas lie dormant as possibilities of the mind in a quantum nonlocal domain of consciousness. Cultivate and be sensitive to nonlocal experiences and interactions.
- Who is creative? All creativity ultimately flows from the quantum self—one universal self. Recognize that you are more than your ego and its agendas. Embrace your wholeness. Accept your power.
- How is creativity? Consciousness, using its creative freedom, self-referentially collapses possibility waves in our brain-mind complex; our minds make quantum leaps, our brains pertake Shiva's dance, bringing a particular creative possibility into actuality. Be open to possibilities and tolerant to chaos to access your freedom to choose the new.

- Why is creativity? The universe is purposive. Align your purpose to cosmic purpose.

The quantum way of looking at creativity gives one answers and yet retains all the mysteries of the phenomenon that computer scientists try to deny with their claim that creativity is algorithmic problem solving. The concepts of quantum leap and quantum self are inherently mysterious; no amount of conceptual understanding can make them mundane. One has to experience them to really know them.

> Where fear does not create barriers impenetrable
> where the mind is free to take risk,
> where neither reward nor punishment
> but honest curiosity motivates,
> where we can listen to the cosmos
> whispering its purposiveness to us,
> into that land of creative freedom
> let my world awake.[4]

---

[4]Following a poem by Tagore (1913, p. 49).

PART THREE

THE CREATIVE ENCOUNTER

I was a little scared when Dr. John Problemsolver showed up on my doorstep. John never shows up anywhere unless there is a problem that he can solve. He seemed to read my mind.

"You are wondering what the problem is that I came here to solve. You, my friend, you are the problem," he said gravely, tossing his hat on a chair as he strode in.

I was not a little surprised. "Now what have I done?"

"There is a rumor going around that you are reviving the old idealist notion that creativity is God's gift to us. What's worse is that you are using science to justify this preposterous notion."

"Read my paper," I tried to conciliate him. "I haven't mentioned God a single time."

"I know, I know," Problemsolver said impatiently. "I've been told that too. You are using Sanskrit names. Atman gives us creativity, you say. What is atman if not God?"

"Atman is our quantum self, our inner self, an identity taken by consciousness because of quantum measurements in the brain. Atman is no emperor sitting on a throne in heaven and ruling the earth beneath. You need not worry."

John did not seem conciliated. "You are doing something fishy, I'm sure of it. Creativity is problem solving. Believe me, I know. But I have never met any atman or quantum self, inside or outside. It is I who does all the work. Why should I give the credit to the atman?"

"Well, John, you have a point. Indeed, the atman does not involve itself with mundane problem solving. Our continuous, local, thinking self is enough for that. But, as the novelist Marcel Proust says, "A book is the product of a different self from the self we manifest in our habits, in our social life, in our vices." When an Einstein discovers the theory of relativity or a T. S. Eliot writes *Burnt Norton*, surely they are not solving a situational problem. Surely you will agree that these people danced to a different drummer altogether. I am saying that the drummer in their case is the quantum self. Their creativity consists of making discontinuous quantum leaps into a nonlocal domain of possibility that is not accessible to the thinking ego, which only ponders the past and its reason-based extensions. Creativity requires an encounter with the quantum self."

"You still don't get it," Problemsolver growled. "Einstein and Eliot are more talented than you or I, so they do more difficult problems. But what they do is still problem solving."

"Is it? When Einstein started his research, he did not even know that the problem was the nature of time. He was worried about the nature of light. He was worried about the compatibility of Newton's laws with the theory of electricity and magnetism that Clerk Maxwell synthesized. And Eliot did not start with the thought, 'Let's see, this morning I'll write about the still point.'"

"You are talking about problem finding. Everybody knows that some people have to find their own problem in order to solve it. That way they don't have to compete. Look, it makes sense. Einstein had a full-time job as a patent clerk. He could not devote all the time that is needed to solve—what did you say?—situational problems that would outdo his competition. Naturally, he looked for a problem that nobody else would be doing. Mere survival tactic. And don't talk to me about T. S. Eliot. Poets are a little peculiar."

"Okay. Let's stick to Einstein. You know, he once said something to the effect that 'I didn't discover relativity by rational thinking alone.' Problem solving is done by rational thinking based on continuity, you must agree. So Einstein himself must have felt that he was doing something beyond rational thinking. Perhaps he was alluding to his encounter with the inner quantum self."

"Look, I'll admit that Einstein was some sort of a mystic. Forget Einstein. Let's take a case history that has been analyzed recently. The story of Alexander Calder's mobile sculpture. One can trace his development of the abstract moving mobile down to every detail, and it's nothing more that solving the Charlie problem."

Now he had piqued my own curiosity. "What's the Charlie problem?"

"You have never done the Charlie problem?" John sounded pleased to get an opportunity to show off his expertise. "Here is the problem. Dan comes home from work and finds Charlie lying dead on the floor. On the floor is some water and broken glass. Tom is in the room as well. Dan takes a look at the situation and immediately knows how Charlie died. Do you?"

"I don't have the slightest idea. You know I am not good at puzzles, especially murder mysteries."

"Why don't you get your inner self to help you? Oh, I know, I know. The inner self won't dirty its hands with such trivia. You might as well not try it. It probably would take you an hour as it did college students. You want to know how they did it?"

"Sure."

"Initially, everybody thought like you. That Charlie was a human being. That did not lead them anywhere. When they realized that it was an impasse, they started asking the question, "Was Charlie human?" When told that Charlie was not human, they immediately figured out the answer."[1]

"Ah-ha! Charlie was a fish." I could not resist.

"See," Problemsolver said proudly, "that's how creativity works—discontinuity, ah-ha experience, and all. You get an impasse with your old context. You ask a new question. The answer makes you shift to another old context, or combine two old contexts, or transfer one context to another. Calder was already doing moving sculptures, regular forms that were moved mechanically; maybe he got bored and was looking to do something different. A problem. So one day, he visited an art gallery that displayed the abstract art of Piet Mondrian. Immediately, he thought of using abstract pieces in his moving sculpture, just as students thought of fish as soon as they were told that Charlie was not human. The source of his discontinuous shift of context was *external*. Eventually, the moving abstract sculpture too became boring. How to make it more interesting?—another problem. So he thought of chucking the mechanical movement and using wind to move his abstract forms. The mobile is born, and it's not boring."[2]

"That's a pretty good construction of Calder's creativity," I said with admiration, "but you are missing something in your equation. Calder is a human being with ego; he has a belief system, a character, a way of doing things that identifies him professionally. Why should he

---

[1,2]For further elucidation, see Weisberg (1993).

change his way, the standard way to create sculptures that represent something concrete in the world, just because he saw somebody's abstract art? You are a scientist with materialist beliefs. To you every phenomenon is a material phenomenon. You know, I think otherwise; I think every phenomenon is a phenomenon of consciousness. Would you change your ways of doing science just by seeing my work?"

"Well, I would have to understand and agree with your view first," said Problemsolver.

"Exactly. You have to explore new meaning. In this exploration, you touch the quantum self. This is what Calder did when he saw Mondrian's abstract art. Calder had a sudden inspired thought—a turnabout, a discontinuous shift from his past thinking on sculpture—when he explored the meaning of abstract art. He had an ah-ha experience involving the quantum self. I am sure of it. Before, he had always thought in terms of sculptures being straightforward representations of things in the world, something that makes sense, a recognizable form. In a sudden flash of inspiration, he discovered the beauty of ambiguity that abstract painting represents, and he realized that he needed this ambiguity in his sculpture in order to bring his message to modern people—the transcendent beauty of moving forms.

But even this change did not satisfy him. There was still something too predictable and mechanical. So he continued his search for a new context. Another day, another encounter with the quantum self, another inspiration. Change mechanical motors to movement by the wind. Not only ambiguity in the form, but also ambiguity in the movement itself—right for our age where ambiguity is something that intrigues people because it helps them jump out of their mundane existence and because it is relatively rare in modern mechanical life."

"Now that is a tall tale if I ever heard one. So how does this encounter with the quantum self work?"

"You really want to know?", I cried, not a little pleased.

"I guess not. If I know how this quantum-self thing effects us, someday I might succumb to its influence. Then I won't be satisfied with solving—what did you say?—situational problems. But I hate to chase those fundamental problems. I hate to chase meaning. There is no money in it."

With that John Problemsolver picked up his hat and left.

11

THE CREATIVE ENCOUNTER

"The creative act is an encounter," said Rollo May (1976), "and is to be understood with this encounter as its center." Indeed so. An act of creativity is the fruit of the sometimes tangled encounter between the self's ego and quantum modalities. Superficially, this "intersection of the childlike and the mature," to quote Howard Gardner (1993), manifests as a product that others can see. But only the creative is aware of the deeper, inner encounter.

Although there are stages of creativity, each is an encounter, an attempt to leap from the simple hierarchy of the ego to the tangled hierarchy of the quantum self. In ordinary experiences the ego seems to be the head honcho of a simple hierarchy of mental programs, the learned representations of the world; in a creative experience, however, it becomes obvious to any introspective ego that there is a discontinuity, an unexpectedness, and that the experience does not spring from the ego's learned repertoire. The researcher Keith Sawyer (1992) wrote about jazz performers that "many describe the experience of being surprised by what they play, or they discuss the importance of *not* being consciously in control" but the comment applies to all creatives.

The creative encounter is the encounter between our human-being-ness (the ego, simple hierarchy, conditioned predictability) and our godness (the quantum self, tangled hierarchy, extended possibilities, and mystery). Michelangelo left us a wonderful archetypal image of this encounter on the ceiling of the Sistine Chapel—Adam and God mutually reaching out to each other.

147

THE QUANTUM SELF AND THE EGO

To understand the nature of the encounter, let's analyze the causal sequence of events that leads to a conscious experience in response to a learned stimulus. In the beginning, there is only the unconscious (consciousness without awareness), undivided from all the possibilities of potential experience. The possibilities, such as the quantum waves of thought, evolve in time like a quantum foam on the ocean of uncertainty.

The collapse of possibility into actuality self-referentially manifests the choosing and recognizing subject simultaneously with the object(s) of recognition and awareness as the undivided possibility world in consciousness appears to divide into a subject-object dichotomy. One part in consciousness sees another, and sees it in its suchness. What is most salient at this juncture is the seeing, the verb, not the subjectness or the objectness, who sees or what is seen. In other words, the relation of the subject and the objects it experiences remains one of tangled hierarchy and dependent co-arising. Self-identity is defined by this beingness of the quantum self, not by the individual ego's object-manipulating doingness. This primary awareness throbs with the possibility of creativity, the experience of new meaning and context, even when the stimulus is old and familiar.

But the causal scenario leading to an ordinary experience continues beyond this primary-awareness event. The time-evolution of the quantum wave-forms continues in the transcendent domain of possibility in response to the memories in the individual brain that play back secondary stimuli. Again there is choice, collapse, recognition, and awareness of secondary mental states. However, this choice of secondary-awareness events is not free, but prejudiced in favor of the learned response (Goswami, 1993a; Mitchell & Goswami, 1992). These secondary-awareness events happen in quick succession as more of the past memories play back their content. Psychologists use the apt term *preconscious* to talk about this shadowy domain of events of muted awareness in secondary processing.

Memories and their playback and conditioned responses imprint their "I" on the mental states of secondary awareness. The learned programs mask the tangled hierarchy of the quantum self with a simple hierarchy in which the top level is experienced as I—*this* personal, doing self separate from all other selves. Figure 11.1 is an artist's rendition of this scenario leading to a personal experience.

Our experience of separateness is due to the illusion caused by the mirror of memory, and our experience of so-called "free will" with-

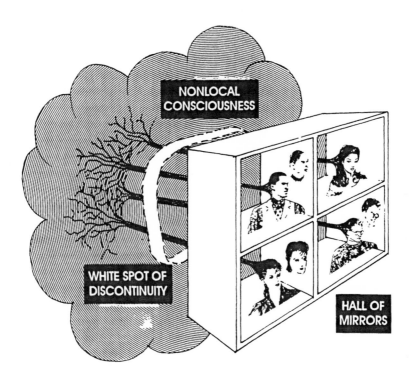

Figure 11.1. Nonlocal consciousness—our inviolate level—is beyond the white spot that signifies discontinuity. Meanwhile, our primary experience is individualized through reflections in the mirror of memory. One experiences a separate, individual I from the cubbyhole of the simple hierarchy that memory creates.

in our own private little cubbyhole is defined by our past.[1] For real freedom and creativity, we have to extend our passage through the twilight zone of the preconscious in order to penetrate through the maze of memory playbacks and conditioned responses to the unconditioned beingness of the quantum self.

Incidentally, the experiments of neurophysiologist Benjamin Libet and his collaborators (1979) during patients' brain surgery give you an idea of the time window of the ego/quantum-self encounter.

---

[1] There are now experiments that indicate that the free will experienced at the ego level when, for example, I raise my arm, is not free at all. An EEG connected to my scalp would show electrical activity in my brain that would inform any onlooker that I am going to raise my arm. Interestingly, however, we retain the free will to say no to a conditioned tendency to act; see Libet (1985).

When, for example, Libet applied a touch stimulus to a patient's hand, the patient was able, in about 200 milliseconds, to press a button to indicate that the stimulus had reached his brain; but it took 500 milliseconds for the patient to report the touch verbally. The extra time is the time taken for secondary-awareness processing. In the ego/quantum-self encounter, this processing time becomes shorter and shorter, and there is "flow," a spontaneity of experience that contributes to the ecstasy of creativity. You very likely have experienced a few enchanted moments of flow when the ego is a mere function and not a structured identity (Csikszentmihayi, 1990). All creatives at such times access a mode of being, the quantum self, in which creative freedom and spontaneity overrule egoic deliberation and slavery to past conditioning.

Often, the encounter begins with the agony of the ego's anxiety. Some experiments on animal training give a provocative perspective on this anxiety. Typically in these experiments an animal is trained in a Pavlovian learning context to discriminate between, for example, a circle and an ellipse. But after the discrimination is learned, the task is made progressively more difficult—the ellipse is made rounder and rounder to look more and more like the circle. Finally, there is no difference at all, and discrimination is impossible. At this stage the poor animal begins to show symptoms of severe anxiety—in short, neurosis. Significantly, naive animals (those not taught to distinguish between an ellipse and a circle) do not show this phenomenon of "experimental neurosis."

Why this neurosis? It seems to me that the smaller capacity of the animal's brain to make representations of the world (the programs of its classical computer) gives it a weak "ego," and it is this weak ego that makes the animal unable to handle creative anxiety and renders it incapable of creative learning. Creativity is the encounter of the ego and the quantum self, and both are important. In contrast, dolphin-training experiments (see Chapter 5) demonstrate that dolphins are able to handle the anxiety of the creative encounter. I am convinced that this is because, like us, they have a bigger brain-to-body-mass ratio, a bigger repertoire of learned programs, and thus a stronger, more secure, more developed ego.

THE ENCOUNTER IN THE PREPARATION STAGE: DESTRUCTURING

In the preparation stage the ego modality, at least outwardly, dominates. We may set ourselves to solve a problem; we may begin by making a survey of what is known about the problem; we may break up the problem into parts to get a grasp on its solvability. But this is all preliminary. The real work begins when we start questioning what we have learned, even questioning the problem itself.

This is because in our ego, as in the central processing unit of a computer, we deal comfortably only with gathering and digesting information; it is in the quantum modality that we deal with the new. It is our quantum self that communicates the new to us, which is felt as intuition in our ego mode. The fact is, preparation always involves an intuition, a vague feeling of something new to be done.

The word *intuition* is used with at least three different connotations. First, to some people, intuition means expertise. An engineer once was called in to fix a machine. He inspected the problem for a few seconds, tapped the machinery a few times, and it started working. Later, when asked to explain why he billed $1,007 for a little tapping, he said he charged $7.00 for the tapping, and the rest was for knowing where to tap. This knowing where to tap is a kind of intuition—an ability to go through problem spaces in the memory very quickly.

Second, some people use the word intuition to mean insight, a sense of the inner nature of things, which includes creative insight. Third, intuition means "a value-anticipatory perception that orients creative work in a promising direction."[2] It is this third meaning that is of interest to us here.

Think of intuition as a summons from the quantum self. The artist Georgia O'Keeffe one day had an emotional crisis. She locked the door of her studio, hung up her recent paintings, and faced the truth. She had been painting other people's ideas. Was there nothing original that she could paint? At that moment she became open to the universe: there were abstract shapes, intuitive glimpses of original images, that no classical computer had collected in any problem space, human or machine. A moment of crisis brought her the crucial intuition of where to go.

One of Rabindranath Tagore's plays about creativity begins with the hero singing a song about this call of intuition from the quantum self—a very appropriate introduction to the preparation stage of the creative journey. When one does not hear this siren song, when one is content with the ego homeostasis, creativity remains quiescent. The poet Robert Browning wrote only one poem during the first three years of his marriage to Elizabeth Barrett. He was too content.

---

[2]This quote is from a paper I refereed for the *Creativity Research Journal*; as is customary, the name of the author or of the article was concealed from me.

Thus, in the preparation stage of creativity the encounter between the ego and the quantum self plays out as alternative intuition and preparation, nonlocal communication and local-information gathering.

The tangled interaction of intuition and preparation eventually leads to a destructuring of the old to make room for the new. (I have already described a possible brain mechanism of how this happens, in Chapter 8.) Experientially, one needs a strong ego to handle the destructuring. In a way, it is similar to entering the world of a surrealistic painting where everything is distorted relative to the comfortable homeostasis of an established belief system.

The creativity researcher Frank Barron (1968) has noted an apparent paradox of highly creative people; in test after test, these people score high both on stable traits of ego-strength, such as coping with setbacks, and of ego-weakness, such as neurosis, anxiety, and deviance. The resolution of the paradox is that the ego-weakness we see in creative people reflects the destructuring of their conceptual world, which causes a partial destructuring of their ego-structures as well, resulting in anxiety and its attendant difficulties.

Carl Rogers (1959) took an important step toward understanding the creative process when he realized that the preparation stage must ultimately end up in creating an open mind. The conviction must grow that existing ideas, programs, and contexts are just not enough. Even the way the creative poses a problem may not be right, and so on. We put to rest what we know, what we have accumulated in our search, and acknowledge, "I don't know." In the words of T. S. Eliot (1943):

> In order to arrive at what you do not know
> You must go by a way which is the way of ignorance. (p. 29)

We reside in this ignorance, this don't-know mind, this "cloud of unknowing," to quote a 12th-century Christian mystic, as we wait for the quantum self to communicate. (Of course, the quantum self is already communicating because there is an intuition that supports the destructuring of the known that is already taking place.)

Some laboratory studies of problem solving indicate the importance of having a large repertoire of contexts— in other words, expertise, the first half of our preparation dynamic; but no similar importance has been found for maintaining an open mind—for example, an ability for divergent thinking (Mansfield & Busse, 1981). What should we make of these studies? Well, problems that can be solved under laboratory situations are problems that require only reshuffling of existing contexts—there is no discontinuous creativity. Because there is no need for a discontinuous shift of contexts or meaning, there is no advantage in developing an open mind. The ability to search problem spaces is enough.

There is another aspect of preparation leading to an open mind. When we prepare, we familiarize ourselves with what is possible. We search for a map in the footprints of great people's work. But, ultimately, our minds can access all the unconditioned mental states of the mental world, if only we are open to the information. We are, in this sense, like a hologram. Each little piece has the information of the whole. Even with libraries, even with the information superhighway, we, in our egos, are privy only to little pieces of the totality, but jumping to the quantum self gives us access to the whole mental world. Da Vinci knew this when he wrote, "This is the real miracle, that all shapes, all colors, all images of every part of the universe are concentrated in a single point."

One of the most crucial aspects of preparedness is the pursuit of a burning question. Have you ever been stalked by such a question? Often people fail to realize the significance of this event and do not act on it. But without burning questions there is no movement toward insight. Everyone understands that stepping into a full bathtub causes the water to overflow. Only an Archimedes, faithful to his burning question, can see in that act the answer for which he has been searching.

An open mind and a burning question are the settings for the next stage of the process of creativity—alternate work and relaxation. Work is more preparation, but what is the relaxation for? The relaxation is needed to incubate the egg of insight in the unconscious processing of new unlearned stimuli, conflicts, and ambiguities.

ALTERNATE STRIVING AND SURRENDER: PERSPIRATION AND INSPIRATION

Before the insight or creative illumination can take place, there are many close encounters between the quantum self and the ego as they alternate between the inspiration of surrender to the quantum modality and the perspiration of the ego modality in which consciousness is trying to capture the insight.

Why so much perspiration? There is perspiration because the mind's superpositions of possibilities, generated in our unconscious processing, are still dominated by our learned contexts with their greater probability weights. The probability weighting of the new is small. For it to have a chance of manifesting, we must bring our will to bear, and we must be persistent (behaviorally, this itself is a big leap because of the strong egoic tendency to escape when the going gets tough; but tough creative people keep going). Persistence is important because it increases the number of collapses of the mind's quantum state relative to the same question, thus increasing the chance to realize a new response.

Marie Curie did her doctoral thesis on the emission of electro-magnetic radiation from uranium, but she got bogged down with the problem of finding the reason for the radiation. Her husband, Pierre, joined her research, and their joint perseverance eventually produced the insight that a new element, radium, was responsible.

The importance of the persistence of the will is noted by the mathematician G. Spencer Brown in words that describe the inexorable quality of having a burning question:

> To arrive at the simplest truth, as Newton knew and practiced, requires years of contemplation. Not activity. Not reasoning. Not calculating. Not busy behavior of any kind. Not reading. Not talking. Simply bearing in mind what it is one needs to know. (1979)

Emily Dickinson called this intensity "white heat." Clearly, the creative individual's ego has to be strong-willed to be persistent and ready to handle the anxiety associated with the quantum jump into the new insight that threatens the ego homeostasis. Thus, the contribution of the ego is justly recognized in Thomas Edison's saying that genius is 2% inspiration and 98% perspiration.

But that 2% inspiration is crucially important. Without it, no creative can happily (yes, creatives by and large are not unhappy people) maintain the persistent striving. Rabindranath Tagore, who understood this alternate play of will and surrender perfectly, puts it well in one of his Bengali songs. Because no translation is available, I am paraphrasing Tagore's experience in the context of my point in the following poem:[3]

> When infinity calls
> I want to fly to its Siren's song;
> I want to hold the infinity in my palm
>   NOW.
> I forget I don't have wings,
> that I am too damn local.

---

[3]The Bengali poem referred to is named *Ami Suduren Piasi.*

This is the stage of striving that all creatives know too well. Tagore understands the stage of relaxation, too, which is different:

> On lazy afternoons, sunshine like butter,
> swaying trees cast dancing shadows.
> I am bathed in the light of infinity.
> Unattended, still it fills my mind's sky.
> I process unaware, in silent bliss.

Tagore also knew that this bliss does not last. Inspiration again fuels the desire for manifestation:

> Oh infinity, oh great infinity—
> go on, play your flute, sing your song.
> Let me forget
> the closed doors of my room.
> I want to be restless with creative energy.
> Will and surrender, surrender and will. Then . . .

THE AH-HA INSIGHT

I vividly remember the day when I came to the realization that all things are made of consciousness, not matter, and that we have to develop an idealist science—a science within consciousness—from this vantage point. For many years, I had been researching the idea that consciousness collapses the quantum possibility wave. I was struggling to write the umpteenth version of this research in book form but always fell short when it came to explaining how consciousness could emerge in the material brain. That day, on vacation, I was explaining the difficulty of understanding the emergent consciousness to a mystic friend. He did not agree with my view and, at some point in the middle of a big argument, made a statement long familiar to me: "There is nothing but God." All of a sudden, without warning, a turning about took place in my psyche. There is nothing but consciousness, *and one can do science on the basis of the primacy of consciousness.* I could already see glimpses of the new science, but I was in no hurry. I stayed in the glow of that ah-ha experience for a long time. The inspiration of that insight was instrumental in the subsequent research and development of the paradigm of science within consciousness that culminated in *The Self-Aware Universe* (Goswami, 1993a).

The discontinuous creative insight is the result of the discontinuous quantum collapse of waves of new possibility into actuality. We bring
them to actuality by recognition. As the Chinese poet Chu Hsi wrote:

> If we simply recognize the face of the eastern wind
> Each of the thousand flowers, red or purple, is Spring.
> (quoted in Chung-yuan, 1970)

Finally, with the alternate play of will and surrender, persistence
and relaxation, conscious and unconscious processing, we *in our primary quantum modality* see the gestalt, the pattern of little insights that
together make up the new breakthrough context. Then consciousness
nonlocally collapses the pattern out of all the uncollapsed superpositions that have accumulated during the creative journey, and we have a
primary experience of our quantum modality—the joy of creativity.[4]

Remember the time lag between primary and secondary experiences? Our preconscious preoccupation with the secondary processes
(indicated by the time lag) distracts us from our quantum self, making it
difficult to experience the quantum level of our operation. A creative
experience is one of the few occasions when we directly experience the
quantum modality with little or no reaction time, and it is this spontaneous encounter that produces *ananda*—the spiritual joy of the ah-ha
insight. It is this spiritual joy that Rabindranath Tagore was writing
about as his experience of the light (of the quantum self):

> Light, my light, the world-filling light;
> the eye-kissing light, heart-sweetening light.
> Ah the light dances, my darling, at the
> center of my life. The light strikes, my
> darling, the chords of my love; the sky opens,
> the wind runs wild, laughter passes
> over the earth. (1913, p. 73)

There is much circumstantial evidence that exalted experiences
occur whenever the time lag of secondary processing is reduced.
Abraham Maslow's (1968) data on peak experiences—direct transcendental experiences of the self rooted in the unity and harmony of a cosmic Being, experiences crucial for inner creativity—provide another

---

[4]There is nonlocality in the collapse of the possibility structure that brings
about insight. Many different uncollapsed coherent superpositions are
involved, as are many different brain areas.

example of reduced reaction time and the resulting glimpse by the experiencer of the quantum self.

ONE BIG BANG OR MANY LITTLE BANGS?

Does the illumination of an act of fundamental creativity come in one big bang when the context shifts discontinuously, bringing clarity to the entire pattern of little clues? Or are there many little insights that together contribute to the moment of final reckoning?

There is evidence for both in the literature of creatives. Music came to Mozart in wholes. The physicist Nicola Tesla saw in his mind's eye his ideas in their entirety. The poet Rabindranath Tagore wrote many of his poems in one inspired session, suggesting that for him illumination was often one big bang. On the other hand, Gruber's (1981) study of Darwin's notebooks clearly reveals that for Darwin many insights—little bangs—eventually contributed to his big breakthrough—the theory of natural selection as the agent of the evolution of life.

What is the explanation for this ambiguity in the evidence? There are two potentially somewhat competing features: conscious and unconscious processing. As noted, unconscious processing has the advantage of a fast proliferation of ideas via the spreading of uncollapsed quantum superpositions. On the other hand, collapsing a particular idea has the advantage of having a bird in hand. Once collapsed, the idea is forever available for subsequent recall, although its premature collapse may hamper the future development of quantum superpositions.

Creatives always walk a razor's edge—to collapse or not to collapse is a difficult question. Obviously, their choice also depends on, and perhaps defines, the style of the particular creative.

THE ENCOUNTER IN MANIFESTATION

The fourth and final stage, the manifestation stage, is the encounter of idea and form. The self in its ego modality has to develop form for the creative idea generated in stage three. It must sort out and organize the elements of the idea and verify that it works, but there is much back and forth between idea and form. Thus the fourth stage of the encounter between the ego and the quantum self plays out as this dance of alternating idea (gained from the quantum leap of insight) and form (from the learned repertoire of the ego).

The importance of form is very apparent in studies done with children's drawings. What is found is that, until children learn certain forms, they are quite unable to express certain creative ideas. And obviously, without the idea, there would be no need to use a certain form.

Even Einstein had trouble making the transition from idea to form. Many times he complained about his struggle to find the right form, the right mathematics, to express his idea of a unified theory of all the forces of the world, the problem that engaged him in the latter part of his life. In retrospect, we know that his idea was right; but even after 30 years of frustrated search, the form eluded him.

The fact is, even after the brain has made a map of a novel mental idea, the unavailability of form in the ego's known repertoire may send one hunting for ideas once again. This is what causes the oscillations in the restructuring process.

And then for many acts of creation, finding form in the outer world is hard work, sometimes literally. An architect's vision may never find expression in the outer world because of economics. Michelangelo's struggle with creative manifestation included the struggle for more marble. Even after their insight about the existence of a new chemical element, radium, it took Marie Curie and her husband Pierre four years and the processing of tons of uranium to isolate it.

When Nikos Kazantzakis first attempted to write *Zorba, the Greek,* he expressed his frustration with form in this way:

> I wrote, I crossed out. I could not find suitable words. Sometimes they were dull and soulless, sometimes indecently gaudy, at other times abstract and full of air, lacking a warm body. I knew what I planned to say when I set out, but the shiftless, unbridled words dragged me elsewhere. . . . Realizing the time had not arrived, that the secret metamorphosis inside the seed still had not been completed, I stopped. (quoted in Malville, 1975, p. 81)

Kazantzakis had to stop for further mini-insights, and the further tangled play of idea and form.

To summarize, the creative process is the encounter of the ego and the quantum self, revealing itself as the alternating play of information and communication, perspiration and inspiration, form and idea (Figure 11.2). The following lines from Rabindranath Tagore (1976) summarize all these aspects of the creative encounter with tailor-made perfection:

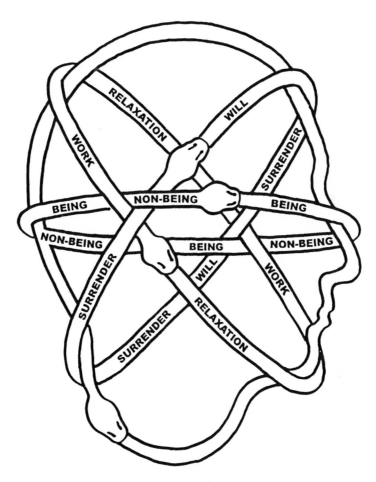

Figure 11.2. The tangled hierarchies of the various stages of the creative process (after Charles-Hampden-Turner, 1981).

Melody seeks to fetter herself in rhythm.
While the rhythm flows back to melody.
Idea seeks the body in form,
Form its freedom in the idea.
The infinite seeks the touch of the finite,
The finite its release in the infinite.
What drama is this between creation and destruction—
This ceaseless to and fro between idea and form?
Bondage is striving after freedom,
And freedom seeking rest in bondage. (p. 34)

12

INSIGHT AND PROCESS IN SCIENTIFIC CREATIVITY

Reader: So now I know *about* creativity. I know definitions. I know what is involved: discontinuous quantum leaps, quantum nonlocality, conscious purposiveness, freedom to choose among the possibilities of the quantum mind, ego-ability to tolerate the destructuring and restructuring of chaotic brain processes, and the openness to a tangled-hierarchical quantum self beyond my ego.

I remember experiencing in my childhood openness to the hidden transcendent order of possibilities. I even glimpsed that the universe has purposiveness and that I personally have a destiny to contribute to that purposiveness.

So why have I not done anything creative that resembles that of a genius? If I am potentially a genius, how do I open the bottle of creativity, let out the genie, and manifest my genius?

Author: Maybe you don't take yourself seriously.

R: On the contrary, my spouse says I take myself too seriously.

A: You know what I mean. Your wanting creativity is more wanting to want because the idea of being famous, being somebody, appeals to you. When you want creativity itself, which is not concerned with fame per se, instead of wanting creativity for its goodies, then you become creative.

R: Just like that?

A: Well, not just like that. Not usually. You enter a process, but actively, you don't just think about it.

R: Oh, yes, the creative process. Preparation, incubation, insight, and manifestation. Does knowing about the stages of the creative process really help me?

A: Definitely. Knowing about the stages of the creative process is important to all creatives or creativity aspirants because, in one way or another, we all tend to ignore the importance of some of the stages. For example, if you go to a "new age" workshop, you may hear the axiom "it does not have to be hard to be good." This philosophy undermines the importance of preparation. Many spiritual seekers seek "enlightenment" experiences (of inner creativity) but ignore whatever experiences they do have. They never arrive at the transformation they really are after and always wonder if they are having the "right" enlightenment experience. Most of us distrust the importance of unconscious processing and go on striving full force when what is needed is relaxation. And, of course, many of us don't believe in sudden insights.

I am convinced that understanding the creative process helps us make the transition from wanting the goodies to really wanting creativity. But there is more to understanding the creative process than engaging the intellect.

R: Yes?

A: Yudhisthira, the crown prince in Mahabharata, was asked under the threat of death, "What is the path?" His life-saving reply was, "The maps are hidden in the cave. Studying the ways of great men and women reveals the path." So let me urge you to study the processes of individual creative people.

We begin our study of individual creative people and their experience with science. Why science? First, the data for creativity in science is abundant and well-studied. And second, this author has intimate familiarity with scientific creativity.

Here are, in brief, the subjects of the rest of the chapter:

- Science is served by all three modes of our investigation of it: fundamental creativity, situational creativity, and problem solving. However, the role of each is different.
- We need not distrust either unconscious processing nor sudden insight. There is much trustworthy testimony in regard to both.
- The study of a couple of case histories will give some idea of how the creative process unfolds over a long time-scale.

PARADIGMS AND PARADIGM SHIFTS

Niels Bohr once said about somebody's theory that it was crazy, but not crazy enough to be right! A creative solution to a problem must be "crazy enough" to open up a new context. Bohr's work on the atom certainly satisfied his own criterion. On the face of it, the quantum jump was a crazy idea; it violated the bedrock notion of the continuity of movement in classical physics. And yet, shifting the context of atomic motion from continuity to discontinuity is revolutionizing our worldview. When Bohr's quantum leap developed into quantum mechanics, the discontinuity remained and obviated the basic assumptions of the old physics; it became the nucleus of what the philosopher Thomas Kuhn (1970) called a paradigm shift from the old physics to the new physics to a new idealist science.

A *paradigm* is a supertheory that acts as an umbrella for new work in a given field of science. A paradigm shift ushers in an entire new worldview, a new conceptual lens through which researchers and eventually all people see. It takes momentous creativity to shift paradigms, as it involves changing the very contexts of how people think within a given field.

It also takes momentous creativity to extend a paradigm to new arenas of experience. Einstein's theory of relativity is an example. The theory of relativity did not change the underlying assumptions of the old Newtonian physics, such as continuity or determinism and causality, but it extended the old physics into the arena of high-speed objects—objects with speed close to the speed of light. Very importantly, this extension led to a new outlook on how we view time. Before relativity, time was seen as absolute; everything happened *in* time, which remained independent of everything else. But relativity cut time down to size; time is relative, after all, and depends on motion.

So this is fundamental about paradigm shifts and paradigm extensions in science—new themes are discovered in the play of the world. The old Newtonian physics that replaced the medieval Aristotelian physics gave us the themes of causal determinism, objectivity, and such—themes that readily showed themselves in the behavior of macroscopic matter once we learned how to look at it and analyze it. The new quantum physics brought quantum jumps and acausality to physics (which, as we have seen, opened the door to understanding creative uncertainty via the current paradigmatic shift leading to idealist science), leaving the old themes only a contingent validity. Similarly, relativity theory replaced the theme of absolutes with the new theme of relativity in every manifest context, even time and space.

The vast majority of scientific work, however, consists of work within a paradigm. Is there creativity in paradigm research? Yes, but it is at best situational creativity. Much of paradigm research is problem solving.

Paradigm shifts and paradigm extensions involve subtle problem finding before problem *solving* begins. The momentous shifts of context bring to the foreground underlying problems—the *real,* though not obvious, ones that have to be solved to eliminate the anomalies of the old paradigm. In contrast, paradigm research is mainly problem *solving* within familiar territory—mere applications of known principles with occasional forays into situational creativity that further clarify the meaning of the paradigm.

To summarize, in the realm of scientific creativity, there is clear evidence (read Kuhn's work) that it is useful to recognize two distinct kinds of processes: (a) transparadigm (fundamental) creativity involved with paradigm-shifting and paradigm-extending discoveries of new contexts; and (b) problem solving and situational creativity within a given paradigm for which one uses a reasoned reshuffle of known contexts or reveals new meaning for the known context(s).

THE CREATIVE PROCESS IN SCIENCE

The creative process is the encounter of our ego and the quantum self and occurs in several stages: preparation, unconscious processing, sudden insight, and manifestation. The importance of preparation and manifestation is fairly obvious; there is also plenty of testimony from scientists themselves as to the importance of unconscious processing and sudden insight.

Einstein once asked a psychologist at Princeton, "Why is it I get my best ideas in the morning while I'm shaving?" The psychologist answered in the vein that consciousness needs to let go of inner controls for new ideas to emerge (cited in May, 1976). This is the point. In ordinary waking consciousness, the ego's inner controls, exerted via secondary-awareness experiences, drown out all preconscious primary experiences through which the quantum self "communicates" to us (in our ego). When we are relaxing—shaving is a good example, dreaming and reverie are others, passively waiting is another—the normally preconscious primary experience breaks through, causing the creative encounter and the resulting insight.

The Bohr atom was conceived in a dream. The chemist Dmitry Mendeleef, who discovered the famous periodic table of chemical elements (a way of classifying the elements), wrote: "I saw in a dream a table where all the elements fell into place as required." The mathematician Jacques Hadamard (1939) reported discovering the solutions of long-sought problems "at the very moment of sudden awakening [from dreams]."

Passive waiting works, too, as in the example of the Nobel laureate chemist Melvin Calvin:

> One day I was waiting in my car while my wife was on an errand. I had had for some months some basic information from the laboratory which was incompatible with everything which, up until then, I knew about the photosynthetic process. I was waiting, sitting at the wheel, most likely parked at the red zone, when the recognition of the missing compound occurred. It occurred just like that—quite suddenly—and suddenly, also, in a matter of seconds, the cyclic character of the path of carbon became apparent to me, not in the detail which ultimately was elucidated, but the original recognition. (quoted in Vaughn, 1979, pp. 75–76)

Creativity during dreams, reverie, or times of relaxation or passive waiting is the best proof that there is indeed unconscious processing and discontinuity in the otherwise continuous stream of consciousness during the process of creativity. However, there are no less impressive reports of discontinuous creative thoughts that occur during the work phase of the work-relaxation dynamic duo. For example, Niels Bohr is said to have discovered the important idea of the "compound nucleus"—a long lived excited state that an atomic nucleus forms when bombarded by low-energy neutrons—while listening to and hassling the speaker at a seminar on a related subject. James Watson and Francis Crick discovered the meaning of diffraction photographs of the DNA molecule in terms of the double-helix structure of the molecule during an intense work session.

Willis Harman and Howard Rheingold, in their book *Higher Creativity* (1984), commented on the frequency with which creatives employ a striking phrase to describe the discontinuity of their creative acts:

> The phrase "like a flash of lightning" occurs again and again in the first hand descriptions [of the creative act]. There is no doubt that this is an observation repeatedly confirmed by independent and reliable sources, a clue to the state in which deep insights occur. (p. 27)

The mathematician Karl Fredrick Gauss provides one example of such a description from a scientist:

> Finally, two days ago, I succeeded, not on account of my painful efforts, but by the grace of God. Like a sudden flash of lightning, the riddle happened to be solved. I myself cannot say what was the conducting thread which connected what I previously knew with what made my success possible. (quoted in Hadamard, 1939, p. 15)

Notice also the insistence on the role of the "grace of God." This undoubtedly reflects the keen sense of acausality felt by the creative, who knew that he did not make the discovery via something he did, such as conscious, step-by-step thinking.

Finally, I would like to emphasize that it is in no way necessary to assume that a creative act is the result of a single moment of insight. One discontinuous sudden insight is part of a series that may well involve additional, important sudden insights.

CASE HISTORY: DARWIN

We are fortunate in the case of Charles Darwin and his discovery of the theory of biological evolution, the idea that nature selects among the random variations of the hereditary material of biological beings on the basis of survivability, because Darwin kept detailed notebooks of his research. These notebooks have been studied intensively by Howard Gruber (1981). For a glimpse of how creative acts *actually manifest* in science, I turn to Gruber's study of Charles Darwin.

First of all, was there a culminating moment of insight? Darwin himself identified a moment that can be compared with Newton's apple experience:

> In October 1838, that is, fifteen months after I had begun my systematic enquiry, I happened to read for amusement Malthus on *Population,* and being well prepared to appreciate the struggle for existence which everywhere goes on from long continued observation of animals and plants, it at once struck me that under these circumstances favorable variations would tend to be preserved and unfavorable ones to be destroyed. The result of this would be the formation of a new species. Here, then, I had at last got a theory by which to work. (pp. 172–173)

Gruber accepts that there may be something special in Darwin's "Malthusian insight," but he also emphasizes the totality of the process. In the introduction to his book, *Darwin on Man* (1981), Gruber says

> The reader may be disappointed if he approaches the subject expecting a tale leading up to one climactic moment of great insight, like the dubious stories of Archimedes' bath and Newton's apple. Although the progress of Darwin's thought is punctuated by many vital moments of insight, each one filling him with the joy of discovery, it is hard to find any single insight which in the living moment really seemed more vital than the others to the thinker himself. (pp. 172–173)

But there is no need to see a contradiction between Gruber's observation and Darwin's comment. Before his final synthesis, Darwin indeed made at least two important shifts of context that were discontinuous from his previous thinking.

Initially, Darwin believed the then-prevalent notion that biological beings are made of simple "living elementary particles" called monads that were being constantly created. Then simple organisms became complex. The turnabout, giving up on the monad theory, occurred when he was confronted with the contradiction that some organisms stay simple—unicellular fossils were found to exist. (However, don't think that simply looking at the data forced the turnabout; the data were not that unambiguous and never are for preparadigm science.)

Darwin also theorized, in line with Lamarck's idea, that changes in the environment produced variation in monads and, thereby, evolution. But his experiences in the Galapagos Islands clearly showed him much contradictory evidence; a great deal of variation existed without any great push from the environment. Another turnabout—giving up on Lamarckian theory.

Behold! These turnabouts are no less discontinuous than reaching a new positive context for evolution, which happened when Darwin read Malthus's essay on population. Furthermore, there were many details, many little but important problems associated with his insights; Darwin had many "mini-insights" to resolve these issues. Thus Gruber is right; there was more than one discontinuity in Darwin's experience.

But Darwin is also right. It takes discontinuous leaps to give up on theories when there is no paradigm to guide you, but giving up on theories does not necessarily produce the same ah-ha as the positing of a new theory. Seeing Malthus's work, Darwin realized the superfecundity of nature—that a lot more offspring are produced than there are parents. Hence he was able to make the bold hypothesis that it is nature, acting on chance variations, that applies the selection pressure that produces evolution.

One can easily identify the various phases of the creative process—preparation, incubation, insight, and so on—in Darwin's work, but the remarkable thing is that these phases did not occur neatly as one problem after another was solved. Instead, Darwin had what Gruber calls a *network of enterprises*—many different issues. The growth of thought in each of these issues formed an interconnected whole. So, ultimately, at least for paradigm-shifting creative work such as that of Darwin's theory of evolution or Newton's theory of gravitation, the creative process that is relevant involves the entire life (or a substantial portion thereof) of the creative individual. "Not only is the individual lightning stroke complex; it is part of a more complex system, the thunderstorm as a whole. And each storm is a part of a still wider worldwide system of storms" (Gruber & Davis, 1988).

CASE HISTORY: EINSTEIN AND RELATIVITY

In contrast to Darwin, Einstein did not keep detailed notebooks. By the time interest peaked in his creative process and people started questioning him, his recollections had become somewhat vague, and therefore he was unable to settle controversial issues. For example, did he or did he not use the famous Michelson-Morley experiment (an experiment that proved crucial in negating the existence of an all-pervading ether as the medium through which light travels) as the pivot of his thinking about relativity? Nevertheless, enough is known about the development of his thought for us to make a good case in favor of the quantum/idealist-science theory of the creative process.

First of all, could Einstein have discovered the theory of relativity by bit-by-bit, rational, algorithmic thinking alone? Indeed, there are researchers who think so (Miller, 1989). And why not? If there is a good case to be made for the power of continuous, conscious thinking, Einstein's is it. As his student and collaborator Banesh Hoffmann recalled:

> Einstein would stand up quietly, and say, in his quaint English, "I will a little think." So saying, he would pace up and down and walk around in circles, all the time twirling a lock of his long grey hair around his forefinger. At these moments of high drama, Infeld [another physicist-collaborator of Einstein's] and I would remain

completely still, not daring to move or make a sound, lest we interrupt his train of thought. [Many minutes later, all of a sudden] Einstein would visibly relax and a smile would light up his face. . . . Then he would tell us the solution to the problem, and almost always the solution worked. (quoted in Holton, 1979, p. 153)

It is easy to theorize that Einstein had access to hidden algorithms unavailable to the rest of us with which he made his unique discoveries, including his theory of relativity.

But alas, such a theory does not hold water if we want to give any credence to Einstein's own musings. Einstein often insisted that he did not make his discoveries by rational thinking alone, and he talked about a sense of wonder and intuition and imagination. As elegantly summarized by Gerald Holton (1979), Einstein's motto was "to live and think in all three portions of our rich world—the level of everyday experience, the level of scientific reasoning, and the level of deeply felt wonder." What Einstein experienced as "deeply felt wonder" is the quantum modality of the self with which he had a not-infrequent encounter. Often Einstein expressed his deep feelings about this encounter in a spiritual fashion: "I want to know how God created this world. I am not interested in this or that phenomenon, in the spectrum of this or that element, I want to know His thoughts, the rest are details." Other times Einstein would say, "God is cunning, but He is not malicious." In the exuberance of his creativity, he would declare, "The most incomprehensible thing about the universe is that we can comprehend it."

I now turn to the creative process that led explicitly to the theory of relativity (special relativity), one of science's most celebrated restructurings. Einstein's preparation stage consisted of a thorough grounding in Newtonian physics, Maxwell's theory of electromagnetism, and the philosophy of Ernest Mach. Especially from Mach's philosophy he acquired a conviction that there is no such thing as absolute motion—the idea that any motion can be independent of other movements. Somewhere along the line he also had the intuition that there were deep flaws in the philosophical conception of space and time.

Alternate periods of conscious and unconscious processing began as early as 1895, when he was only 16-years-old and had an intuition that the nature of light is very special, and continued until 1905 when he wrote his relativity paper. Like Darwin, Einstein also had a network of enterprises. During this period he also researched the idea of the quantum of light (the photon) and did fundamental work in deciphering the statistical movement of molecules.

Einstein's first mini-insight toward relativity theory resulted from his teenaged gedanken experiment: If he traveled at the speed of light, how would light waves appear to him? The thinking answer that light waves would be found frozen from a frame of reference that was moving at the speed of light did not make sense to young Einstein. He had a mini-insight: Light *is* special, and Maxwell's theory, which suggested that light waves move at a speed of 300,000 km/s but did not specify a frame of reference, means that the speed of light is a constant, irrespective of any reference frame.

At some point during this period of alternate work and incubation, Einstein might have heard about the Michelson-Morley experiment, which proved that the earth's motion through the supposed all-pervading ether did not cause any wind. This confirmed his vision that there was no all-pervading ether with respect to which absolute motion could be detected—no ether, no absolute motion.

If there is no absolute motion, and motion is relative, then a postulate that physical laws are the same in all reference frames in relative motion made sense to Einstein. But combining this notion with his other insight—that the speed of light does not change due to the motion of a reference frame—led only to paradoxes. As Bertrand Russell said later, everybody knows that your speed goes up if you walk on the escalator.

A few lines from Einstein's (1979) autobiographical notes is very telling about the next significant step:

> By and by I despaired of the possibility of discovering the true laws by means of constructive efforts based on known facts. The longer and more despairingly I tried, the more I came to the conviction that only the discovery of a universal formal principle could lead us to assured results. (quoted in Bergia, 1979, p. 84)

Einstein had in mind a formal principle such as the laws of thermodynamics (e.g., "There is no perpetual motion machine"). His breakthrough came during "two joyful weeks" when Einstein discovered that time is not absolute, as postulated by Newton, and is "unrecognizably anchored in the unconscious." This was Einstein's big turning about, the pivotal, discontinuous, quantum-leap insight around which the whole gestalt of his fragmented findings made sense without giving rise to any paradoxes. Now he could connect his thoughts to those of his contemporaries (such as H. Lorentz and Henry Poincare), not that Einstein necessarily did so. His two postulates, mentioned earlier, could now be used logically to make predictions (the famous $E = mc^2$ was one). All of that Einstein did in the process of restructuring not only his own psyche but also physics (Bergia, 1979).

The picture just presented is essentially the same as that of other science historians (Miller, 1989; Wertheimer, 1959) who, however, did not emphasize the discontinuous nature of Einstein's insight. The point they missed is that nothing in previous data or thinking, even Einstein's own, pointed toward seriously posing the postulate that the speed of light is independent of reference frame or questioning the idea of absolute time. These are gaps that bit-by-bit, continuous thinking could not fill. The gedanken experiments for which Einstein is celebrated were devices for heuristic (after the insight) verification of his quantum leaps of insight.

One final comment on Einstein. Einstein excelled in his drive toward creativity (called *sattwa* by Easterners). The following poem by Louis Zukofsky makes the point beautifully:

> Said Albert—where?—in infinite diapers:
> The bitter and sweet come from the outside,
> The hard from his own efforts.
>
> For the most part I do the thing which my own nature
> Drives me to do.
> It is shameful to earn so much respect and love for it.
> I live in that singleness painful in youth,
> but delicious in the years of maturity.
> (quoted in Friedman & Donley, 1985, p. 77)

The reference to infinite diapers is particularly telling, symbolizing that Einstein retained a childlike sense of wonder all through his life. The rest of the poem refers to Einstein's true modesty: Why should he be honored for things that came naturally to him (namely, creativity)? If the work was only "hard from his own effort" (that is, problem solving) perhaps Einstein could take credit.

An Einstein story celebrates his modesty. Once he went to see a movie at the local theater (in Princeton) with an associate. During the intermission, the two wanted to go outside, but Einstein was worried that without their ticket stubs (he lost them) the gatekeeper would not recognize them and let them back in. So he insisted that the gateman take a good look at them. The gatekeeper, of course, was highly amused. "Yes, Professor Einstein," he said smiling, "I will recognize you."

A CONVERSATION WITH A YOUNG SCIENTIST

Young Scientist: Okay, you convinced me. The acts of great scientists, the paradigm shifters and extenders, involve creativity in all its important aspects—developing a burning question, destructuring, a journey into transcendence, discontinuous quantum leaps, and restructuring. Isn't it the case that paradigm shifts are rare in the history of individual fields of science? Even paradigm extensions are relatively rare. So what if there is no paradigm shift going on in a field? Should young people like me stay away from such fields?

Author: You make a good point. Paul Dirac once said something to the effect that during the quantum revolution in physics (the 1920s), even second-rate physicists did first-rate work. I think what he meant is that during a paradigm shift, many scientists engage in creativity because of the simple availability of great problems. But conversely, in times of stable paradigms, even first-rate scientists must perforce work on second-rate problems, that require only traditional problem solving. Should we then discourage creatives from science as their primary enterprise during times of stable paradigms?

YS: I guess that's what I am asking. After all your encouragement to engage creativity, isn't it a shame to get bogged down by a mere contingency? If there is no new paradigm on the horizon, there is little scope for creativity. In science, we cannot manufacture paradigm shifts at will, can we? Maybe creative young people should concentrate more on the arts, leaving science to the problem solvers, except in special times like the quantum revolution.

A: We need not be overly pessimistic. There is always the possibility that there is a paradigm shift or major paradigm extension around the corner. An example is the recent development of the Gaia hypothesis in biology. Just when biologists were becoming convinced that life can be reduced to genes, two scientists, chemist James Lovelock (1982) and biologist Lynn Margulis (1993), theorized and found evidence that the earth itself is a living system. How much more holistic can you get? Those who depend on their intuition—and most creatives do—will find a way to gravitate toward where the creative action is, even if it means going outside their fields.

YS: For young people there is the question of financial support.

A: True. The ubiquitous power of economics, money over mind. It is true that most scientists who have a lot of grant support tend to emphasize the status quo. But look at their predicament if young people refuse to join them in their business-as-usual work. In the 1960s, many young people abandoned that economic loop. Some of them became hippies and never returned to the loop. But for many, a revolution happened in academe—a liberalization of attitudes. After all, what would the movers and shakers do without able people? If the able, the talented, insist on creative opportunities, society must respond. On the other hand, when you are lulled into accepting the good life, you get caught in the noncreative trap.

YS: It is easy for you to say. You come from a country where material needs are underemphasized. In this country, one grows up with certain social conditioning, material as it is. We are only human. So we accept a good job even if it means inane, repetitive work.

A: Never compromise your creative freedom. That's where you must draw the line. Hold out, meditate, be open to the creative opportunity. It will come. Not in the way you expect it, but in some way or other.

YS: Alright. Say for the sake of argument that I hold out and eventually land a postdoctoral job in a great research lab. The problem of dealing with the establishment remains. There are always people who will tell me what to do and what not to do.

A: But do you really have to comply? Heed Nobel laureate physicist Isidor Rabi's advice:

> We don't teach our students enough of the intellectual content of experiments—their novelty and their capacity for opening new fields. . . . My own view is that you take these things personally. You do an experiment because your own philosophy makes you want to know the result. It's too hard, and life is too short, to spend your time doing something because someone else has said it's important. You must feel the thing yourself. (1975)

If you don't feel that a certain question is worth investigating or is important, then don't do it. Period. Have you ever tried not compromising your freedom? There are subtle movements of consciousness, synchronicities, to help us. We are not alone in our striving for creative freedom.

YS: Okay. For the sake of argument again, let's say that the lab director let's me carry out my own novel experiment (or theory). But creative work takes enormous time (think of Darwin's and Einstein's works). My publications dwindle. In the current economic model for scientific activity, which literally measures success in terms of quantitative production, I am no longer satisfying the criterion of excellence. But I don't have tenure, so I get fired. What good does that do?

A: Good point. This is why the Buddha talked about skillful means many eons ago; it is still good advice. You have to work on some conventional stuff on the side, be helpful to others, that kind of thing. Until you get tenure.

YS: Even tenured people are not given raises if they don't produce, if their work doesn't earn their peers' approval. What if my creative work is not appreciated anytime soon?

A: That's the risk you have to take. If you do, you will find that it is worth it. You will be able to better live with yourself. Creativity is its own reward. It may sound trite because it is so often repeated, but it is true.

Meanwhile, as a society we must change. We must allow young scientists to devote time toward developing and pursuing·burning questions. The current economic model of productivity encourages only problem solving at the expense of creativity. This, too, has to change in favor of a greater balance between fundamental and situational creativity and between creativity and problem solving. Science and society need them all.

YS: I wish movers and shakers would hear you.

A: They will. They don't live outside consciousness. As we enter the new era of a science within consciousness, there will be unprecedented opportunity for creativity, both fundamental and situational. This will sweep away much of the red tape of the current system.

YS: Ah, science within consciousness. Do you anticipate that when we include the subjective in science, when we change the metaphysics of our science, then how we do science, its epistemology, will also change?

A: I am glad you asked that. Young scientists like you need to be aware of a major change in the way science is done, the basic epistemology of science. Hitherto, science has been largely objective except in the creativity of scientists, which has always been subjective, as I have amply demonstrated. But even so, because of the objective nature of science within the Newtonian paradigm, scientists could take themselves out of the equation and be aloof and objective. The demand of science within consciousness—idealist science—is going to be quite different. The idealist scientist must be prepared to let consciousness transform him or her during the investigation.

YS: What do you mean, transform? You are not suggesting that we all become spiritual, practitioners of inner creativity?

A: It is inevitable for the truly great scientists of science within consciousness. Listen to what Willis Harman and Christian de Quincey (1994) say:

The point is that the transformation in experience which the scientist would undergo while exploring consciousness is essential for the kind of direct and deep insight required to gain knowledge of the psyche. Without that, the scientist would be blind to the phenomena and processes under investigation. Such "inner vision" is the starting point—the *sine qua non*—of any true consciousness science; it is the source of data which, later, the scientist can build into a communicable model. (p. 47)

Do you comprehend?

YS: I never thought about it before, but I think I do. It is exciting.

A: Let me add one more thing. Not all young scientists will end up working on the problems of idealist science, of consciousness. And not every scientist, realistically speaking, will work on creative enterprises, either. But even if you are engaged in tasks that require only problem solving, there is one way that even problem solving transforms into creativity. And this is by using problem solving to serve the world—humanity and its environment. Action in the service of others always touches the quantum self—it is inner creativity at its purest, and it will even transform you in the process. There is no better incentive for action.

> The idea of Einstein's space
> is beyond Einstein's space.
> The laws of Newton are not written
> on the bodies they govern.
> Ideas and laws, oh creative,
> are your transcendent companions.
>
> Earthbound, scientists may be,
> but when they discover the laws of nature,
> they soar in heaven.
> Problem solving is satisfying, to be sure,
> but don't you wish to mount the quantum catapult
> just once? Your own encounter
> with this new context, this new meaning of science,
> will launch you too into heaven.

13

CREATIVITY IN THE ARTS

How does one know anything? First of all, we can observe. If we closely watch someone in the act of creation, we can learn a lot about creativity. This is how some of the research data on creativity are gathered. Second, we can read about other people's data (which are almost always mixed with their theories and ideas). This is knowledge on the basis of somebody's authority. Third, we can use reason and concept to figure things out. And last but not least, we can know from the "inside," from direct experience; we can know about creativity by being creative.

I personally have very little direct creative experience in the arts, so I have to depend on anecdotal accounts, observation, authority, reasoning—quantum theoretic as it may be—and intuition. What do artists—musicians, novelists, painters, architects, poets—say about their creativity? Quite a bit. When we analyze these accounts with observation, authority, intuition, and reasoning, the picture that emerges is quite similar to that from the study of scientific creativity, but there are also differences.

SUDDEN INSIGHT AND UNCONSCIOUS PROCESSING

The way artists talk about their work clearly suggests sudden acausal insight—quantum jumps of thought. "It is like diving into the pond—then you start to swim," said the novelist D. H. Lawrence. "Once the instinct and intuition get into the brush tip, the picture *happens*, if it is to be a picture at all."

177

The novelist Gertrude Stein, in a conversation with the author John Preston (1960), said the same thing. "Think of the writing in terms of discovery, which is to say that creation must take place between the pen and the paper, not before in a thought or afterwards in a recasting."

The English romantic poet P. B. Shelly expressed the acausality and discontinuity of writing poetry succinctly: "Poetry is not like reasoning, a power to be exerted according to the determination of the will. A man cannot say, 'I will write poetry.' The greatest poet even cannot say it" (quoted in Harman & Rheingold, 1984, p. 35). (Obviously, he was not talking about computer poetry.)

Often the acausality is expressed in terms of help from God. The composer Brahms described his creative experience in composing his most famous music with these words:

> Straightaway the ideas flow in upon me, *directly from God*, and not only do I see distinct themes in my mind's eye, but they are clothed in the right forms, harmonics, and orchestration. Measure by measure the finished product is revealed to me when I am in those *rare, inspired moods*. (quoted in Harmon & Rheingold, 1984, pp. 38–39; emphasis added)

Next is a compelling quote about the suddenness of creativity from the great composer, Tchaikowsky:

> Generally speaking, the germ of a future composition comes suddenly and unexpectedly. . . . It takes root with extraordinary force and rapidity, shoots up through the earth, puts forth branches and leaves, and finally blossoms. I cannot define the creative process in any way but [by] this simile. (quoted in Harmon & Rheingold, 1984, p. 45)

Obviously, Tchaikowsky knew that a creative act bursts forth from a transcendent unconscious realm; the underground is his metaphor for a transcendent world.

There is also ample evidence of discontinuity, acausality, and unconscious processing in the use of altered states of consciousness in the discovery. The novelist Rudyard Kipling often "drifted" into reverie to find his creative ideas. Similarly, the romantic poet William Wordsworth was reported to make use of a trancelike state of consciousness when "the world around him seemed unreal." The great composer Beethoven wrote about finding a canon while in a dream:

I dreamt that I had gone on a far journey, to no less a place than Syria, on to Judea and back, and then all the way to Arabia, when at length I arrived at Jerusalem. . . . Now during my dream journey, the following canon came into my head. . . . But scarcely did I awake when away flew the canon, and I could not recall any part of it. On returning here however, the next day, . . . I resumed my dream journey, being on this occasion wide awake, when lo and behold! in accordance with the law of association of ideas, the same canon flashed across me; so being now awake I held it as fast as Menelaus did Proteus, only permitting it to be changed into three parts. (quoted in Harman & Rheingold, 1984, p. 46)

The poet Henry Wadsworth Longfellow puts his experience of writing a ballad this way:

Last evening I sat till twelve o'clock by my fire, smoking, when suddenly it came into my mind to write the "Ballad of the Schooner Hesperus," which I accordingly did. Then I went to bed, but could not sleep. New thoughts were running in my mind, and I got up to add them to the ballad. I felt pleased with the ballad. It hardly cost me any effort. It did not come into my mind by lines, but by stanzas. (quoted in Harman & Rheingold, 1984, p.45)

Note the words "not . . . by lines, but by stanzas"; not bit by bit, but the whole, discontinuously. This wholeness is characteristic of the quantum nonlocality of creative insights (see also the earlier quote from Brahms). Even when an idea is only part of a whole solution, it acts as a "germ" for the wholeness that follows.

The novelist Isabel Allende had an amazing experience while writing her second novel, *Of Love and Shadows*, about the political crime in Chile in 1973. The military killed 15 people and hid their bodies in an abandoned mine, where they were discovered five years later by the Catholic church. Unable to find any clue from her research as to how the discovery happened, Allende filled in the details from what she thought to be her imagination: A priest heard the details of the killing in a confession, went to the mine, and took pictures, wrapping them in his blue sweater. Years later a Jesuit priest came to her and corroborated her "imagined" story even to the last detail—wrapping the photos in his blue sweater. "I think there is a prophetic or clairvoyant quality in writing," Allende said, based on her experience (Bolen, Walker, & Allende, 1993).

Similarly, the novelist Alice Walker, while writing *Temple of My Familiar,* felt "connected with the ancient knowledge we all have, and that it was really a matter not of trying to learn something, but of remembering" (Bolen, Walker, & Allende, 1993). Here is a shade of quantum nonlocality over time.

The key to nonlocal experiences in creativity is the unconscious processing that precedes it. This is why they come so often in dreams (as for Beethoven) or at least in silence (as for Allende and Walker). William Butler Yeats (1960) put it well when he wrote this about a creative person:

> Like a long-legged fly upon the stream
> His mind moves upon silence.

PARADIGMS AND PARADIGM SHIFTS IN THE ARTS

Kuhn articulated the concept of a paradigm shift in science, but I submit that all creative acts, whether in art, music, or science, embody the potential to change the current paradigm of any field in a major way. The quantum revolution of Bohr, Schroedinger, Heisenberg, and company has changed the way we look at classical physics; the same thing happens in the arts, according to Malraux (1951):

> After Van Gogh, Rembrandt has never been quite the same as he was after Delacroix. (Nor has Newton been the same since Einstein.) Each genius that breaks with the past deflects, as it were, the whole range of earlier forms. (p. 38)

The fundamental feature of a paradigm shift is the discontinuity, the gap that exists between the old and the new paradigms. It is true that some aspects of the old paradigm remain useful, but we can never look at the old in the same way. The new context shapes our understanding of truth. A discontinuous change occurs in the way we look at the world.

But there is a fundamental difference in how the concept of a paradigm shift applies to the arts. Science is progressive in the sense that new laws replace old ones. The validity of the old laws, although still functional in the old arena (this is the correspondence principle), is only approximate. In contrast, in the arts, be it painting, music, or literature, the validity of the old is never in question. The old and new paradigms coexist peacefully, each in its own right.

As an example, Picasso initiated the new paradigm of cubism, looking at an object from different perspectives in the same piece of art.

This new paradigm reflects the multidimensionality of 20th-century culture and forever changes the way we appreciate all art, present and past, but it never diminishes our appreciation of the old.

In dance, until the 20th century in the West, there was only folk dance and classical ballet, the dance form that could be considered anything close to a paradigm. When Martha Graham in the late 1920s developed a new paradigm—modern dance—she broke with tradition and she brought a new context. In her own words:

> Once we strove to imitate gods—we did god dances. Then we strove to become part of nature by representing natural forces in dance forms—winds—flowers—trees. . . . [Modern dance] was not done perversely to dramatize ugliness or to strike at sacred tradition. . . . There was a revolt against the ornamental forms of impressionistic dancing. (quoted in Gardner, 1993)

But modern dance did not affect our appreciation of either ballet or folk forms.

Science is progressive also in Newton's sense of seeing "so much because I could stand on the shoulders of giants." In the arts, strictly speaking, there is no need to stand on the shoulders of giants. Of course, the old can teach techniques, but how technique is applied to capture the meaning of an archetypal theme depends entirely on the sensitivity of the artist to the theme and to his or her contemporary social environment. As Gertrude Stein said, "What is seen depends upon how everybody is doing everything."

ORIGINALITY IN THE ARTS

In one episode of the comic strip *Calvin and Hobbes*, Calvin says to Hobbes, "The problem with fine arts is that it's supposed to express original truths. But who wants originality and truth?", he complains. "People want more of what they already know they like."

Calvin has a point. We do like to encounter over and over again what we already know; the new can challenge us too much, and we take comfort in the familiar. But even so, few of us would call movie sequels, TV soap operas, or romance novels creative art.

So what is creative in art? Is Calvin right when he says that fine art expresses original truth? What is truth, and what is original? This is more subtle than meets the eye.

Unlike the sciences, the discovery of new themes, new truths, is not the objective in the arts—that is, the originality of artists does not lie in the originality of the truth or themes they express. Art throughout all ages revels in the same transcendent themes—love, beauty, justice, and so on.[1] These themes are so profound in content that no one artist can ever express them completely.

However, there is a sociocultural context corresponding to every time and place. The challenge to the artist in exploring "new truth" is to build a bridge between the eternal themes and the specific context of a particular place and time. According to author John Briggs, "So though the 'truth' . . . for Homer, Cervantes, Balzac or Faulkner may be at some level the same, evidently that truth must be constantly remade through different historical contexts—so it is many different truths as well" (1990). Creativity in the arts is manifested whenever such a bridge between a timeless truth and a given historical context is built. Even postmodern art, whose avowed motif is to "deconstruct" all logos from art, ends up pointing us to the transcendental nature of all truth. This art is an appropriate bridge between postmodern pessimism and the end of the societal euphoria of the industrial age, which gave us the problem-solving image of the can-do human.

Transparadigm fundamental creativity in the arts—the discovery of new paradigms or a radical new extension of the old one—goes one step further. There are artists or groups of artists who are way ahead of their time; they anticipate a sociocultural change that has not yet broken through the inertia of the old. This is the arena of the great: Homer, Kalidasa, Shakespeare, Michelangelo, Bach, Dostoyevsky, Picasso, Van Gogh and his impressionist friends, Rabindranath Tagore, Martha Graham, and the Beatles, to name just a few. Being ahead of their time is one reason why we find many cases of creativity overlooked by an artist's contemporaries (Van Gogh is a tragic example). With the context not yet clearly manifested, they fail to recognize the new sociocultural context from which to judge the work. But the artist who has heard the siren song of creativity has to take the risk that his or her contemporaries will not understand.

Most people in the arts, however, engage in activities within the limits of a well-defined paradigm (as Calvin says, people want more of what they know they like). But engaging in popular art is not necessarily uncreative for the artist. So long as artists are not using reasoned, programmed steps that can be anticipated (canned poetry, formula

---

[1]In music, the transcendent themes have further structures of melody and harmony—for example, the East Indian ragas. Most, if not all, of these archetypes of music may already have been discovered.

movies, or art as problem solving), they are engaging in creativity; they are still taking risks because there is no guarantee that will succeed in building a bridge between their audience and timeless truth in any particular attempt.

This risk taking is one of the things that separates the wheat from the chaff, creativity from problem solving. In a telling conversation between John Preston and the novelist Gertrude Stein, the issue of the originality of American novelists came up. Preston asked why most writers "start gigantic at first" but, by the time they are 30 or 40-years-old, "repeat according to formula." To this Stein's answer was that, as they age, American writers tend to become professional and compartmentalized. In other words, they become practitioners of writing as problem solving. "If Mr. Robert Frost is at all good as a poet," said Stein, "it is because he is a farmer" (Preston, 1960). I agree completely.

Professionalism in the arts, as essential as it is, also tends to breed mediocrity. Professionals have to produce a certain number of "successes" in order to maintain their professional standing. Also, professionals breed more professionals through writing schools, poetry conferences, and that sort of thing. It is not all bad, but creativity can suffer, as the critic John Aldridge (1992) notes in regard to the "fraternity" of the contemporary American writing scene:

> What is at issue here is a professional fraternity so obsessed with turning out writers that it has lost all regard for the purpose they are supposed to serve and the skill with which they are expected to serve it. It is rather as if the medical profession were to produce physicians whose ability to treat patients is considered irrelevant when weighed against the fact that the medical profession must be kept going and that the training of physicians is a vital source of revenue and prestige. (p. 25)

Most importantly, many professional American writers have lost sight of the primary law of creativity in art: cosmic vision. Take the work of novelists of a previous genre: John Dos Passos' *USA* or Norman Mailer's *An American Dream*. In the first, the author describes the destruction of transcendent values in modern American culture; in the second, the archetypal battle between good and evil is truthfully played out in New York City. Thus, these stories are of cosmic vision, fundamental truths. There is hardly anything equivalent on the current American writing scene with few exceptions, such as the work of black women writers Tony Morrison and Alice Walker. The new paradigm in writing is taking place in South America at the hands of such powerful writers as Gabriel Garcia Marquez (author of the Nobel winning *One Hundred Years of Solitude*) and Isabel Allende.

Unfortunately, the defects of professionalism are engulfing not only the writing scene but all endeavors of human creativity, including the sciences. What we need is a balance. Can a professional in the arts give up the extra security that the training of other artist-professionals brings? Can a professional set aside time for creative projects that are not as efficiently produced as those that require only problem solving? After all, if making money is the primary objective, why be involved with the arts instead of the stock market? If the joy of creativity is what attracts one to the arts, how can one not notice that the joy dries up in projects that require only problem solving? How can one turn from the encounter with the quantum self when, even once, one has heard its call—"the flute of interior time"?

In an interview, the artist-poet Carolyn Kleefield, put it well: "Most artists are like engineers reproducing the familiar. This type of art, from the outside in, is not the same art as art that is being created as part of an emerging consciousness."

The novelist D. H. Lawrence (1971) reminded us of what the job of the creative is with these powerful words:

> Man fixes some wonderful erection of his own between himself and the wild chaos, and gradually goes bleached and stiffened under his parasol. Then comes a poet, enemy of convention, and makes a slit in the umbrella; and lo! the glimpse of chaos is a vision, a window to the sun. (p. 430)

THE IMPORTANCE OF PROCESS

In prehistoric India, there lived a cruel man named Ratnakar who was the leader of a band of robbers. This band, among other acts of cruelty, offered human sacrifices to the goddess of their worship. The myth is that one day a young woman was brought in to be sacrificed, but looking at the pain-filled, appealing face of the girl, Ratnakar was overwhelmed by compassion. Ratnakar was deeply hurt at having interfered in the girl's life, and from his pain a verse came out of his mouth unrehearsed and in a language (Sanskrit) that was unfamiliar to him. According to the myth, this was humanity's very first poetry. Later Ratnakar became the great poet Valmiki, who is credited with writing the great epic *Ramayana* in the same inspired and perfected form that his first verse displayed.

In another version of the same myth, Ratnakar saw a hunter kill two birds who were making love. He became so moved with grief that lines of poetry came out of his mouth. Later he became Valmiki.

Whichever Valmiki myth we subscribe to, we must note that this is the archetypal story of how poetry comes to poets: suddenly, writing itself as though dictated by a higher power. Also note that this is not different from Puccini's claim that the music of *Madame Butterfly* "was dictated to me by God; I was merely instrumental in putting it on paper."

But it is wrong to get the impression that all is sudden inspiration in the arts—between inspirations there is a lot of perspiration. (As Brahms noted, his moments of inspiration were rare). Like the sciences, the arts are also the result of creative processes that involve more than the original inspired insight. The French novelist Balzac, his contemporaries said, wrote with huge spaces between his lines that he would fill in later. All artists have to fill in a lot of empty space between original breakthroughs. And this part of the process of creativity in the arts is no different from problem solving. Picasso did not create his masterpiece *Guernica* in one brilliant sitting. He made an inspired sketch when the idea first came to him; after that came gradual work and unconscious processing with occasional insights. Even after his big insight came—using a broken statue of a warrior in the center of the painting (see later)—it took several days to finish the picture. Wordsworth used to write three-page segments that he would later expand and connect—sort of writing backward.

Great creatives also make use of preparation and practice. Picasso often disassembled faces of people and assembled them back again. Musical composers spend hours practicing. Poets often like to translate other people's poetry.

Bertrand Russell provides an excellent example of the habitual use of alternate work and relaxation, of striving and unconscious processing, in his writing. He said:

> When I was young each fresh piece of serious work used to seem to me for a time—perhaps a long time—to be beyond my powers. I would fret myself into a nervous state from fear that it was never going to come right. I would make one unsatisfying attempt after another, and in the end have to discard them all. At last I found that such fumbling attempts were a waste of time. It appeared that first contemplating a book on some subject, and after giving serious preliminary attention to it, I needed a period of subconscious incubation which could not be hurried and was if anything impeded by deliberate thinking. Sometimes, I would find after a time,

that I had made a mistake, and that I could not write the book I had had in mind. But often I was more fortunate. Having, by a time of very intense concentration, planted the problem in my subconscious, it would germinate underground until, suddenly, the solution emerged with blinding clarity, so that it only remained to write down what had appeared as if in a revelation. (1965, p. 195)

Thus even in the arts, the sudden illumination and original insight—the encounter with the quantum self—are parts of a more involved process. Although Picasso used to say, "Je ne cherche pas, je trouve" ("I don't look, I find"), perhaps that meant only a lack of deliberate thinking on his part. But the intelligent brain activity behind painting is not thinking; didn't Susan Langer say that art is a form of feeling? (This is not to say that painting does not use intelligent concepts, only that such concepts are not amenable to purely rational treatment.)

Finally, artists do not necessarily go about their work systematically through a process directed straight toward the product. Often they do not even know when to call it quits. Consider Thomas Wolfe's (1960) description of the completion of his first novel, *Of Time and the River*. Wolfe began the project trying to write a book called *The October Fair*. The more he wrote, the more he felt that he was nowhere near finishing the project and that he was not doing such a good job of writing. After a couple of years, his editor told him that the project was done and that he should put together all the bits and pieces of writing. Wolfe did and began to see for the first time that the editor was wise—there was a book already there, after all. But the book was too big, more than a million words. Cutting it down to size was another huge task for the author, even after realizing that he had the material for not one but two books. In the end, when Wolfe asked his editor for another six months and the wise editor told him that the book was finished as it was, Wolfe finally realized that he did not have to be a perfectionist.

In both science and the arts, the actual process of the act of creation is quite complicated. The stages and encounters in actual case histories are not necessarily neat, linear, and progressive. Ultimately, one has to carve out for him- or herself a unique process that works. This is true for every creative; there is an essential individuality in the act of creation.

CASE HISTORY: PICASSO'S GUERNICA

We have discussed *Guernica* before, but now we do so in some detail, taking advantage of the fact that Picasso left notebooks that have stimulated comments by many researchers (Gardner, 1993). Picasso was commissioned by the Spanish Government to do a mural for the Spanish exhibit at the Paris World Fair in 1937. Originally, Picasso planned to paint a scene in an artist's studio. But after the Nazi bombing of Guernica, Picasso changed the subject to a portrayal of the bombed town.

And what an impressive painting it is (see Figure 13.1). We can recognize a horse and a bull, torn up and in agony. We can see women: a mother grieving the dead child in her arms; a woman, lamp in hand, looking out the window of a burning building; a woman falling from a burning building in burning clothes; a woman running into the scene. Amazingly, there is no man in the mural except for a lifeless, mechanical statue of a warrior that is torn apart.

The brutality of the bombing certainly comes through, but was Picasso trying to express much more? Perhaps he saw in the pain of the bombed people of Guernica the pain of all humanity, which the women and animals of the scene are displaying. It could not be a coincidence that the lone male figure of the painting is a shattered statue of a warrior; Picasso was inspired to choose this image in the final days of the painting. The warrior represents the hero within us—torn apart, mechanical, mind and body split, stony matter frozen away from spirit. Guernica is a portrait of our own fragmented psyche.

Art historians have debated the location of the scene of the painting, whether it is an exterior scene or an interior one. There is ambiguity. The woman leaning out from a window seems to suggest exteriority, but there are lines in the upper corner of the canvass that suggest interiority. Can it be that the ambiguity is purposeful and the painting represents both exterior and interior? As an exterior painting, it pictures the horrors of the bombing in Guernica. As an interior painting, it pictures the equally horrible fragmentation of our psyches.

The discontinuity in Guernica is much more than the changing of the physical context of the picture from a studio scene to the scene of the bombing, as has been suggested (Weisberg, 1993). The real discontinuity took place in Picasso's psyche, a discontinuous shift of context that enabled him to use a local event to portray global truth in a yet-to-come context—a fundamental fragmentation of the human psyche. The painting of *Guernica* was an act of fundamental creativity because, while painting it, Picasso became one with the universe.

Figure 13.1. Artist's rendition of the themes of Picasso's *Guernica*.

Professional or amateur—neither
is sufficient for creativity.
You must embrace responsibility, Oh creative.
Do not stop short of the goal as amateurs often do.
And forswear the self-limiting of the ego's career needs;
they too often dominate the professional's drive.
Rather, heed your quantum self! It speaks through you
whenever ego-you is in abeyance.

Here, now, the whole, all at once,
You never thought you could write it down, did you?

But you are a professional. The eternal archetypes
bloom anew in the fresh forms you discover to clothe
the ever-changing context of your again-new age.

Like an amateur, you move on
from context to context, from meaning to meaning,
ever ranging ahead of your professional self.

14

PROCE// IN INNER CREATIVITY

The process of inner creativity is similar to that of outer creativity. There is a burning question, there is preparation and incubation, there is illumination, and finally, manifestation. The product of manifestation is a shift of one's center of being in the world—a change of conscious identity from ego toward the quantum self.

The intuition that becomes a burning question in the inner journey of creativity may arise from a general dissatisfaction with inner conflict in the ego-identity. Ego-agendas are laden with desires, and desires are often conflicting. For example, suppose I have a desire to succeed, and I work very hard to that end; but I also want to enjoy life, spend time with my family, and so forth—the two desires are not compatible. This kind of conflict brings about an unending tension, an unease that the Buddha called *dukkha*. The inner-creativity initiate is motivated to end dukkha.

Another intuition is that there is more to the self than the ego. This leads to the burning question, the intense desire, to know the self— the nature of consciousness itself. This fuels the inquiry—who am I? What is the true nature of my self?

Still another deep inquiry is, How can I love? When I am ego-centered, I live in a web of solipsism—only my consciousness is real, and all others exist only in relation to me. As one man said to his wife when she expressed dissatisfaction with their marriage, "I don't get it. Your job is to make me happy; I'm happy, so what's the problem?"

There is a cartoon that perfectly describes the situation with the ego. Calvin says, "I am at peace with the world. I'm completely serene."

191

When pressed by Hobbes, he clarifies, "I am here so everybody can do what I want." From the superior level in a hierarchical relationship we can love only magnanimously. But this is not love and leads to a feeling of isolation. When we become aware of our loneliness, in spite of having friends and partners, we begin to inquire why we are lonely, why we do not feel loved, and why, in truth, we cannot give unselfish love either.

Inner creativity can also begin with a spontaneous experience of oneness with the whole universe—a primary-awareness event. We wonder what created the joy of that experience. We want to know the source of that unblemished joy.

The beginning of the journey beyond ego is as varied as the variation we find in the ego-characters of people. But the goal is the same—the shift of the ego-identity to a more balanced being in the quantum self. I call this shift the awakening of *buddhi* (Goswami, 1993a). Buddhi is a Sanskrit word meaning intelligence. Etymologically, intelligence comes from the root word *intelligo* which means "to select among." This is appropriate. Indeed, with the awakening of buddhi, we begin to become aware of the quantum self and to take responsibility for the choices it/we make. In our ego level of being, the selection process from among the possibilities that the quantum mind presents to consciousness is entirely preconscious.

There is a lasting myth in some spiritual traditions that to be truly initiated into a path of inner creativity, you must have a guru, an enlightened teacher. But the quantum self, the atman, is the guru, as some of these traditions explicitly acknowledge, and it is not separate from us. If you are sinking into quicksand, you cannot pull yourself up by your own bootstraps; a law of Newton prevents you. But it is possible to bootstrap yourself out of the quicksand of ego-identity. This is because the ego - identity is not real. The ego's simple hierarchy and its solipsistic perspective is an aberration on the clear consciousness that is the atman. To expect another, guru or not, to do your creative work for you is to perpetuate the aberration.

The problem is that in inner creativity you are trying to lift yourself beyond the simple hierarchy of the ego-identity to the tangled hierarchy of the quantum self. You cannot reach a relationship based in a tangled hierarchy through one that demands a simple hierarchy, as in some power-based guru-disciple relationships. If perchance you encounter one of those rare individuals who understands and engages in tangled-hierarchical relationships, that is different. In India, such a guru is called a *sadguru*.

Now comes the quintessential question. How do the stages of inner creativity catapult us into the exalted buddhi level of being?

INITIAL PREPARATION

Part of the preparation for the spiritual journey of inner creativity is the study of the literature in order to achieve an intellectual understanding of the philosophy of consciousness, of the essence of the work done by philosophers and mystics through the ages. If you are part of a religious lineage, you study the scriptures with the motivation of understanding the meaning behind the form. You also investigate the meaning of particular rituals and practices. Rote learning will not do. Routinely carrying out ritual practices will not do. This, of course, is the same as in the journey of outer creativity.

Today there is a tendency to discount intellectual study and understanding and to overemphasize experience. Note the case of Ramakrishna. Ramakrishna initially attained "high" altered states of consciousness by sheer devotion. However, to go further, he underwent a traditional training in Vedanta philosophy with a teacher.

Once you arrive at an intellectual understanding of the basic idealist ontology that there is only one consciousness and that you are that one, preparation takes a different thrust. Now the goal is to cultivate the receptivity of an open mind (notice the parallel with outer creativity). Literally, you must loosen the identity with the memory that forms the ego by challenging the automatic tendency to respond to stimuli in an habitual way.

ALTERNATE WORK AND INCUBATION: WILL AND SURRENDER

As with outer creativity, much of the work of inner creativity is unconscious. In outer creativity, we relax from actively pursuing the problem at hand. In inner creativity, we become quiet, silent. We surrender to the flow of life rather than try to push the river.

Moudgalyayana came to Buddha with many questions that he had asked of all the teachers he had encountered. But Buddha saw that the striving student was ready for the next stage. He asked, "Do you want to know the answers or know the questions?" Moudgalyayana was startled. He did not know what to say. Buddha elaborated, "All worthwhile answers have to grow inside you [from your burning questions]. What I say is irrelevant. So stay with me in silence for a year. After the year, if you still want to ask, I will answer." Moudgalyayana went into silence. After the year, when Buddha asked him if he had any questions, he remained silent. He had understood the importance of silence—unconscious processing.

At this stage of incubation, you let unconscious processes do their work. You must invite ambiguity into your life (remember the role of unlearned stimuli in outer creativity). You may try to solve a Zen koan (a puzzle, such as what was your name before you were born?), read spiritual texts, write poetry when inspiration hits, contemplate spiritual paintings, or take walks in nature.

Supplementing these unconscious processes with conscious striving to exercise the will is often advantageous. Meditation helps cultivate awareness that enables you to see your pattern, your conditioning. You may sit in concentration pondering the universe. You may stand with one arm raised for an hour a day to increase the power of your will. The Sanskrit word *tapasya,* the generation of heat (intensity) through practice, describes this aspect of the process well.

So how hard do you have to practice? It depends. Some people are so entrenched in their egos that the heat of hard practice is needed for them to jump out of their trenches. Others find it easy. In a Zen story, a spiritual seeker meets an extraordinary spiritual family in which all members have awakened to their Buddha nature. In answer to the seeker's question, "Is it difficult to awaken to our true nature?", the father says, "It is very, very difficult." But the mother says, "It's the easiest thing in the world." The son says, "Neither." Finally the daughter says, "If you make it difficult, it is. If you don't, it's not."

THE ENCOUNTER IN INNER CREATIVITY

I also want to stress the encounter aspect of inner creativity. As with outer creativity, inner creativity is an encounter between our ego and quantum modalities. The existentialist philosopher Martin Buber called this the I-thou encounter; the encounter is even more intense than in outer creativity because your purpose in inner creativity is transformation of your self-identity, a radical change in the familiar homeostasis of your adult ego. And radical change requires a tremendous intensity.

The following story gives an idea of the kind of intensity that may be brought to bear. A young man did not understand how it was possible to concentrate on a mantra even for a few minutes. So his teacher, who happened to be the king, ordered the young man to carry a vessel full of oil three times around the palace. "And while you carry the oil," cautioned the king, "be careful that not a single drop falls to the ground. A swordsman will follow you, and he will instantly cut off your head if any of the oil spills." While carrying out the command, the young man easily understood the intensity that is involved in successful concentration.

Such intense concentration as the young man mastered is normally quite beyond us unless we too are faced with a similar urgency. As in outer creativity, the heat of our inquiry must burn off our resistance and indolence in order for us to experience the primary awareness of the quantum self. And yet we must also relax into unconscious processing. It is the same game again, will and surrender.

If you are attentive, ordinary life situations can give you rich and immediate opportunities for change. These situations may involve suffering, but the very intensity so often found in suffering is what can be transforming.

The physician/spiritual teacher Richard Moss (1981) recognizes impending surgery as fostering the meditative intensity that I am talking about. When the mystic/psychologist Richard Alpert worked on a prison Ashram project, he was impressed with the level of awareness of the inmates on death row (Dass, 1977). Hospice workers, too, find that high levels of intensity become available to people facing death. Such intensity can forge the bedrock commitment to your spiritual quest that is required.

Nonlocal correlations are characteristic of quantum functioning and primary awareness. Group activities tend to produce nonlocal correlation even in people who are not meditating consciously—at a football game or a rock concert, for example. Not surprisingly, then, group coherence can intensify our own meditative encounter. Hence the saying of Jesus, "When two or more are gathered in my name, there I am in the midst of them."

It is important to realize that a meditative context is not essential to bringing the intensity of a nonlocal relationship to inner creativity. Other contexts may be equally effective, for example, the love relationship between intimate people. In my own case, I began my journey of inner creativity with meditative practices, both solo and group. I had some exalted experiences, but no real transformation came until the question, "How can I love my wife unconditionally?", became a burning question. From then on, my relationship with my wife became an encounter between my ego (where I was subject, and she was object) and the quantum self (where she and I were one).

The effectiveness of psychotherapy has often been questioned (Garcia, 1974). I think psychotherapy is much more effective in breaking up the homeostasis of a neurotic situation when the therapist and patient approach therapy from an encounter point of view. So long as the therapist and the patient meet as separate individuals within an established simple hierarchy, the interaction is all local. But when they meet as one, their separateness dissolved in the tangled hierarchy of a nonlocal encounter with the quantum self, there is room for creative insight. And it is these personal creative insights that enable people to change. If psychotherapy is done in such a way as to foster this kind of encounter, inner creativity for both therapist and patient can be enhanced. Their nonlocal correlation helps them both to rise beyond their conditioned fixities (and then the therapist surely would be less susceptible to burnout).

Even business relationships can be used as encounters (Ray & Myers, 1989). If the idealist worldview is lived, business becomes more than a vehicle for making money; it becomes an engaging and self-transformative way to serve people. At the least, it is an arena within which to confront the inner conflict between personal ethics and business practices.

Even when we are alone, it is not difficult to build intensity. Many of us know this from such "negative" experiences as brooding or anxiety. What prevents you from looking into your patterns with the intensity that develops from these states? We escape with television or light reading or squander our energy on imagined scenarios of triumphs and failures, retaliation and vengeance. Instead, suppose you vigilantly observe whatever comes up as precisely as possible? This was the basis of the teaching of the mystic Krishnamurti.

Ultimately, we are afraid of intense practice (*sadhana* in Sanskrit). It is like the hungry chicken and the pig who were traveling together. They saw a diner with a sign advertising a bacon-and-egg special, and the chicken wanted to stop there. But the pig balked, protesting, "You have to make only a contribution. But for me, that's total commitment." The mystic Ligia Dantes (1990) suggested watching our fear and learning to discriminate between fear as a natural survival instinct and fear as fantasy to perpetuate the illusions of the ego-identity. When you shed fantasy fear, you can more readily invite intensity into your practice.

"If I give up my ego, what is left of me?" This is the eternal question, formed entirely from our desires, fears, attachments, and so on, that makes us shy away from honest self-scrutiny and prevents us from surrendering to the quantum self. Is there life after the shift of your center of being beyond the ego? You have to ask the question with intensity and perseverance, to take a risk with no surety of reward, and to accept the anguish of waiting for the "new life" to spring forth:

The travail of the night
Will it not usher the dawn?
In the night of sorrow, under death's blow,
When man bursts his mortal bounds,
Will not God stand revealed
In His glory? (Tagore, 1976)

MINI-INSIGHTS AND BIG INSIGHTS

In outer creativity, illumination comes with the discontinuous collapse of a previously uncollapsed gestalt that expresses the scientist's or the artist's truth. What is the equivalent of this "truth" for the inner creative? First of all, it is the abiding truth or truths by which we can live with ourselves in inner harmony.

Spiritual beliefs often consist of ethical precepts such as "love thy neighbor." But when we try to practice such a precept, we often find it too difficult, and we rationalize our failed attempts. Alternatively, we make unbreakable rules for what we think it means (or would look like) to love our neighbors and try to follow these rules (an outside-in approach), always afraid that the slightest deviation from our disciplined practice will prove our unworthiness. In search of freedom, we become slaves to rigid practices, lost in the attempt to recondition ourselves.

The reality is that each of us has to discover creatively the truth of "Love your neighbor as yourself." Only when, in an acausal direct quantum leap (a mini-insight), you experience your oneness with your neighbor can you really live this truth with some genuine effortlessness and consistency. Love then becomes an ongoing renewal of relationship—grounded not in rote fixity but in present creative fluidity. You must similarly discover all spiritual themes of life—respect, humility, justice, and other time-honored values—if you want to live them.

Such discovery of living truth becomes subtler and subtler. Once while driving on the freeway, I heard a preacher on the radio talking about "giving your gavel to the holy spirit." He was urging us to give up being the chairperson of our lives and to surrender to what, in my terminology, is the inner quantum self. But, we cannot surrender until we have discovered the truth of the holy spirit. And we cannot discover that truth until we surrender! There is that tangled hierarchy again.

There is a story of a young Westerner visiting Calcutta for the first time who is looking for the famous "round pond." He flags down a cab and asks to be taken there. The cab driver gives him a surprised glance but sets out to do his bidding. The driver, an amateur tour guide, points out various tourist sights on their drive through the city. The Westerner is delighted, but after a while he asks how much farther the "round pond" is. The cab driver says that it's right ahead, then continues to point out more sights. Finally, the Westerner has had it. "I want you to take me to the round pond now," he demands. The driver immediately returns to where their journey began. "Why have you brought me back to where we started?", he asks the cab driver angrily. "This is the round pond, sir. It's the name of this area," says the cabbie. The young man is stunned. "Why didn't you tell me that before? It would have saved me the trip." "You wouldn't have believed me before," answers the cabbie, smiling.

You may question the cabbie's motive, but as far as the spiritual search is concerned, he is absolutely correct. The object of the search—the quantum self and its archetypal themes such as love, humility, and justice—is unwaveringly present to you all the time; you are it, I am it, we cannot be anything but it. As the mystics say, "You are already enlightened," or, "You are love." And yet, we simply don't experience it, so compelling are the secondary-awareness events in the illusion of separateness. But to fail to recognize the quantum self is also part of the illusion—maya—hence the roundabout trip in the cab of worldly distractions until we are really serious about knowing ourselves. According to the East Indian mystic Ramana Maharshi (1978) *Sadhanas* [practices] are needed . . . for putting an end to obstacles. Finally, there comes a stage when a person feels helpless notwithstanding the sadhanas. He is unable to pursue the much cherished sadhana also. It's then that . . . the [quantum/atman] self reveals itself.

In other words, what we normally call *practice* in inner creativity—the preparation and incubation, the will and surrender—itself hides the experience of truth from the inner creative: our quantum-self identity.

The American mystic Franklin Merrell-Wolff (1973) practiced the path of wisdom (he was a trained mathematician/philosopher) for years with high intensity. One day, he realized that there is nothing to seek. To his amazement, this realization was followed by an experience of the quantum self.

What actually takes place in awareness in this direct encounter with the quantum self? Franklin Merrell-Wolff is quite specific:

> The first discernible effect on consciousness was something that I may call a shift in the base of consciousness. . . . I knew myself to be beyond space, time, and causality. . . . Closely associated with the foregoing realization there is a feeling of complete freedom. . . . I did not attempt to stop the activity of the mind, but simply very

largely ignored the stream of thought. . . . The result was that I was both here and "There", with the objective consciousness less acute than normal. (1973, pp. 38-40)

In the moment of spiritual illumination of this kind, primary awareness floods the field of attention; secondary-awareness processes continue but are given no attention or importance.

Not everyone, however, has so striking an experience of the ah-ha in inner creativity. After all, it is a subtle event. The women's spirituality researchers Sherry Anderson and Pat Hopkins (1991) found that many spiritual women do not identify their awakening to the truth of their being beyond ego with one big bang; many little bangs contribute to their turning about in self-identity. (This is, of course, the same point that Howard Gruber makes about many people's outer creativity.)

Some people declare that they are "enlightened" as a result of the insight experience of inner creativity. But there is a fallacy here. As Lao Tzu said, "the one who knows cannot say, the one who says cannot know." The one who knows is the inner quantum self, but speech unavoidably employs secondary-awareness processes involving the ego. The one who says "I am enlightened"—the ego—cannot know enlightened being.

So here is a genuine difference between inner and outer creativity. In outer creativity, at the manifestation stage, the ego is the central player. Thus, the subtle ego-boosting that is inherent in regarding a product as an accomplishment does no harm to the product. But in inner creativity, any such inflation of the ego is a detriment to the process and must delay or distort the manifestation of the wisdom of the insight.

The American mystic Richard Alpert (a.k.a. Ram Dass) went public with his "enlightenment" only to realize years later how the declaration had interfered with the manifestation of the buddhi level of his being. After he corrected his mistake, his flowering resumed.

In other words, humility is a necessary ingredient of the inner journey. Humility is the recognition that a transpersonal consciousness beyond ego is in charge and is the source and repository of the wisdom of that universal self, not the ego-I.

MANIFESTATION

During the earlier stages of the process of inner creativity, a moving away from the world, a renunciation, takes place. During manifestation, there is a reentry into the world, but from a new center of self-identity that has shifted beyond ego to buddhi. This reentry is alluded to in the Zen saying, "Before awakening [of buddhi], mountains are mountains and lakes are lakes. Then [during the creative process], mountains are not mountains, lakes are not lakes. After awakening, mountains are mountains, lakes are lakes."

There is some difference from outer creativity in this stage of the process. In outer creativity, manifestation is mostly at the level of the ego, which is the main player. But inner creativity involves a surrender of ego dominance. Instead of being the decision maker, the ego more and more becomes merely a function. The ego as function is clearly necessary to carry out worldly chores, but the distinction of "I" from others is merely an operational convenience. It is a little like a patient with multiple personality disorder—a fragmentation of the ego into many selves. As integration proceeds, the function of each of the fragments is incorporated, making separate identities no longer necessary. It is the same with the relationship of the quantum self and the ego. With the awakening of buddhi, the identity with the ego more and more gives way to the quantum self from which comes real choice and creativity in action. The ego now serves more and more as the functional agent that carries out the choices of this greater, nonpersonal identity.

The East Indian mystic Ramakrishna used the analogy of a salt figurine dipped into the ocean to make the same point. The figurine dissolves. Its function, the saltiness, remains even though merged with the ocean, but its separate structure and identity no longer exist. This is the goal. The challenge is not to run away from ambiguities that arise during living toward this goal or to escape into an action-oriented approach but to remain aware of the movements of consciousness as they manifest reality.

All three great East Indian mystics of recent times—Ramakrishna, Ramana Maharshi, and Sri Aurobindo—spent long years in silence *after* their ah-ha insight. The sixth patriarch of Chan Buddhism, Hui Neng, was a humble cook for 12 years after his enlightenment before circumstances catapulted him to public life. The well-documented American woman mystic known as Peace Pilgrim (1982) went through severe oscillations of self-identity before arriving at a new homeostasis at the buddhi level of being.

As the center of the self shifts beyond ego and buddhi awakens, action increasingly comes from the quantum self—primary awareness. Its signature is spontaneity which creates the sense of wonder that the poet Walt Whitman (1972) celebrates in these lines:

> To me every hour of the light and dark is a miracle,
> Every cubic inch of space is a miracle,
> Every square yard of the earth is spread with the same,
> Every foot of the interior swarms with the same.

The buddhi level of being brings a welcome freedom from compulsive self-preoccupation. One may sometimes feel this freedom when singing in the shower or walking in the woods. But imagine feeling that kind of freedom during what one calls chores, boredom, or even suffering? It would be like dancing through life. "Will you, won't you, will you, won't you, won't you join the dance?" This exuberant invitation from Lewis Carroll is always open to all of us.

DOES INNER CREATIVITY END WITH THE AWAKENING OF BUDDHI?

Here is another source of confusion. Many people regard the ah-ha experience of inner creativity, such as the experience of atman, as the culmination of spiritual work. Afterwards, they are empowered to become a guru and to enjoy the fruit of their accomplishments. But they have not even begun living in buddhi because they have not completed the most important manifestation stage. Instead, inner creativity continues, even after the manifestation of a shift of the center of self-identity—even after joining the "dance."

Remember, being a dancer is not being free; being in buddhi is not being free. One may still be attached to the glamour of dancing, to the romance of experiencing the limited freedom it represents. Can this ultimate romance be sacrificed?

The fact is that within the buddhi level of identity, there are several bands (Goswami, 1993a; Goswami & Burns, 1993; see also Wilber, 1977). It is not a hierarchy because as the identity shifts away from the ego, hierarchies also dissolve in the growth of profound humility. The first such band may be called the *creative/psychic/mystic band*; people of this band have discovered the potency of the quantum self, primary awareness, and quantum leaps. They thrive on creative, parapsychological, or mystical powers (i.e., they continue exploration of outer creativity and reap the rewards in these domains).

The next band can be called *transpersonal* because the psychosocial context of living is no longer appealing. In this band, the creativity of people who have discovered the nonlocality of relationship is more dedicated to love and service to others. This contrasts with an identity with the local ego in which one literally falls prey, to a greater or lesser extent, to solipsism, the delusion that I am the only conscious being and that other people are objects of my projections. They are mere appearances, forms to whom I cannot attribute an inner life as valid as mine.

To the extent that I identify with the atman, the quantum non-local self, I "real"ize the consciousness of others in relationship with me. Through my relationships I appreciate the "otherness" of others in their unique individuality, with their own unique perspectives and problems, at the same time experiencing that it is the same consciousness that we share. This experience of otherness is crucial to this band of self-identity.

The third band can be called the *spiritual band,* in which one surrenders even the idea of creatively serving the world and, thus, of inner creativity itself. People of this band see the wholeness of the quantum self. They experience the seamlessness of consciousness and recognize apparent individuality as a purely functional aspect of manifestation. Life is firmly anchored in appropriate action—creative or not.

As the saying goes, the journey to buddhi has an end, but the journey in buddhi never ends. Giving up the romance, the excitement of the dance of inner creativity itself, occurs when the dancer more and more becomes the dance and not separate from it; deeper and deeper shifts of self-identity take place and a profound humility permeates being as more and more weighting toward the quantum self occurs.

At the cremation grounds in India, an attendant stands by the pyre with a stick to see that no part of the body escapes the fire. When the job is done, the attendant throws the stick on the pyre. This is the destination.

PROCESS IN INNER CREATIVITY: A SUMMARY

The following is a summary of the important points raised here regarding the nature of inner creativity:

- Inner creativity is a journey of the creative fulfillment of the adult human potential: It is creativity directed inward to shift our identity beyond the ego. As such, the process has the same four stages as outer creativity.
- In the beginning, it helps to have an intellectual understanding of the literature, the philosophy, and of how other people

have traveled their journeys. It also helps to have an understanding of the contexts of any formal rituals and practices that you undertake (e.g., the rituals and practices of the great religious traditions).

- Along with active striving, it is imperative to make room for unconscious processing. In the encounter of inner creativity between the ego and the quantum self, the will of the ego is paradoxically brought to bear toward the surrender of the ego's dominance. Spiritual practices must become creative encounters that helps one discover the truth behind those practices. Only when one directly experiences the truth of a practice can one live that truth.

- Insight or illumination, the discovery of living truth or an experience of the quantum self, is by no means the end of the spiritual journey. It is the blooming of the possibility of a transformation of the center of one's being. To stop at this point, to cease to foster your continued development in the creative process, is to forego transformation.

- Manifestation in inner creativity consists of a shift of the context of living from the ego to the buddhi level of being, with greater and greater weight accruing to the quantum self. Thus, much of the manifestation process requires an inward silence in which unconscious processing continues as the ego increasingly surrenders its dominance to become only a necessary function. This is the stage in which inner creativity radically differs from outer creativity.

DOES INNER CREATIVITY LEAD TO LIBERATION?

Inner creativity is a journey of transformation. Every time we realize a truth about ourselves that manifests as a shift of our identity toward buddhi and away from our ego or to grow in buddhi, we are engaging in inner creativity. But we can also realize one truth, "knowing which all truths are known." This is the truth about our real nature. Does knowing this truth comprise inner creativity?

Knowing this truth is called liberation and is paradoxical. Truth *is,* and everyone is always liberated. Ignorance is an illusion. Knowing the truth does not change anything. In this sense, this is not inner creativity. Creativity itself is transcended in liberation.

However, we should not fall into the mistake of thinking that this knowing the true nature of the self is a continuous process. It is not.

Like creativity, it is also a discontinuous quantum leap. In this sense, it is similar to insight in inner creativity.

What can be confusing is what happens to the body-mind individual after liberation. Whereas in inner creativity, transformation is a compulsory part of the creative act, in liberation, in principle nothing *needs* to be done. What we find empirically is that God's will—the will of the whole—plays out in at least two different ways in these individuals who have arrived at liberation while living. For some, life is lived in an easy-without-effort way while the karma—the cause-effect propensities accrued in the course of many lifetimes—runs its course. For others, especially for those who become teachers, the universal will manifests in further training of the body-mind, but this is not transformation in the same sense as inner creativity: There is no personality surrendering, no personality transformed.

> What brings you to the path of inner creativity,
> Oh traveller? Do you seek
> to know yourself? Perhaps you want
> to realize your full human potential.
>
> Read, meditate, practice—until,
> your striving exhausted, you surrender
> in utter humility.
> Then, enfolded in your experience
> of oneness with the universe,
> do you think you are enlightened?
> Is this your new identity?
>
> In the journey of inner creativity
> you travel from separateness to unity.
> When all your identity structures give way
> to a profound fluidity,
> only then is there unending celebration.
> This bloom has no name, only fragrance.

PART FOUR

GENIUS?
OR CAN ANYONE BE CREATIVE?

You finally have arrived at the quintessential question: Does it take a genius to be creative or can anyone be creative by making the right effort? Can this book guide you to the answer to this question?

That is the purpose of this section. But first, I advise you to take a little tour of the wisdom that is available. To do this I return to the school of creativity research.

You turn with hope to the researchers; there have to be some data with clearcut, objective answers.

According to Barron (1955), there is, says one researcher, "one can come to the conclusion that original responses, it would seem, recur regularly in some persons, while there are other individuals who never depart from the stereotyped and the conventional in their thinking. If, then, some persons are regularly original, whereas others are regularly unoriginal, it must be the case that certain patterns of relatively enduring traits either facilitate or impede the production of original acts" (p. 478).

"Barron makes sense, and how can I debate you when you talk about data?", you say sadly. "I myself most times feel quite unoriginal, but sometimes, at moments of great enthusiasm, I sure feel original."

"But are you able to transfer your feeling to acts of creation?"

"Not yet. But who is to say I never will?"

"We do. If you don't have the right traits, and that includes acting promptly on your creative hunches, you are hopeless."

You look disappointed but don't be too easily disappointed. Creativity is fundamentally a phenomenon of consciousness; subjectivity is inherently associated with it. Barron belongs to the class of creativity researchers called *trait theorists,* who believe that creative behavior is caused by certain antecedent character traits. In other words, it takes a genius to be creative, and geniuses are people with certain personality traits in common. But other creativity researchers see it differently.

On your way out you notice that inadvertently you did enter the den of trait theorists; there was a sign that you didn't see at first on the other side of the hallway saying "Developmental theories."

The receptionist explains. "We, and that includes behavioral theorists and the organismic and even idealist theorists, warn you not to listen to the trait theorists. We maintain that *all* normal children are born creative—everyone is a potential genius."

But just when your eyes light up and your mind begins to hum a tune of happiness that, because you were born creative, perhaps creativity is within your reach after all, you hear a voice.

"But there is a caveat." The voice belongs to a behaviorist, as a card on her lapel indicates. "Creative behavior has to be conditioned like all behavior, and only those who have been so conditioned end up creative in their adult lives. So what is your history of developmental conditioning? Show it to me, and I'll tell you in a jiffy if creativity is a legitimate aspiration and pursuit for you."[1]

But before you can answer, somebody else wearing a T-shirt with the insignia "Think Organismic" attracts your attention. "The behaviorists are too narrow in their interpretation; don't waste your time with them. Yes, development matters, but it's effect on the creative potential of a person is more subtle."

You are noncommital this time. You are not going to get your hopes up only to be crushed once more. The organicist continues.

> It is true that the key to why some adults retain their creativity in their adult years has to be found in the history of their development. The clues are there. We contend that the creative is an individual who manages a most formidable challenge: to wed the most advanced understandings achieved in a domain with the kinds of problems, questions, issues, and sensibilities that most characterized his or her life as a wonder-filled child. It is in this sense that the adult creative draws repeatedly on the capital of childhood. (Gardner, 1993, p. 32)

---

[1]This extreme behavioral stand is due to Skinner (1971).

"But what if I did not accumulate any such capital in my childhood?" Your voice shows dismay once again.

"That's your tough luck. Sorry, fella."

But another person vies for your attention. "Don't give up yet. Let me ask you. When you were a child, did you ever experience nuance?"

"What's nuance?" You are curious.

"You know, an experience of the subtlety of things. It is from these experiences that we develop a sensitivity to the subtler connections of the world, which then expresses itself in our creative acts."[2]

You have to think about that one, you tell her.

Moving on, you find another group of people. "You look pensive," one of them comments to you.

"I am trying to decide whether I have a special sensitivity to subtle things." You explain your encounter with the nuance theorist.

"Creativity is problem solving," he says. "Problem solving requires only ordinary thinking, nothing special. No sensitivity, no subtlety. Anyone can do it, anyone can be creative, including you.[3] Look, computers can do it. And, as everyone knows, computers are anything but subtle. They solve everything by brute force."

"I am not sure I have that much brute force as a computer. Perhaps, for us humans, a little subtlety would be helpful?"

"Oh, baloney!" The man loses interest in the discussion.

"Disappointed?"

"Yes!"

"Don't be. Of course, there are opposing worldviews, opposing ideas. As a matter of fact, this is the old nature (traits, mechanistic) versus nurture (development) debate in which there is never a clear winner. Did you have a chance to talk to an idealist?"

"No."

"Idealists, most clearly Carl Jung, add a further twist to the debate. Jung introduced the idea that creativity itself is a factor in our becoming; according to him, creativity is a drive from the collective unconscious that, along with nature and nurture, shapes what we become."

"But what determines who will have more of this unconscious drive, or an adequate amount at least? The only important question for me is, Do I have it in enough quantity?"

---

[2]You can hear Briggs (1990) here.

[3]He is speaking the voice of Weisberg (1993).

"Easterners say that that question requires an analysis of not only your development of this life, but past lives as well."

"It looks hopeless then."

"Don't make up your mind so fast. Why don't you read this section and see if you can see through each of these positions and find the loopholes in them?

"I believe that all these views have grains of truth. Our genetic traits, the environment in which we grow up, our childhood experiences, the drive from our collective unconscious—all can be seen as grist for the mill of adult creativity. And more. Even the role of chance and coincidence must be acknowledged."

"But is creativity restricted to a few geniuses? Certainly, geniuses exist; in them, the confluence of these factors is remarkable. But, paradoxically, it is also correct to say that anyone can be creative. Everyone is potentially a genius not only when they are young but at all ages because genius factors are available to virtually every human being, irrespective of age."

"So the study of the question, Can anyone be creative?, will also show us what the genius factors are, and what factors we should strive to acquire no matter what age we are. These factors will not make us creative, only we can do that. But these factors will help us manifest solutions to our burning questions when we are creative."

15

I/ CREATIVITY A QUE/TION OF TRAIT/?

All material realists believe in local causes for every effect, and creativity is no exception. Trait theorists assume that certain stable traits cause creativity—for example, the ability to visualize and imagine, the ability to take risks (manifested as self-confidence and originality), the ability to be persistent, the capacity for divergent thinking, and a good memory.[1] In some empirical studies and surveys, creative people as a group are indeed found to be imaginative, self-confident, original, to be risk takers, divergent thinkers, and hard workers. Trait theorists maintain that it is these traits, among others, that separate creatives from ordinary folks.

Two boys were given the task of taking a short trip and then coming back and reporting on it. When they returned, the first boy was asked, "So, what did you see?" The boy shrugged his shoulders. "Nothing much," he said. Sound familiar? But the second boy, in answer to the same question, said with luminous eyes, "I have seen so much." Then he proceeded to describe what he saw. The first boy could not see past the mundane world. The second boy grew up to be the renowned novelist Victor Hugo.

This is a good story for trait theorists, who would say that Victor Hugo was a genius because he had the traits (among others)—

---

[1]Guilford (1959); for a recent compilation of other references in the field, see Tardif and Sternberg (1988).

even as a boy—of a special eye that saw possibilities and a mind that thought divergently.

Most trait theorists think that the traits connected with creativity are measurable traits, so they develop tests to measure people's creative potential (Torrance, 1988). These creativity tests are reminiscent of IQ tests for intelligence, but to their credit they are much more elaborate and often cover many dimensions of personality such as thinking, emotions, and values (whereas IQ tests tend to be one-dimensional—they concentrate on mostly thinking abilities).

Some trait theorists believe that traits may be latent in many people—many more people than the number of active geniuses. They believe that some of the traits can be enhanced via training and techniques and many such techniques are available now (Davis, 1975).

THE MEANING OF MACKINNON'S SURVEY

There are many surveys, as mentioned earlier, that support the trait theorists' claims that personality traits are cause-effect related to creativity. There are, however, surveys that negate the trait theorists' claims.

One of these surveys was carried out by Donald MacKinnon (1962), who studied 40 of the most creative architects in the United States in the 1950s. There were two control groups. One control group was chosen at random from a directory of architects—call it the unrelated group. The second control group also consisted of noncreative architects, with one difference: Each of the members of this group had worked with one of the members of the creative group for at least two years—call it the associate group.

The tests were multidimensional. And the creatives came out to be significantly different from the unrelated group in many of the personality dimensions. In the dimension of value, the creatives scored much higher on appreciation of aesthetics and much lower on the appreciation of economics. The creatives also scored much higher in sensitivity to feelings and emotions, and they were significantly less social.

But this was the good news for trait theories. The bad news was that in 39 of 40 personality measures, the associate group performed similarly to the creative group (the one exception was that the associate group preferred economics to aesthetics). How can we say that personality traits are unique to creatives when, clearly, noncreatives also have them?

However, we would be too hasty in making the negative conclusion that there is no such thing as a creative or genius personality. The only reasonable conclusion is that creative personality traits do not guarantee creative achievements. The associate group, perhaps because of their association with the creatives, emulated the right personality, but that did not make them creative—not because the personality traits are not helpful to the creative but because they are not sufficient.

The problem is this. Trait theorists assume that creativity is an objective phenomenon and, to them, talking about a strict "cause" of creativity makes sense. In contrast, if we accept that creativity is always subjective, then we can easily understand MacKinnon's survey results. Are personality traits important? Yes, the difference in traits between the creative and the unrelated noncreative group is too striking to ignore. But having these traits does not guarantee creativity exclusive of the essential subjective components of creativity—purposiveness and a willingness to explore meaning and discover contexts. Sensitivity to aesthetics is essential for a creative architect; when this sensitivity gives rise to a burning question of exploration, it translates into a creative piece of architecture.

DIVERGENT THINKING

Widely used tests by the creativity researchers E. P. Torrance (1988) and J. P. Guilford (1959) emphasize how one learns and thinks, and whether one has the tendency to think about a problem in many ways or to focus quickly on one particular way; that is, whether one's cognitive style is divergent or convergent. Suppose you ask a child to name two days of the week that begin with "T"; at first, he or she says, "Tuesday and Thursday," then on second thought, he or she adds, "also today and tomorrow." You know this child is a divergent thinker. More seriously, Edward de Bono (1970) gave an excellent example of divergent thinking (which de Bono called *lateral thinking*). When debtor's prisons were prevalent, a money lender was able to manipulate a borrower to consider the following offer while the borrower and his daughter walked along a gravel path. "Here are two pebbles," said the money lender as he picked up two pebbles from the gravel path and dropped them in a bag, "a white one and a dark one. If your daughter, without looking, can pick the white one from the bag, your debt will be excused. But if she picks the black one, then she is mine." In convergent thinking, one would expect a 50-50 chance of retrieving the white pebble, so the borrower agreed, with hope, for his daughter to try. But his daughter, thinking divergently, knew better than to trust the lender. She suspected that both pebbles might be dark ones. What should she do? She put her hand in the bag. But as she withdrew her hand, she dropped the pebble, exclaiming, "How clumsy of me. But, of course, you can tell the color of the pebble I drew by looking at the one remaining in the bag."

On the face of it, how can we doubt the relevance of divergent thinking to creativity? Creativity is the exploration of possibilities to discover the new. How can you discover the new without an open mind to consider many possibilities before homing in on one? But there is more subtlety here. In a survey, when real-life creative scientists were asked if they use much divergent thinking, they said that, on the contrary, they use convergent thinking, narrowing down the possible answers.

Are Torrance, Guilford, and company wrong then? Not necessarily. I think that creatives engage in divergent thinking but process it in the unconscious. They allow unresolved ambiguities to proliferate via unconscious processing (as in the earlier story, in which the doubt of the debtor's daughter proliferated into quantum superpositions that contained the answer). Then when the time is ripe, when creative ideas pop out, they use convergent thinking to manifest the creative act.

WHAT ABOUT GENES AND BRAINS?

One important question for aspiring creatives is, are creativity traits, if such exist, genetic? Are we born with them? This is the underlying assumption that many trait theorists share.

Francis Galton, an eminent scientist of the 19th century, published a book in 1869, *Hereditary Genius*, in which he attempted to show "that a man's natural abilities are derived by inheritance, under exactly the same limitations as are the form and the physical features of the whole organic world." Indeed, if you go through Galton's list of the genealogy of talented people (whether they are all geniuses can be debated), you will be impressed.[2] One of the claims he made, for example, is that "at least 40% of the poets (number studied: 56) have had eminently gifted relations."

Galton conceived his list even before we knew how heredity works. When genes were discovered, that was considered a great support for Galton's hypothesis of the inheritance of creativity traits. But gradually, with more understanding, the excitement subsided. No creativity genes were ever found. Genes do not express themselves in any kind of one-to-one correspondence with the macroscopic traits of a per-

---

[2]For an excerpt from Galton's book, see Rothenberg and Hausman (1976, pp. 42-47).

son, especially personality traits. These latter result from complicated interactions between the genetic inheritance and the development of the person—it is very difficult to separate the genetic and environmental influences. Moreover, the glaring fact is that it is extremely rare for a creative's children to also be creative.

In the same vein, more recently, there has been a lot of attention to creativity being a property of the right-brain hemisphere, which is holistic in its processing, as opposed to the left hemisphere, which is mundane, calculating, and reason-based. It was theorized that people, conditioned by society to develop only the left brain, fail to become creative because they have not cultivated their right brains. But research has failed to identify any physical location such as the right brain where creative ideas congeal.[3]

If you want to attend a workshop on how to act with the right side of your brain, go ahead. Most likely, the leader of the workshop is only trying to enhance your creativity. But be careful to take any right-brain talk as strictly metaphorical.

SOME CONCLUDING REMARKS ON TRAIT THEORIES

Undoubtedly, there is some substance to the idea that traits, including personality traits such as self-discipline and divergent thinking, contribute to creativity. However, it is a fact that having these traits does not alone guarantee creativity. And not having them as children does not prevent creativity as an adult; that too is fact. Thus it is hard to make a cause-effect connection between traits and creativity. I doubt that Einstein as a child would have passed many of the trait theorists' tests.

In truth, it is virtually impossible to make a definitive cause-effect connection between the possession of traits and actual acts of creation.[4] Hence the debate—does creativity belong only to an elite group of geniuses with traits, or is everyone capable of creativity—continues. The psychologist Robert Weisberg claims to have debunked the myth of genius. According to Weisberg (1993), there is nothing special about creative thinking; plain, ordinary thinking of which everybody is capable has all the ingredients that lead to creative acts. Hence, argues Weisberg, everyone is capable of creativity.

---

[3]Nevertheless, authors keep assuming that creativity has something to do with right-brain activities; see, for example, Edwards (1989).

[4]See the review by Gardner (1993, p. 20).

Like Weisberg, I believe that everybody has the potential to be creative. Creativity is not limited to the talented and gifted. I do not believe that special genetically (or behaviorally) conditioned traits cause creativity, although such traits certainly can help. This is why creative people acquire these traits on the job.

But is creative thinking the same as ordinary thinking? To Weisberg, all thinking is machine thinking, nothing but computing, and, therefore, algorithmic. As we have seen in previous chapters, creativity involves nonalgorithmic jumps in conscious thought. But all of us, by virtue of being conscious, are capable of making such jumps. So creativity is potentially universal, not because all thinking is the same but because we all are potentially capable of both ordinary and creative thinking.

We know that as children our creativity is practically universal; without it, there would be little learning. If it is not the lack of traits, then, can it be the developmental process that constricts universal creativity in all but a few adults? This question is taken up in the next chapter.

Habit says, "Believe the data
that fit your model of the world
and ignore the rest."

The world says, "Ignore the habit
and extend your model
to fit the world."

16

CREATIVITY,
EARLY CONDITIONING,
AND DEVELOPMENT

When I was a 7-year-old boy in a small town in British India, I once entered a poetry recital competition. I was not satisfied with reciting the little, 10-line poem they assigned to us. So instead of reciting the assigned poem, I began reciting a well-known, long poem. Some people in the audience objected and tried to stop me, but the chairman of the session was amused and let me go on. Eventually, I ended with thunderous approval from the audience and received a special prize.

Behaviorists say that my behavior on this occasion was creative behavior. To them, any behavior that redefines any or all of the "givens (the initial problem), goals (the intended solution), gateways (methods), and gremlins (obstructions against reaching the goal)" of solving a particular problem is creative behavior (Boles, 1990). It can be arrived at deliberately (as I did) or appear by chance. If reinforced, people become conditioned to behave in this manner on certain occasions. Creative people are those people for whom creative behavior has been conditioned early on. This is the essence of the behavioral theory of creativity (Skinner, 1971).

However, the "creativity" that behaviorists usually permit in their worldview is problem solving, not fundamental creativity and not situational creativity dedicated to the pursuit of meaning (there are exceptions[1]). Unacknowledged by behaviorists, meaningful creativity

---

[1]Boles (1990) is one.

requires the freedom of the quantum self. Even so, appropriate behavioral conditioning engenders such mechanical aspects of creativity as problem-solving ability, accomplishment orientation, and the ability to redefine a problem. Our current university curricula, particularly in science, are ample proof of that.

Environmental conditioning and some types of self-images (e.g., perfectionism and lack of self-worth) can have a negative influence on people's creative potential. Creativity is fostered not only by what people do but also by what they don't do. The Japanese Nobel-laureate physicist Hideki Yukawa, no doubt speaking from his own experience, suggested that creativity is nurtured as much by dissolving fixed ideas as by the ability to question assumptions. Often creativity is not a positive thing to be pursued aggressively but a process of gently working around the barriers of environmental conditioning that block our creativity. Geniuses are first of all those people who are capable of pursuing the creative journey in spite of their detrimental conditioning. "It is not the perfect but the imperfect that is in need of our love," wrote the novelist Oscar Wilde. The genius accepts his or her imperfections and, by so doing, becomes the vehicle for perfect actions of creativity in the imperfect world of manifestation.

A Zen story is worth citing here. Two traveling monks came across a shallow stream. A pretty woman, beautifully dressed, arrived there at the same time. The stream was walkable, but the woman hesitated lest her dress get wet. One monk picked her up and carried her to the other side; she thanked him, and they parted ways. The other monk was bothered by all this because monks were not supposed to touch women. After a while, he could no longer keep his aggravation to himself. "Brother. You carried a woman", he accused. The other monk looked at him and said gently, "Yes. But I carried her only across the narrow stream. You are carrying her even now."

FROM UNIVERSALITY TO THE CREATIVE INDIVIDUAL

How does creativity, a phenomenon so universal in children, become so rare in adults? Piaget, whose study established that child development takes place via processes called equilibration (see chapter 7), also proposed that the definitive step, hierarchical equilibration—the jump of internalizing a logical context—is a creative leap accomplished via what he called *reflective abstraction*. It is the same process that Gregory Bateson called Level II learning and that I have termed creative learning which involves a quantum leap.

Perhaps the average adult individual, limited to mundane activities in the world, always stays at the level of the activities themselves. They look at a movie as a movie, a job as a job, never bothering to find abstract (and meaningful) relationships among the various acts or in their relationship with the self. Perhaps creative people continue their childhood discontinuous quantum processes of Learning II, or reflective abstraction, to find the deeper context of things, whereas most people succumb to the continuity of adult conscious experience. But why? Why do some people retain the use of the creative process, whereas others lose it? Developmental theories of creativity suggest partial answers.

The creativity researcher David Feldman (1986), who did a definitive study of child prodigies, found that prodigies succeed because of a remarkable early match between their talent and their field of activity. Perhaps those children who end up as creative adults receive (by plan or by accident) special attention and training to develop a special talent. Indeed, adult creativity often requires mastery or developed talent in a field, and the earlier the mastery, the better.

Perhaps so for mechanical, problem-solving ability, perhaps not for creativity when pursued meaningfully. Not unless people retain a childlike curiosity in matters pertaining to the field of their special talent do they continue to make fundamental and meaningful creative contributions to the field as adults. The biologist Edward Wilson, who founded sociobiology—the idea that genes control human culture—based on his observations of the behavior of ants, retained his childhood curiosity about bugs. "Every kid has a bug period," he said at age 64. "I just never grew out of mine" (1975).

But how does this childlike curiosity continue in a few, whereas many people burn out under the barrage of early training and discipline? Retaining curiosity is not a matter of conscious will.
It may be the other way around—perhaps it is better not to have childhood expertise in a variety of fields (although some familiarity is certainly helpful). Said Einstein about why he was the one to end up making discoveries about the nature of space and time:

> The reason, I think, is that a normal adult never stops to think about problems of space and time. These are things that he has thought of as a child. But my intellectual development was retarded, as a result of which I began to wonder about space and time only when I had already grown up. Naturally, I could go deeper than a child with normal ability. (quoted in Clark, 1971, p. 27)

Einstein retained a curiosity about things that are mundane to most adults because he was a "retarded" child. (The principal of Einstein's school once told Einstein's father, that Einstein would never make a success of anything.) Einstein's case is not isolated; apparently, the novelist Virginia Woolf was also "retarded." But most creative people are not retarded children in the same vein. How do they manage to retain curiosity and not burn out with the burden of expert knowledge?

CREATIVITY AND NUANCE

The author John Briggs (1990) thinks that creative people have an extreme sensitivity to nuances; they see a subtle world of meaning in events that ordinary people miss. Take the case of the novelist Henry James. He was at a dinner party when a woman made a comment about a mother-son fight over an estate. Was this just a mundane conversation piece? Not for James, who experienced a nuance—a certain feeling in which a whole story line came to him, and he proceeded to write *The Spoils of Poynton* as a result of his sensitivity. If this ability to observe, to see the subtlety of events (there's-more-to-it-than-meets-the-eye and I-am-going-to-investigate attitudes), starts early, this may explain why only a small fraction of people retain their natural childhood creativity.

The Harvard physicist Gerald Holton (1973), who studies creativity on the side, found that children who are imprinted early with a theme or themes for their lifelong investigation end up creative. For example, Einstein may have developed an abiding sensitivity to nuance and found one of his lifelong themes of research—continuity—when he was 5-years-old, ill in bed, and his father brought him a magnetic compass. Similarly, Briggs says that the tree of life, the recurrent image found in Darwin's notebooks, expressed Darwin's nuance—the doorway to the subtle world.

Virginia Woolf described her first childhood experience of nuance with vivid imagery:

> If life has a base that it stands upon, if it is a bowl that one fills and fills and fills—then my bowl without a doubt stands upon this memory. It is of lying half asleep, half awake, in bed in the nursery at St. Ives. It is of hearing the waves breaking, one, two, one two, behind the yellow blind. It is of hearing the blind draw its little acorn across the floor as the wind blew the blind out. It is of lying and hearing this splash and seeing this light, and feeling, it is almost impossible that I should be here; of feeling the purest ecstasy I can conceive. (quoted in Briggs, 1990, p. 36)

Those waves of Woolf's early experience spread their gentle influence on the greatest of her novels, *To the Lighthouse and The Waves.*

What happens in these experiences of nuance? They are events of primary awareness—a momentary encounter with the quantum self, a glimpse into quantum nonlocality. Such an encounter leads to a wider vision (producing images of wide scope). Indeed, such an event would have the ecstasy of a peak experience, inciting a personal sense of purpose in tune with the purpose of the universe (see chapter 9).

When you were a child, you experienced nuance many times, but perhaps you don't remember. Nobody told you the importance of that kind of sensitivity to the world, and you kept it secret until you forgot. Briggs believes that early experiences of sensitivity to nuance is crucial.

But the important question is can you redevelop that sensitivity now? I think you can. You are the quantum self but you misidentify with the ego. To be sensitive to the world, you must give sway to your quantum self again, as when you were a child. This re-enchantment is the goal of inner creativity.

There are many examples of late starters in creativity. Personalizing the purpose of the universe is the key, and I intuit that it can be done at any age if one is properly motivated.

TRANSCENDING CONFLICT AND AMBIVALENCE

Conflict is in the nature of the ego modality. We want to perpetuate the ego, to look after the numero uno that we think we are. But we also want those things that make being numero uno so pleasurable—love, creativity, beauty. But the latter are not in the ego's domain; they reside in the quantum modality. We want to love, but we also want to hold on to our separateness and control. We want to be creative, but we don't want to surrender the security of our bit-by-bit, continuous-reasoning mode of operation built from past conditioning. We want the fruit of a creative act but do not want the agony of a burning question or the uncertainty of waiting in absorption. We want to appreciate beauty but do not want to give up the judging mind that quantifies it. This ego-dynamics driven by separateness and ambition conflicts with our quantum dynamics and sets up ambivalence. We are torn between two lovers, we cannot act freely.

But there is energy in conflict, there is intensity in the engagement with ambivalence. We cannot act in the quantum modality simply by wishing it, but the energy and intensity of conflict can catapult us into the quantum being. This is what creative people manage to accomplish from their conflicts—where other people see conflict, they see possibility.

Where other people are caged in their separateness, creative people retain faith because they have discovered nuance; they have experienced the unity of their quantum self in past creative acts. And they remember; this ability is called *omnivalence* by John Briggs (1990) and *negative capability* by the poet John Keats. The faith of the creative is usually rewarded by the creative act that brings integration, a synthesis both in the object of creation and in the mind of the creator. The result is transformation.

It is amazing what the creative act can transform—even cruelty. The Russian film director Sergei Eisenstein was compelled to depict cruelty in his films. He grew up as an abused child, and cruelty became a nuance for him. He saw a French movie that further crystallized his vision. In the film a prisoner, a sergeant, working on a farm was branded on the shoulder as punishment for making love to the farmer's wife. A strange transformation took place in how Eisenstein looked at cruelty—he no longer was sure who was being cruel to whom:

> In my childhood it [the film] gave me nightmares. . . . Sometimes I became the sergeant, sometimes the branding iron. I would grab hold of his shoulder. Sometimes it seemed to be my own shoulder. At other times it was someone else's. I no longer knew who was branding whom. (quoted in Briggs, 1990, p. 117)

This is the thing—in the quantum modality, even evil is not separate from us. When we realize this creatively, then evil can be transformed. The integrative transformation that took place in Eisenstein's own psyche eventually enabled him to use the ugliness of cruelty to achieve great beauty in the totality of his films.

Shakespeare knew about this transformative aspect of creativity when he wrote Ariel's song in the *Tempest*:

> Full fathom five thy father lies
> Of his bones are coral made;
> Those are pearles that were his eyes;
> Nothing of him that doth fade
> But doth suffer a sea change
> Into something rich and strange;
> Sea nymphs hourly ring his knell;
> Hark, I hear them; Ding-Dong Bell.

Creativity can metamorphose the horrible stuff of a cadaver into "something rich and strange." But our rational ego must yield to the alchemy of our quantum modality.

So why do only a fraction of children—all with creative potential—grow to adult creativity? Briggs (1990) says that only those who
are able to allow their ambivalence and omnivalence to cross-catalyze
each other are the lucky ones. But here again, this is not necessarily a
trait that only children can acquire.

Like most children, you probably reacted to crisis as danger and
missed seeing an opportunity. (The Chinese epigram for crisis stands for
both danger and opportunity. Still how many Chinese children acquire
omnivalence as a trait?) But can you change your ways now?

WHY ISN'T EVERYONE CREATIVE?
THE DEVELOPMENTAL PERSPECTIVE

The picture that emerges from the behavioral and organismic frame-
works is that the way we grow is important in our staying creative as
adults. The primary problem we face as adults is the all-pervasiveness of
the ego identity—our proclivity to identify exclusively with certain tendencies to which we have been conditioned, some of which are counter
to creativity. Why can't we escape these tendencies? Because in our ego,
we don't want to. We say that these tendencies define our character, our
uniqueness. If I lose my character, what will be left of "me?"

We are very defensive about our ego, our character. We say, with
age my brain has lost its plasticity; there is no more room in it for new
learning. If one thinks of the brain even as a classical computer, it certainly is not a space problem; we use perhaps as little as 20% of our brain.

Sometimes we say there is nothing new under the sun. But it is
not a question of not having anything left to discover. With the quantum mind contributing its vast number of states (the primary mental
states of all people at all times) to our "library" in potentia, and with
the brain's equally unlimited power to make maps, we could not
exhaust our discovery potential in a million lifetimes, let alone in one
lifetime. Our society becomes more and more complex with time, continually giving rise to new social contexts to be discovered for the creative expressions of eternal themes, if only we would do so.

So why don't we? Organismic theorists believe that what makes
the difference are the details involved in growing up. Once you grow
up, you cannot do anything about your condition. (These theorists do
not acknowledge the power of inner creativity, which is really about creative adult development; see chapter 4.)

Carl Jung (1971a) had a different idea (and millenia ago the
ancient Hindus had a similar notion) of what the problem is in the concept of *unconscious drives*. This is the subject of the next chapter.

Can you be creative?
If you stay with your burning question
and your inadequacies don't lead to despair . . .
then you are free.

Can you be creative?
If your sensitivity to possibilities
reflects universal purpose in you . . .
then you are free.

Can you be creative?
If conflict reveals opportunity to you
and you can transform poison into nectar . . .
then you are free.

Can you be creative?
If you can tolerate uncertainty
inviting the encounter with your quantum self . . .
then you are free to create.

17

CREATIVITY AND THE UNCONSCIOUS

Eastern psychology makes reference to three *gunas,* normally translated as "qualities" of the mind. The three gunas are (in Sanskrit) *tamas, rajas,* and *sattwa:*

1. *Tamas:* literally translated as darkness, it means inertia. Clearly, tamas refers to our tendency to follow the inertia of our environmental conditioning.
2. *Rajas:* meaning activeness, it refers to our tendencies to engage in activities driven by desire; sexual desire is chief among these.
3. *Sattwa:* meaning illumination, it refers to our quality to illuminate—in other words, creativity.

Easterners clearly realized that the first two gunas, rajas and tamas, are detrimental to creativity because they obscure sattwa like clouds hide the sun. Interestingly, ideas similar to theirs are now being revived in modern psychology, thanks to the work of Freud and Jung on the unconscious.

Because of the dominance of materialist thinking, there is considerable reluctance on the part of many researchers to accommodate the idea of the unconscious in their philosophy (although most ordinary people use the idea quite freely). However, evidence has now accumulated in favor of the unconscious (see chapter 10).

IS CREATIVITY A DRIVE FROM THE UNCONSCIOUS?

Once we recognize that consciousness is the primary reality in our worldview and that the unconscious (i.e., absence of awareness) can be defined and even be studied experimentally, the role of the unconscious in creativity is easy to recognize. We have already explored the importance of unconscious processing. Additionally, according to Freud (1961/1963), we develop a personal unconscious, a repository of repressed instincts. To what extent does the existence of this repository affect our creative outbursts?

For Freud, the ideas that come from the unconscious are mostly socially undesirable. They consist mainly of libido, a drive that fuels people's sexuality, although in his later writings Freud enlarged his concept of libido to that of the life force, the force that stimulates all action in the world and not merely sexual action.

According to Freud, creative people are those who put their socially undesirable, repressed instincts to good use. They have an unusual capacity to sublimate the sexual drive and to process unconscious images into socially acceptable forms that may appear novel and creative. However, these unconscious images originate in conflict; for example, Leonardo da Vinci's particular style of portraying women originates, according to Freud, in the repressed feelings of what his mother's smile meant to him in his childhood. But the unconscious drive that motivates a creative solution to the conflict may also motivate, a neurotic solution. Therefore, Freud saw creativity as a close cousin of neurosis:

> An artist is once more in rudiments an introvert, not far removed from neurosis. He is oppressed by excessively powerful instinctual needs. He desires to win honor, power, wealth, fame, and the love of women; but he lacks the means for achieving these satisfactions. Consequently, like any other unsatisfied man, he turns away from reality and transfers all his interest and his libido, too, to the wishful construction of his life of fantasy, whence the path might lead to neurosis. (quoted in Woodman, 1981, p. 45)

Freud saw a connection between children's imagination and adult creativity but insisted that the "freely rising" fantasies and ideas of adult creativity were nothing but a continuation of childhood play and daydreaming. The power of the creative person lies in accepting these daydreams and putting them to good use whereas the noncreative suppresses the fantasy. For Freud (1961, 1963), a person arrives at "achievements of special perfection" when his unconscious processes become adaptive to normal ego-functioning.

But creativity is not just play and daydreams; in fact, such identification probably excludes the vast majority of creative acts (e.g., scientific creativity) from the applicability of Freud's theory. Freud's theory also excludes the many occasions when a creative person uses creativity to catapult beyond ego—an act of inner creativity.

And Freud's theory that creatives convert unconscious neurotic images to socially acceptable ones does not hold water either. When Van Gogh painted *The Starry Night* as a swirling mass of cosmic energy, he may have been painting what he saw with neurotic eyes, but he was also painting what he saw with transcendent eyes. The first gave his painting mere form, the second gave it formless, universal emotion that connects directly to the viewer.

It was Jung (1971a) who recognized that sublimation of the sexual libido is only a partly necessary criterion for creativity, not a sufficient one. He identified the motivation for creativity as a drive from the collective unconscious—a realm of the unconscious that is universal and not bounded by space, time, or culture: "The creative process, so far as we are able to follow it at all, consists in the unconscious activation of an archetypal image, and in elaborating and shaping this image into the finished work." Thus, for Jung, creativity is a result of an unconscious drive, but not one that drives up images of conflict from the personal, repressed unconscious of Freudian vintage; instead, it drives up archetypal images that reside, according to Jung, in the collective unconscious.

Consider the chemist Fredrick von Kekule's discovery of the structure of the benzene molecule. A benzene molecule is made of carbon and hydrogen atoms; the question was how carbon atoms bond with one another and with hydrogen atoms. All then-known bonding occurred in open, linear arrangements. Within this rigid context the solution eluded everybody. Kekule's famous solution was circular bonding, an idea that came to him during a reverie state in which he saw a snake biting its own tail. According to Jung, the dream image of a snake biting its own tail, which triggered Kekule's insight, is a prime example of an archetypal image.

Jung always emphasized the fact that it is conscious awareness that gives meaning and value to unconscious images; creativity is an interplay of the unconscious and the conscious. Surrealistic painting is a vivid and most obvious example of such an interplay, but, according to Jung, all creative acts are a bit surrealistic.

Jung also put considerable emphasis on inner creativity, which, he said, leads to "individuation"—a stage of development in which the person's individuality is firmly established within a cosmic unity. According to Jung, individuation takes place when the archetypal drives of the collective unconscious become integrated with conscious awareness.

Freud's and Jung's works are important because, once we accept the concept of the unconscious, our own empirical experience certainly resonates with the importance of the unconscious in creativity. Materialists, of course, are extremely uncomfortable with the concept of the unconscious; if a theory denies consciousness, except as an epiphenomenon, an unconscious that has a causal exchange with what is conscious cannot be given recognition either. But in idealist science, using ideas of the quantum theory, unconscious repressions can be easily understood.

If we are conditioned to avoid certain mental states—for example, because of childhood trauma—the probability becomes overwhelming that these states are never collapsed from the superpositions containing them. Such superpositions may, however, influence the collapse of subsequent states, collapses that will seem to be without any apparent cause and thus produce neurosis.

Similarly, we can understand Jung's repressed archetypal themes of the collective unconscious. For example, a male would tend to suppress mental states that pertain to the experiences of a female body, for which he has no context. This may be the origin of the anima archetype repressed in males. Correspondingly, the repressed male archetype in females is the animus.

Any human being, in the quantum picture, is potentially capable of manifesting all the primary-awareness states of all human beings, irrespective of space-time restrictions. This is a consequence of the fact that we share the same mind and similar brain mechanisms to make maps of the mind. As we become conditioned, a preference for personally experienced states develops, as mentioned earlier, and transpersonal states become repressed from our experience. Thus, creativity becomes an unconscious drive because conditioning leads to the repression of the new in preference to the old, learned states.

UNCONSCIOUS PSYCHOLOGICAL DRIVES AS GUIDES OF OUR ACTIONS

In the new idealist science model of the self, we are capable of acting in two very different modalities. One, ego, we have called *classical*—this is the conditioned modality, reflecting our habitual patterns and character. The other, atman, we have called the *quantum modality*—this manifests in the act of creativity.

We should recognize that all of our actions, conscious and unconscious, are guided by one or the other or both of these modalities. However, it is not that we choose what modality to invoke for a particular act, it is more that we are driven toward certain acts that require one or the other or both modalities. Normally, we are not particularly conscious of either our conditioning or our creative facility. Is there a terminology that we can develop to account for this normal unconsciousness we have about who we are, how we are motivated, and why we do what we do?

As mentioned previously, Freud initially thought that most of our actions are driven by unconscious, genetically programmed, sexual urges that he called the *libido*. But later he realized that the unconscious drive of libido is far more generally rooted than the sexual motif— genetic and body programming go much deeper. So according to Freud, libido is a psychological drive that defines our *life force*. In this perspective, we can see that what we conventionally refer to as the *contribution of nature* to our being is what manifests as the psychological drive of libido.

Behaviorism gives us another perspective on psychological drives. According to behaviorism, our actions are conditioned by past learning; they result from extensive conditioning at the personal, family, social, and cultural levels that shape our ego-identity. But the ego has no causal power in behaviorism (a strict behaviorist would not even entertain the concept of the ego), so it is quite accurate to say that our actions are driven by our unconscious conditioning, although, admittedly, behaviorists would never use words such as the unconscious. We normally refer to this unconscious drive due to environmental conditioning as the *contribution of nurture* to our being and mode of action.

Thus, what we call the classical modality in our model and what is normally expressed unconsciously can be thought of as the two unconscious psychological drives of environmental conditioning and libido. Where does quantum modality and creativity fit in this description?

The drives of environmental conditioning and libido are the drives of our personal unconscious. They reflect quantum mental states that have gained greater probability weighting as a result of environmental and genetic conditioning. In contrast, quantum modality and creativity involve Jung's collective unconscious. Jung thus added a definite third component—creativity— to nature-versus-nurture debate of human development, and the idealist science developed here supports Jung's contention.

The similarity of the concept of psychological drives to that of the Eastern gunas should also be obvious. Behavioral conditioning is the psychological drive that the Easterners referred to as *tamas*. Similarly, one can recognize that libido is rajas, and the Jungian drive of creativity corresponds to sattwa. There are, then, three important drives that guide our actions:

1. Behavioral conditioning, nurture, or tamas
2. Libido, nature, or rajas
3. Creativity, or sattwa

Looking at the human condition from the point of view of the psychological drives or the gunas is helpful. All people have these drives; however, the influences of genetic conditioning, ego-development, and culture may manifest in a dominance of one of these drives over the others.

If tamas dominates, the person is not likely to engage in creativity. If the dominant drive is rajas, creativity will find expression in outer accomplishments that require, at best, problem solving or situational creativity—as in the movers and shakers of the world. If the dominant drive is sattwa, only then are people motivated toward acts of creativity. This is another reason why adult creativity is not universal—most people are dominated by tamas and rajas, their environmentally and genetically conditioned unconscious drives. Little room is left for sattwa—the creative drive from the collective unconscious.

Why are some people born with sattwa as the dominant drive, so dominant that tamas and rajas, nurture and nature, are unable to obscure it? Easterners think that this can be understood only within a reincarnational framework. People of sattwa are "old souls," so to speak; they have accumulated strong good propensities through a vast number of previous lives.

I hope you see the enormity of the idea of the collective unconscious driving our creativity. The totality, consciousness, seeks to know itself through this drive of the collective unconscious, so its movements are often intricate, even bizarre—so much so that we tend to see them as mere coincidences or chance events. Close scrutiny may reveal them to be otherwise. Carl Jung thought so; he called acausal, meaningful coincidences events of *synchronicity,* and he saw an important role for synchronicity in creativity. I discuss Jung's idea of synchronicity in the next chapter.

Care to take a fantasy tour?
See yourself approaching a forest dense and dark.
A path disappears into it.
What is your tendency?
Do you follow that path or clear your own path?

You are now well into the forest.
The deep shade thins to reveal a great boulder
sprawling across your path, obstructing it.
    What is your tendency?
Do you climb or vault it? detour around it? tunnel through?
dynamite it to gravel?

What's down there? An underground house,
dark and mysterious, evoking childish
memories of witches scary.
    What is your tendency?
Take risk, go down, explore?
Or stay in the filtered light of safety?

Is that a blue ocean yonder?
Do the sparkling waves beckon you?
Is their surging surf a rhythmic call?
    What is your tendency?
Stay where you are—or plunge naked into the water?

18

CHANCE AND SYNCHRONICITY IN CREATIVITY

An interesting case involving chance events that trigger creativity is Alexander Fleming's discovery of penicillin, as reconstructed by his biographer Gwen MacFarlane. While Fleming was on vacation, a michologist on the floor below Fleming's lab happened to isolate a strong strain of the penicillin mold, which found its way on the wind to a petri dish in Fleming's lab. Unusual weather for that time of the year (a cold spell) helped the mold spores to grow and simultaneously prevented the growth of bacteria. Then the temperature rose, and bacteria grew everywhere except in the petri dish. This was what attracted Fleming's attention: What was in the petri dish that prevented bacteria from growing? This is a case in which "an incredible string of chance events" gave rise to momentous creativity.

If chance can work its miracles by accident, then why not use chance deliberately to manifest creativity? The musician John Cage experimented with the role of chance in musical creativity. The archetypes of music are quite thoroughly investigated by now, and musicians know what works and what doesn't. Even improvised music like jazz or East Indian music follows known patterns. Cage felt that to discover truly new music in the 20th century, he had to give chance a chance. So he began to mix in quarter tones, synthesized music, and used all sorts of natural and artificial sounds to create his music. At one of his concerts, no musical instrument or voice greeted the listeners, but only the chance sounds of somebody's sneeze or people's restless movements.

231

In the realm of art, a similar experiment was done by Robert Rauschenberg. Rauschenberg in his youth became disillusioned with expressionist art—art that tried to arouse emotions in the viewer via the representation of archetypes. Instead, Rauschenberg felt that paint on a canvas could be treated as an object on the canvas, and then the idea came: Why not use just any objects? So he created some interesting paintings of New York City by pasting little bits and pieces of real New York on a canvas.

Gertrude Stein once said something to the effect that what changes from age to age is not who we are but what we meet on the road, the chance contingencies. There is ample evidence in the history of human creativity that a special kind of chance, coincidence, also plays a role in many acts of creation. *Synchronicity* is the name Carl Jung gave to acausal but meaningful coincidences (Jung & Pauli, 1955).

Creativity is an encounter of the universal quantum self and the creative's personal ego. The movement of nonlocal consciousness in the quantum self that manifests in a creative act can involve more than one person, and events can conspire to give the appearance of blind chance—this is synchronicity. Multiple creativity, the birth of a creative idea coincidentally originating with more than one person, is a well-known phenomenon (Lamb & Easton, 1984). It could be an example of synchronicity.

The meditation teacher Jack Kornfield (1993) gives a wonderful example of synchronicity in inner creativity. At a meditation retreat that Kornfield was teaching, a woman was struggling with wounds and emotions arising from childhood abuse inflicted on her by a man. At this retreat, she finally found forgiveness in her heart for this man. When she went home from the retreat, she found a letter in her mailbox from the man, her abuser, with whom she had had no contact for 15 years. In the letter, the man asked for her forgiveness. When was the letter written? The same day the woman had completed her act of forgiveness, an act of inner creativity.

I discussed Calder's development of the mobile sculpture in the prelude to Part 3. A seemingly chance coincidence played a momentous role in Calder's work. The abstract artist Piet Mondrian visited Calder at a circus, and Calder in turn visited Mondrian at his art gallery the next year. In a sudden insight, Calder saw the value of abstract sculpture. Was it pure chance that Mondrian visited Calder? I think it was more than chance; It was synchronicity. Anyone who has engaged in creative work can find such seeming coincidences—opening the right page of a book, looking at a picture at the right moment, hearing something at the right time.

After attending a seminar on the wave-nature of matter that Louis de Broglie discovered, the chemist Peter Debye commented to the physicist Erwin Schrödinger that if matter is a wave, there must be a mathematical "wave equation" that applies to matter. Debye himself forgot about his quip; but his comment synchronistically inspired Schrödinger to the discovery of the equation for matter waves (the Schrödinger equation, which Heisenberg also discovered independently) that is the basis of quantum mechanics.

Even a chance slip of the tongue can actually be an event of synchronicity (call it the Jungian slip of the tongue). The Nobel laureate physicist Murray Gell-Mann was giving a lecture on some strange elementary particles when he committed a slip of the tongue only to realize in a sudden insight that the idea conveyed by the slip was the answer to the problem he was considering.

I agree with Jung: Coincidental events in creativity may often be events of synchronicity. Creativity is nourished by our interconnected roots in the collective unconscious (Figure 18.1). Like Kornfield's forgiving woman, when we are involved in a creative insight, we become aligned with the movement of the whole, the nonlocal consciousness. That movement has no local boundary; it neither originates nor ends in one particular brain-mind complex.

So here one can find another reason why only a few children end up as creative adults; some are favored by chance or synchronicity or both!

WHEN JANE MEETS KRISHNA: A CREATIVE ENCOUNTER

The famous *Bhagavad Gita* is a dialog between the human Arjuna and the divine Krishna. It is one of the best metaphorical depictions of the creative encounter between the ego and the quantum self, an encounter that is at the heart of all creative acts. The following dialog takes place with an average American citizen (Jane) who meets Krishna on the road to creativity.

Jane: Here we are.
Krishna: Here, indeed.
J: I am a little disappointed. The research seems to show that geniuses are those people who get a lot of help from the confluence of a lot of factors. Without those factors, what is an average Jane or Joe to do? How does she or he go about excelling in creativity?

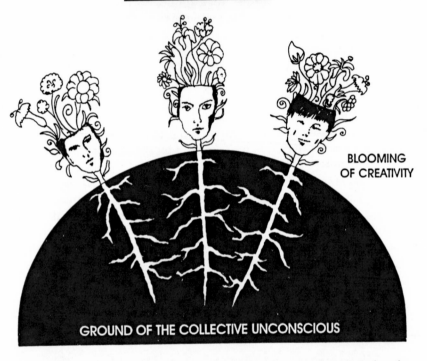

APPARENT SEPARATENESS
OF THE IMMANENT REALM

BLOOMING
OF CREATIVITY

GROUND OF THE COLLECTIVE UNCONSCIOUS

Figure 18.1. The apparent separateness of the immanent realm arises from the unitive ground of the collective unconscious. Our creativity is nourished by our interconnected roots—quantum correlations.

K: Maybe you are interpreting the data too pessimistically. You are looking at the glass as half empty when it is really half full.

J: Well, there isn't really much scope for misunderstood pessimism. Take personality traits, for example. Creatives are found on the average to be risk takers, divergent thinkers, and so forth. Although the research also shows that having such traits does not guarantee creativity, that is small consolation. Clearly, having the traits is an important step toward creativity. So people like us, who don't have them, may as well pack our bags.

K: You are being too hasty in your conclusions. What if I tell you that creatives develop these traits *because* they are creative. Suppose the traits are not causes but effects.

J (startled): What do you mean?

K: Consider the study done by the creativity researchers Jacob Getzels and Mihalyi Csikszentmihalyi (1976), who followed a group of artists from their art school days through the beginning of their adult careers. As a group, these artists seemed to have definite character traits that stereotypically one associates with the creative artist. And yet, when the researchers tracked down 31 of the students five or six years after they had left art school, only one had unequivocally become what can be called a creative artist.

J: So, what does that mean?

K: Simply that the traits are not the cause of creativity. That one case was just a statistical fluctuation.

J: All right, forget traits. Take transforming poison into nectar, conflict into omnivalence. I had many bad experiences in my childhood. My father never gave value to anything that I said or did and consistently intimidated and humiliated me. He rigidly believed the dictum, children are to be seen and not heard. I have never been able to transform my resulting despair into something constructive and meaningful. I don't have Eisenstein's ability to convert childhood cruelty into movie ideas. Instead, even today I get nervous when anyone pays much attention to me. Maybe I'll say something stupid if I speak. So Eisenstein was a creative, I am not. Case closed.

K: Don't be fatalistic! What I am saying is this: suppose Eisenstein developed this omnivalence after he became creative.

J: What do you mean? When was the first time Eisenstein made a movie?

K: Wait a minute. You are treating creativity only in association with a product. The product is important, but creativity starts with an attitude about the subtle nature of the world.

J: You mean one of those childhood experiences, those experiences of the subtle world, that nuance thing? Well, I never had one of those experiences. So you see, it was settled early on that I was not going to be a creative adult.

K: Was it? What prevents you from discovering the subtle world even now?

J: My ego?

K: But your ego has no substantiality. It is just an identity you put on, like clothes. If human beings were completely and irrevocably identified with their egos, no one would ever be creative.

J: Are you saying that one can discover this hidden reality at any age, that even I can do it, even now?

K: Yes. Whose is the subtle world? It is yours! It is not outside you. Nothing is outside you.

J: It is easy for you to say. You are Krishna, the quantum self incarnate. You don't carry the burden of conditioning.

K: But I am not separate from you.

J: Oh, no? Then why don't I have your creative attitude, your purposiveness?

K: Because you limit yourself to the service of the ego—relative purposiveness. Be free of trivial pursuits.

J: How can I be free? I am conditioned, remember?

K: Hear me again. Your identity with this ego, this slavery to conditioning, is no more complete than any creative's. But creatives are not stymied by their negative conditioning. Why are you attached to yours?

J: You are sidestepping the issue. Can anyone be creative? I say not. To be creative, one has to have traits, or develop them anyway. One has to bypass negative conditioning. Of course it is nice if one has a coincidence between one's talents and one's intended field of creativity. One has to discover nuance—sensitivity to a subtle world that ordinary people cannot see. One must align one's purpose to cosmic purposiveness, whatever that is. One must turn poison into nectar. (Teach me that trick, and I will be a millionaire.) One has to have sattwa dominance. Did I leave anything out?

K: Chance and synchronicity.

J: Right, synchronicity. Creatives have the ability to recognize and respond to synchronicity. So it boils down to chance, doesn't it? Chance is my only chance to be creative!

K: Chance is not necessarily so chancy, you know. It is said that chance favors the prepared mind.

J: There you go, my last chance at creativity shattered.

K: Jane, you insist on missing the message. You enjoy your pessimism too much. Of course, creatives have all or many of these factors working for them. But they don't begin with most of them; they develop them.

J: But they have to begin somewhere. What is the starting point?

K: I'll give you a hint. Creativity is a quantum leap, right? What does that entail?

J: It is discontinuous.

K: Of course. What else?

J: Creativity is not a space-time, local thing. It involves quantum nonlocality.

K: Good. What else?

J: The quantum leap is acausal.

K: Exactly. You cannot assign causes to creativity. You cannot even give a starting point to it. You cannot say, I became creative at such and such a date when I had such and such an experience. You are already creative.

J (sarcastically): That is good news!

K: I'll tell you a story. Narada, the great celestial angel, was passing two mortals. One was a sadhu, a renunciate who was meditating. He asked, "Oh, Narada, when shall I arrive?"

To this Narada said, "I have an appointment with God soon. I'll find out."

The second man was inhaling deeply from a marijuana pipe. But he had the same question, "When shall I arrive?"

Narada laughed but promised him also that he would ask God.

When Narada returned, he first went to the renunciate. "Well, what did God say? How many years longer need I meditate?"

"You have to meditate three more births," said Narada.

Well, if nothing's going to happen in this birth, I may as well give up and have some fun, thought the renunciate, and he gave up his practice.

The marijuana addict was also eager to hear from Narada.

"Well?"

"See that tree over there? See all those leaves? That many lives it will take you to arrive," said Narada.

"Really? I'll arrive, too?" exclaimed the man, who then began to dance. At that moment he arrived.

What do you think happened, Jane?

J: He really believed. So if I believe that I am creative at this very moment, I can break through?

K: Yes and no. It's not a thinking thing. You have to lose yourself to recognize your potential, you have to intuit your power.

J: Isn't that hard?

K: It is, and it isn't. Most people are like you. They "want to want" creativity, believing that creativity is something nice to have because it brings this and that—nice things, fame, sex, money. When you truly want creativity, those other things become insignificant. But there is a circularity in the transformation from wanting to want to truly wanting creativity. Without an intuition of the subtle world, without recognizing that the possibility is already within you, you cannot want creativity. But if you don't want creativity, you don't get to intuit.

J: That sounds like a tangled hierarchy.

K: It is. This is why creativity means encountering the quantum self, longing for it, surrendering to it, which is synonymous with tangled hierarchy.

J: I have to give up the idea that I am the doer?

K: Yes. But again, you cannot give up the idea that you are the doer until you intuit the quantum self.

J: And I cannot intuit the quantum self until I give up the idea that I am the doer. So what do I do?

K: I will give you a hint. What did Jesus mean when he told his disciples, "Be ye as little children?"

J: Practice inner creativity?

K: Surveys show that some of the same processes that people employ in their pursuit of inner creativity can help outer creativity as well.

J: But you are not giving me any guarantee.

K: No. You have to take the risk.

J: I have never taken risks, let alone the risk of losing myself. I want to be there when I arrive.

K: That is your problem. Intuition is when you aren't. Creative recognition is when you don't cognize in your usual rational ways. You really have to leave the cocoon of your simple hierarchy and enter the tangled hierarchy. Study tangled hierarchy. Devour tangled hierarchy. Become tangled hierarchy.

J: Okay. You convinced me. I will do it.

K: You have to do it out of your own free will, not because I persuaded you.

J: But I don't have free will. I am conditioned, remember? Wait a minute. You and I aren't separate, so I do have free will. I . . .

K: You and I are not separate. Say no to the conditioning. Let the sattwa shine forth. Awake, arise, understand. Be committed to creativity and enter the process. Let the process transform you.

J: I can't wait.

I see creativity expanding
   beyond mechanism
   beyond organism
   beyond idealism
integrating them all
with the quantum leap.

I see genius sprouting
   beyond traits
   beyond childhood experience
   beyond drives from the unconscious
integrating them all
with a growing awareness of the quantum self.

I see the creative process
   beyond preparation
   beyond unconscious processing
   beyond insight and manifestation
integrating them all
with purposiveness.

From being to becoming,
the great chain of being links
the creator and its creation. The awakening of buddhi
integrates both in consciousness.

PART FIVE

PREPARATION FOR THE NEXT CENTURY

What can we say about the future of creativity as we approach a new century and a new millennium? As the worldview changes from material realism to monistic idealism, the focus of the new century will be us—the human condition and its potential—in contrast to recent centuries in which the focus was the material domain. And the central motif of our inquiry into us in the new century will be creativity.

The novelist Ursula Leguin wrote, "Everything dreams. The play of form, of being, is the dreaming of substance. Rocks have their dreams, and the earth changes. But when the mind becomes conscious, when the rate of evolution speeds up, then you have to be careful. Careful of the world. You must learn the way. You must learn the skills, the art, the limits. A conscious mind must be part of the whole, intentionally and carefully—as the rock is part of the whole unconsciously." In the new century we will have to be creative as never before if we are to assume the planetary responsibility being demanded of us. Can we integrate inner and outer creativity and the methods of the East and the West toward the common goal of enhancing planetary creativity. We will need both these kinds of creativity in large quantity. Additionally, we will need fortification of each by the other, which only integration can give us.

The Bhagavad Gita is written as a dialog between the divine Krishna and the human Arjuna, but many philosophers interpret it as an inner dialog between the human ego and the atman, the quantum self. The Bhagavad Gita is the song of the inner encounter of creativity, according to this traditional interpretation. But the philosopher-sage Sri Aurovinda (1955) added a timely twist to our understanding of it; he said that for our age the encounter is not only inner but also outer. In this he seems to be echoing Jesus, who said, "when you make the inner as the outer . . . then shall you enter [the kingdom of God]."

The emperor Akbar of India was a great connoisseur of music and supported a great many musical virtuosos in his court. The most famous of them was Tansen. It is said that when Tansen sang the appropriate raga, he could make the rains come from nowhere. Naturally, he was Akbar's favorite; but even the best of music loses its charm under the erosion of familiarity. So one day the king wished to hear someone new. Tansen pondered the matter for quite a while—it is not easy to think of somebody who is better than the best. Finally, Tansen thought of his own teacher. "But there is a problem," said he to the emperor. "My teacher does not come to the city. All the grandeur of the emperor's court, all the wealth it offers means nothing to him. If you want to hear his music, you have to go to his ashram." The emperor agreed. "Another thing," said the venerable Tansen, "my teacher plays only for God. You have to listen from the background." Akbar reluctantly agreed to that as well; his curiosity had been aroused.

The next morning at dawn they came to hear Tansen's teacher. The emperor listened enraptured, becoming totally lost in the spirituality that the music touched in him. When the music stopped, Akbar sat quietly for a long time. Finally, he asked Tansen, "Tell me, why did this man's music move me so? You are the best; but perhaps your teacher has not taught you everything?" To this Tansen's reply is famous. "Oh noble emperor, the difference between my music and what you've heard today is a profound one. You see, I create my music and play it for your satisfaction. But the music my teacher creates is for God's satisfaction. My music resonates with your mind, his music with your soul."

This is the thing. When creativity flows from a psyche in which the inner and the outer have been integrated, the creative product resonates with the entire cosmos. Can you imagine the force of such creative acts?

Let's begin collectively to direct the force of our inner-outer integration and bring it to bear against the arms race, consumerism, bigotry, ignorance, violence, and scientific and other orthodoxies. Let's direct that force to the healing of the environment, to peace, to freedom for all colors, sexes and preferences, to values and ethics, to creative education of our children.

A major arena for our integrated creativity must be the social sciences, in which the existing theories must undergo no less than a quantum revolution under the auspices of idealist science in order to deal with the responsibilities of the new century. With revolutionized social sciences, we can transform those problems that we have avoided so far—equity and justice, sharing equitably and conserving dwindling resources, the environment, war and peace, and so on. Art and music will flourish, creating new forms to go with the changing contexts of our societies.

In India, people say that when the old ways of doing things no longer work, a *yuga* is ending and a new one is coming. The new yuga arrives with the help of specially gifted, creative, and integrated individuals, or *avataras*. Let me reiterate my exhortation in *The Self-Aware Universe* (1993a)—become an avatara or help to grow an avatara. Let the 21st century be the century of a world-wide renaissance facilitated by an unprecedented number of avataras, creative all, together serving co-creatively the purpose of the creative universe.

Millennia ago, in India, a sage was departing after retirement to dwell in the forest (a metaphor for looking inward). He had two wives, as custom permitted in those times. When he asked the first wife, she didn't want to go with him; she would rather have his worldly possessions, she said. The other wife, Maitreyi, said, "Of things that will not help me be immortal, what use are they?" She joined her husband in search of immortality which only inner search, inner creativity can bring. And the immortality she sought was not transcendent immortality but immortality in life on earth.

Can one find immortality on earth? Subjectively, yes, by living timelessly in the moment, by letting one's acts flow effortlessly from timeless being. The last 70 years (since the discovery of quantum mechanics) have taught us that it is not necessary to retire to the forest. The search for and fulfillment of immortality can go on right here, in a growing balance of modes of creativity, situational and fundamental, inner and outer. But we have to learn to do it. This is the subject of Part 5.

> Follow the music of Tansen's teacher
> into the forest of self-discovery.
> When your body becomes the forest,
> your soul becomes the music,
> and naught else remains—
> then shall this living immortality
> breathe the infinity of heaven
> into your creative future.

19

CULTURAL POLARIZATIONS

Every autumn in India, where I grew up, hundreds of sculptors mold beautiful and diverse clay statues of the goddess *Durga* and dress them in extravagant apparel, only to throw them, still clad in their finery, into the river Ganges at the end of a 4-day festival. Through my studies, I was quite taken as a teenager by the values of Western culture—where all art is preserved for the future—and this traditional Indian custom did not make sense to me.

More recently, while teaching a course on the physics of sound and music, the same issue came up in the contrast of Western and Eastern music. Western classical music is clearly progressive. Every piece of music is written and can be traced to a particular composer, and every performer must be fairly faithful to the written music. In contrast, in Indian classical music the same music (certain basic scales, a few thousand, actually, called *ragas,* are combined with a number of rhythms called talas) is passed on from generation to generation. There is often no written music, seldom does any one composer get credit for any score, and the artist plays with a considerable amount of originality. So what is going on?

One simplistic but common answer is that Indian music (and Eastern music, in general) is "primitive" compared to Western music, which is "sophisticated." This way of categorizing may sound derogatory to Eastern music, but it contains a grain of truth. If you compare Eastern music with Western, very soon you see that Easterners are basically playing simple melodies in a succession of separate, individual notes. In contrast, Western music abounds in complex combinations, consonance, and harmony, which require considerable scientific sophistication, if nothing else. But this is not the whole story.

A more sensitive assessment of Indian music reveals that there is considerable sophistication in its performance as well. The sophistication consists in the ability to play a particular raga in just the "right" way so that it elicits a profoundly "right" mood from the listener (in Sanskrit, the word raga means mood). A vocalist, especially, may practice a particular note used in a particular scale for years to perfect it so that its psychology is properly represented. (The mythical story is that the vocalist Baiju, whom people fondly referred to as Baiju bawra [Baiju the madcap], practiced one note for 35 years before he found what he was looking for.)

The Eastern musician is considered "sophisticated" only when he or she has discovered the psychological basis of the notes of the scales (the ragas). The raga seems to have a prior existence that is connected with a particular psychological mood; the musician's job is to "discover" this connection—the context of the music, if you will—and arouse the resonation of the context, the mood, in the listener. It is this discovery and its conveyance to the listener that is "creative" for the Eastern musician.

In contrast, the Western composer of music has a better crack at fundamental creativity than the performers and conductors. Because the music is written down, the latter cannot change it. And only a few composers "discover" the psychological essence of music in the way that Easterners do; these are the great composers, the Bachs, Mozarts, and Stravinskys. (People who conduct and play such music have the opportunity to rediscover this psychological essence and hence for inner creativity in transformation and outer creativity in communication).

Others invent music in a way that is comparable to the role of technology in clarifying the message of scientific paradigms to society at large. If the invented music explores new meaning in the discovered music of the masters, the music will still psychologically move us. But if the "invented" music is mere "professional" shuffling of the old, it is fundamentally different in quality from "discovered" music. I think that many modern composers of classical music in the West are primarily inventors in this latter sense; they are coasting on the discoveries of the classical composers and focusing not on meaning but on professionalism, one reason why their own names don't stand out. As Beethoven said, "Music must strike fire from [the musician's] mind." Many modern composers shy away from striking fire and settle for merely the mechanical and mundane music of "problem solving," what Roger Sessions called "the associative element of musical expression."

What I am saying is that it is possible to cultivate music and art with the spirit of discovery, in which case you can stay creatively in the same old tradition and it does not seem to matter. This is what the sculptors of Durga do; the discovery of Durga every year is spiritual creativity for them. Recent materialist Western culture, on the other hand, is primarily inventive and worse. It is driven not by a search for meaning but by incentives such as money, prestige, and patents.

The spirit of discovery that characterizes "primitive" music, of course, continues in the West in such forms as jazz, in which the artist explores the psychological essence of music rather than learning formal scores.

In summary, in music or art or science, creativity expresses itself most grandly in discovery, which is fundamental creativity—finding transcendent themes or contexts of consciousness, themes that we call, following Plato, *archetypal*. In contrast, worthwhile inventions consist of new applications and clarifications of a discovered theme, and they involve situational creativity. Inventions are based on the exploration of meaning of the contexts of human discovery, and in that exploration of new meaning, they also often involve greatness. An example is the Wright brothers' invention of the airplane; the human spirit soared along with their airplane. Only when invention becomes mechanical, devoid of inspiration and subjective motivation, does it become as meaningless and uncreative as a "new" perfume or a "new" hairstyle.

In science, discovery gives us laws that govern nature. If scientific laws guide the behavior of material objects, they must exist before matter, transcending the material world. Invention gives us technology. We need both discovery and invention. There is creativity in both. A society can keep its purity, as in Indian music, and emphasize only fundamental creativity; in that case there will be little development in its civilization, which needs history, memory, and situational creativity. The Balinese culture is an example of such purity (although it is now changing).

The power of a culture arises from balancing the emphasis on discovery and invention. The West now dominates the world because it was recognized early that civilizations need inventions to manifest fully the meaning and value of the discoveries as active influences in societies. However, with the current dominance in the West of a materialist worldview, there is a tendency to stress invention over discovery; invention seems more like problem solving, and thus less challenging to the material-realist worldview. But dominance of either of these polarities is undesirable; neither polarity by itself allows us to explore our full potential.

CREATIVITY EAST AND WEST

In a slightly different vein, the distinction of outer and inner creativity helps us understand why creativity traditionally has manifested differently in the East and West, so much so that the two peoples inhabit radically different cultures: "East is East, and West is West, and ne'er the twain shall meet."

The West, in general—in fact, the entire Judeo-Christian culture—has emphasized outer creativity, whereas the East has delved more into inner creativity. Let's return momentarily to Hamlet, who is torn between ego-ethos and higher truth. The Western resolution is tragedy, a haunting view of the possibility and nobility of inner creativity, but no more. There is no leap to creative transformation. Compare this to the case of Arjuna in the *Mahabharata* on the eve of war between rival factions, who are cousins. Arjuna, like Hamlet, is also torn by a similar conflict between the ego-ethos, the duty to fight for the kingdom that is rightfully his, and the higher ethos—how can one kill one's own relatives? But the Eastern resolution is not tragedy. Arjuna talks to his spiritual teacher, Krishna, who encourages him to transcend his moral dilemma via inner creativity (this is the theme of the *Bhagavad Gita*). Arjuna transforms and fights victoriously from this transformed context.

As a result of the emphasis on outer creativity, the West has made great strides in science, technology, and even in the arts. On the other hand, the East has made major contributions to the understanding of our spiritual nature and the development of techniques for inner creativity—the technology of transformation of the psyche.

The de-emphasis on the outer in the East has led to a general disregard of outer well-being, but the emphasis on the inner has made the East much more harmonious with its natural environment (until the recent advent of materialism). On the contrary, emphasis on outer creativity has increasingly made the West rich in science and industry but poor in moral values and kinship with nature (a poverty that is now being diffused all around the globe).

INTEGRATION

Let me repeat a Sufi story. Mulla Nasruddin, the perennial Sufi teacher-fool, was found one day searching for something under the street light near his house.

A passerby asked, "What gives, Nasruddin. What have you lost?"

"My key," said Nasruddin.

The good Samaritan began helping Nasruddin search, but to no avail. After a while, the passerby asked, "Nasruddin, where did you lose your key?"

"In my house," said Nasruddin.

Now the good Samaritan became angry. "If you lost the key in the house, why are looking for it here, you fool?"

Nasruddin answered with a sly grin, "There is more light here."

There is more light to see with in the exploration of outer creativity over inner, of situational creativity over fundamental. No doubt it is this light that attracts us. Unfortunately, often the key is in the house—a metaphor for the unconscious, unexplored, vast regions of consciousness.

The great creatives among us know this. The Indian poet Rabindranath Tagore took leave from his outer play in poetry, which was becoming somewhat frivolous. His inner exploration brought him close to the spiritual heart of India, which he began realizing and reinterpreting, and culminated in *Gitanjali* for which he won the Nobel prize. Similarly, the American poet T. S. Eliot, after creating the Nobel-winning *Wasteland,* the saga of the disintegration of the West, went into hibernation. When he came out, he gave the world *Four Quartets,* poetry rich in spiritual insight and inspiration, and a proper aftermath to *Wasteland.* The music virtuoso Yehudi Menuhin gave up playing the violin from age 40 to 52. He needed a long regrouping in which inner creativity was his principal helper.

So what about the "twain shall ne'er meet" pessimism? I believe that the twain parted in the first place due to a misunderstanding of the full human potential. The truth is, outer and inner creative experiences often complement one another. Engaging in outer creativity for the expression of the inner (and not for accomplishments) is something that we have almost forgotten in this culture (do the people of Bali still do that?). In general, spiritual traditions tend to negate the worldliness of outer creativity. On the other hand, materialist science, the bastion of outer creativity in today's culture, denigrates spirituality. I am convinced that understanding the nature of our self and the nature of creativity on the solid basis of idealist science will encourage a balance of outer and inner creativity in people.

As we begin to understand the breadth of our potential and to appreciate that outer and inner creativity can work harmoniously within each of us, we can proceed—the entire human family—on both fronts, both inner and outer. Then the twain shall come together in each one of us, and also collectively.

And, of course, the same integration needs to happen with fundamental and situational creativity, individually and collectively. Inventions depend on the contexts discovered through fundamental creativity. Heinrich Hertz would not have invented the apparatus for the demonstration of radio waves without knowing about Clerk Maxwell's prediction of their existence. Likewise, as more readily appreciated, fundamental creativity—the discovery of a new context of value—must be followed up with inventive work that augments the new with already-known, old contexts to bring out the final product. Copernicus' heliocentric system was gathering dust until, with the newly invented telescope, Galileo looked at the heavens and found Jupiter with four satellites. Inventions often act as the scaffolding for new discoveries, especially in science.

Up to now, we have unwittingly polarized these different expressions of creativity. The coherent theory of creativity that is developing gives us the key to integrate the polarities. The integration will require a thorough understanding of the quantum nature of creativity, the relation of creativity and consciousness, and the creative process. When we integrate outer and inner, situational and fundamental, on the basis of a fuller understanding, we will be able to fulfill our creative potential to a hitherto unprecedented extent. Only then shall we be properly prepared for the challenges of the 21st century.

Oh mind, how slow you are to integrate.
You cultivate one little field.
Be you a situational-outer creative
or fundamental-inner,
do you never face the horizon beyond?

As far as your consciousness reaches,
so can your husbandry,
else the Great One, without your cultivation,
remains barren, unconscious.

Oh mind, integrate,
until, infinitely fertile,
your field is lush with creativity.

20

CREATIVITY AND YOUR SELF

What do you remember of all the data, theory, examples, and world-views in the preceding pages? The following is a summary of the basic facts of the phenomenon of creativity:

- *Four-fold nature:* Your creative acts are classified broadly as outer or inner, depending on whether you produce something in the world or accomplish a shift in your self-identity beyond ego. Within each category, there is a further classification—fundamental and situational creativity. If your act involves the discovery of something new in a new context of value, it is fundamental creativity. Acts of situational creativity involve finding new meaning in old context(s).
- *Process:* When you bring an act of creativity to fruition, you engage in a process involving four stages—preparation, incubation, insight, and manifestation of the product.
- *Discontinuity:* Your creative acts involve discontinuous jumps from your usual continuous and conditioned thinking mode.
- *Acausality:* You cannot assign a strict cause-effect sequence to an act of creation.
- *Nonlocality:* In an act of creativity you manifest nonlocal themes of consciousness that involve at least one new ingredient not in your local repertoire.
- *Purposiveness:* Your creative acts stem from universal purposiveness.

- *Freedom:* Creativity requires your uncompromised freedom to act. And, vice versa, in creativity you experience true freedom.

The role of theory is to empower you, to enable you to understand what obscures your creative power. So what should you take with you of the integrated theory of creativity developed in this book? This list may be helpful:

- *The fundamental importance of consciousness and the quantum:* To explain the discontinuity, acausality, nonlocality, and universal purposiveness of an act of creativity requires the idealist metaphysic that consciousness is the ground of all being and the hypothesis of a quantum mind. Creativity is fundamentally a subjective process and a play of consciousness. The purpose of creativity is for consciousness to see itself.
- *The discontinuous and self-referential collapse of the possibilities of the quantum mind:* The new contexts and meanings of creativity are manifested when a person, in his or her quantum self-reference, collapses appropriate states of possibilities of the quantum mind via choice and recognition and the correlated brain follows through by making a map of the new through destructuring and restructuring itself.
- *The importance of unconscious processing:* Unconscious processing involves processing (without awareness) uncollapsed superpositions of quantum possibilities of the mind in search of the new. This stage precedes the quantum leap of insight. In practice, unconscious processing takes place when you relax in the midst of striving to solve a problem. Ambiguities and unlearned stimuli help the job of unconscious processing.
- *The quantum self and the ego:* Self-referential collapse splits one consciousness into an experiencing subject (the universal quantum self) and object(s) of primary awareness. Primary-awareness events always have the potential to stimulate creativity. Repeated experience produces conditioning and memory. Memory playbacks of learned stimuli bring about secondary-awareness events that obscure the primary experience. Identification with the secondary-awareness processes leads to the personal ego. Experiences in the quantum self are tangled hierarchical—the experiential emphasis is on the verb, not on the subject or the object. The ego-experience, in contrast, is simple hierarchical; the ego is the boss. Remember, however, that the ego itself is not the obstruction to creativity but only

one's identity with it. One needs the ego function as well as the quantum self in the creative act.

- *Outer and inner creativity:* Creativity is the result of the encounter of you in your ego (with which you normally identify) with you in your quantum self (with which you normally do not identify). When the product of this encounter is outwardly directed, one engages in outer creativity; when the encounter is directed toward a transformation of one's self-identity, one engages in inner creativity.

- *The encounter of the ego and the quantum self in the creative process:* One can think of one's ego as acting with causal continuity from past conditioning and its algorithmic extensions. The quantum modality, in which one has unlimited freedom and universal purposiveness, is what takes one quantum-leaping beyond one's conditioned patterns of behavior. The creative encounter between one's ego and the quantum self is expressed in a tango of alternating doing (conscious striving) and being (unconscious processing), conditioned algorithmic thinking (perspiration) and quantum nonalgorithmic leaps (insight), and insight from the quantum modality (idea) and manifestation employing the ego's learned repertoire (form).

- *Creative drive:* Along with nature and nurture, creativity is a natural drive in all of us. This drive enables a person to engage in the various activities that we call creative: learning and understanding, outer acts of fundamental and situational creativity, and inner creativity that propels our identity beyond ego. Creativity was naturally present in us as children and helped us to discover and develop personal contexts of living that we call ego, or your adult character. As adults, our creative drive is partially muted by the fixity and homeostasis of the adult ego. We can recognize in ourselves and others the three gunas (qualities) or unconscious drives: sattwa (creativity), rajas (libido or nature), and tamas (behavioral conditioning or nurture).

- *Synchronicity:* Nonlocal correlations, sometimes manifesting as synchronicity—acausal but meaningful coincidences—play an important role in a creative quantum leap. One is wise to be alert for them.

THE BALANCING ACT

Current creativity research indicates that creative people have more than an ordinary share of encounters between their egos and the quantum modality. The profile of creative people shows them to be unconventional, spontaneous, open minded, willing to live with uncertainty and to entertain doubts, good in divergent thinking, emotionally involved with their quest, strong willed, capable of intense concentration, and independent. In other words, they excel in balancing the ego and quantum modalities—and this, in my opinion, is the key for excelling in creativity, both inner and outer. Moreover these are not genetic traits. Creative people become this way through their practice of creativity and their response to their creative encounters.

It doesn't mean *doing* a lot of unconventional things, either. At one point in my life, I was heavily engaged in the methods of inner exploration, filling up my life with meditation, chanting, service, reading spiritual books, and so on. You name it, I did it if it had anything to do with spirituality. And quite a bit of what I did involved the new and unconventional. Then one night I dreamed of some vague and abstract entities. The thought arose in my dream that I was seeing two kinds of entities—those of being and those of doing. I was told that my job was to integrate the two kinds. When I woke, I realized that I had been going about my spiritual quest in an unbalanced way. Even too much meditation is doing. One really has to heed Frank Sinatra's ad lib—do be do be do—quite literally. One must not let the doing of the ego modality overshadow the being of the quantum modality of consciousness.

The best part of creative experiences is that they give us a taste of real freedom. The occasional creative jump from the ego modality encourages some of us to consider a bigger jump, that of personal transformation. Jung once said, "It is not Goethe who creates Faust, but Faust that creates Goethe." This is literally true. Every creative act, every encounter with the quantum modality, has the potential to set one free for more quantum acts. The more one lets go of limits, the more limitless one becomes.

I hope that the infant science of creativity sketched in the previous chapters makes one thing clear; creativity is a drive for all of us. If one is able to give up the constriction of one's consciousness to which one's ego—expressed as artfulness—often leads and to gamble instead on one's uncharted genius, if one is willing to accept the creative anxiety that accompanies the play of will and surrender in the creative encounter, then the light of the quantum self breaks through the cocoon of ego-imposed mediocrity.

As children, we were naturally creative. But the price of ego-development is a desire to win approval from others and a certain reluctance to engage one's creative drive for creative acts. The tendency is to rationalize or intellectualize; in the intellect, creativity is used largely to further egoic tendencies. Instead of engaging creativity to discover new contexts and meanings, the temptation is to engage your problem-solving abilities to fortify old ones. Intellect is valuable; it develops some of the wonderful things of civilization. But overemphasis on intellect thwarts creativity.

How do you break through adult intellectualizing tendencies? Through self-observation and a modicum of positive self-criticism—a discontent. One should develop an ego habit of openness to the conditions of creativity, of not backing away when conventional problem-solving ability fails, as paradoxical as that sounds (behaviorists are right in asserting that we can learn such behavior; see Chapter 16). One has to respect one's intellect and yet be able to disregard its dictates when the situation demands it. In other words, one must be cognizant of the appropriate roles of the ego and quantum modalities in the creative process.

As a playful approach to looking at your own patterns in terms of this dual-modality that you are, I hope you will have fun with the following questionnaire. It is meant only to give you food for thought and to guide you toward seeing your patterns. It is not a creativity test for determining your creative potential. As we have noted previously, everybody has creative potential; it is our patterns that prevent us from realizing it. As the poet said:

But we know ourselves least; mere outward shews
Our minds so store
That our soules, no more than our eyes, disclose
But form and colour. Onely he who knowes himself knowes
more. (quoted in Zolla, 1981, p. 113)

It is by knowing ourselves that we can explore—beyond the forms and colors that the physical eyes can see—the realm where creativity is our guide.

HOW OPEN IS YOUR EGO?

1. Your friend reports that she was in a car accident and the car was wrecked. What is your more likely response? (a) I hope you have insurance; (b) I hope nobody was hurt.

2. At a crossroad, you unconsciously take the wrong turn. Would your likely response be (a) light-hearted, perhaps to look for a new route; (b) to be irritated or to berate yourself?

3. When somebody asks your advice about a personal problem, are you more prone to (a) suggest a solution; (b) discuss alternatives?

4. When your opinion is rejected in a discussion with a friend, are you more likely to (a) lose interest in the discussion; (b) remain engaged in the dialog?

5. When working on a difficult problem, are you more likely to (a) persevere for long hours on it; (b) give up if you don't find a quick answer?

6. When you have to wait while your child gets a check-up, do you (a) get bored; (b) remain alert?

7. When you cannot find a quick answer to a problem that is important to you, do you (a) allow yourself time; (b) get upset?

8. Are you more likely to define happiness as (a) a new car; (b) a lively discussion?

9. Is most of your reading confined to (a) all sorts of things; (b) your own special interest?

10. Given the choice of watching a situation comedy on TV or playing a board game with a friend, would you usually choose the (a) game; (b) TV?

11. As an onlooker to an argument do you tend to support (a) the tried and the familiar; (b) the "weird" and the original?

12. When you work on a complex problem for a long period of time are you more likely to (a) throw out information that doesn't seem to fit; (b) redefine the problem as you learn more about it?

13. In a heated argument are you more likely to (a) take everything personally; (b) keep your cool?

14. If your boyfriend or girlfriend breaks a movie date, are you more likely to (a) immediately look for a replacement; (b) enjoy the movie by yourself?

15. In telling a friend about a creative idea, are you more likely to say (a) you figured it out; (b) it came to you?

16. In working with a problem, are you more likely to (a) follow a logical step-by-step approach; (b) play with analogies and metaphors?

17. In regard to moral values, do you tend to (a) accept some differences in values; (b) be intolerant about a friend's violation of your values?

18. In solving an ethical dilemma, are you more likely to (a) stick to the rules; (b) consider the specific factors?
19. Do you think it is possible to love other people unconditionally? (a) possible; (b) not possible.
20. When following instructions, (a) do you follow them to the letter; or (b) do you follow the spirit?
21. Would you describe your cognitive style as (a) spontaneous, willing to take risks; (b) methodical, cautious?
22. When you know you are wrong, are you more likely to (a) justify your reasons nevertheless; (b) explicitly admit it?
23. People who are unpredictable are more likely to be (a) disturbing to you; (b) interesting to you.
24. When you feel things are out of control, are you more likely to (a) panic or fix blame; (b) remain open to a new order?
25. When learning a new game are you willing to (a) start only after you know all the rules; (b) start playing even though you may not know all the rules?
26. When life is full of uncertainty, do you (a) feel uncomfortable but alive; (b) feel uncomfortable and down?
27. In the middle of working on a difficult problem, a friend asks you to accompany him or her for a walk. What is your tendency? (a) to talk shop or think shop anyway; (b) to welcome the relaxation afforded by the walk and the company.
28. In challenging situations are you more likely to (a) become intimidated or disoriented; (b) remain committed and motivated?
29. When people don't agree with you, do you (a) judge them; (b) respect them regardless?
30. Do you put a lot of energy into planning for the future? (a) seldom; (b) often.
31. If a friend does something unexpected, are you more likely to feel (a) intrigued; (b) uneasy?
32. When with a friend, do you like mostly (a) to talk about yourself; or (b) to listen to him or her?
33. If you have had a paranormal experience (regardless of what you believe about ESP), have you (a) acknowledged it even though you don't understand it; (b) denied it or explained it away, for example, as coincidence?
34. Have you had any mystical experiences? (a) yes; (b) no.
35. Do you enjoy myth and allegory? (a) no ; (b) yes.
36. On the dance floor, do you (a) tend to concentrate on your style, or compete; (b) just enjoy yourself?

37. In your love relationship do you (a) allow for some inconsistencies of character; (b) feel insecure or intolerant about inconsistencies of character?
38. Do you tend to follow your synchronicities? For example, if acausal, meaningful coincidences begin occurring for you to move to a certain city, would you?
39. Do you usually see things (a) as black and white; (b) often as gray?
40. In your mate relationship, do you prefer (a) intensity; (b) restraint?
41. When you are doing a necessary chore, do you often (a) enjoy yourself; (b) resent it?
42. Is your life worth living (a) because you have a purpose; (b) because you keep yourself amused?
43. Suppose you meditate a lot and gain paranormal ability. How do you think you will use your ability? (a) helping people without fanfare; (b) demonstrating to your friends that you have power.
44. Do you like singing in the shower? If so, do you do it regularly? (a) yes, frequently; (b) no, never.

DISCUSSION OF THE QUESTIONNAIRE

Now that you have answered the questionnaire, you may realize that there are no right or wrong responses. Ultimately, there is only one very personal criterion: Does this choice make me more free and help me fulfill my creative potential? We must all personally be the judge of that. However, I offer some comments on the questions. Again, remember that this is a questionnaire to consider inwardly; the idea is really to look at your patterns.

1. The egoic tendency (especially when grounded in a materialist worldview) is to value objects and to conserve the physical—do you have insurance, can you repair your car, can you replace all your possessions? In contrast, concern for people signifies a lessening of the ego boundary.
2. The challenge of taking "the road less travelled," even if unconsciously, is always welcome to the open mind.
3. Suggesting a solution, except for purely objective problems, is a response that often only reinforces the ego.

4. A dialog can take place only when, in some real sense, the issues begin to answer themselves. Whose opinion prevails is irrelevant except to your ego.

5. Staying with a problem increases the probability of discovering a creative answer.

6. Getting bored is our mental state when we want to escape the present moment—definitely a tendency of the classical mind.

7. Getting upset is an ego-neurosis reaction to creative anxiety.

8. A lively discussion can lead to creativity.

9. Reading all sorts of things is a way to combat the egoic tendency to specialize and compartmentalize.

10. A game provides a chance to interact with another person and to look at yourself in the interaction.

11. The tried and familiar, the past, the certainty of knowledge— these are all egoic tendencies. Creativity often expresses itself through apparent weirdness.

12. Creativity, remember, depends on the ability to shift contexts or find new meaning; if you know what is irrelevant from the beginning, you arbitrarily close out potentially creative solutions. On the other hand, redefinition of a problem often leads to a creative solution.

13. It is the ego's self-justifying tendency to be offended. Do you want to understand the issue or to reinforce your ego superiority?

14. What ensures more freedom for yourself? That is the question. The automatic assumption that you can only enjoy yourself in company constricts your self.

15. Always taking ego credit reduces your openness to the extent that it reinforces the ego-"I." In complete truth, have you ever "figured out" an idea that belongs to fundamental creativity as defined in this book? (Admittedly, the case of situational creativity is somewhat ambiguous on this point.) Think about it.

16. Analogies and metaphors assist us in making creative quantum jumps beyond ego.

17. It is the ego's tendency to judge others, thereby solidifying relative values into rigid belief systems that obscure more universal values.

18. The solution of an ethical dilemma is not a question of applying absolute rules, but a question of a living conscience. An open mind considers the specific factors of a situation.

19. Conditional love is the terrain of agenda-bound, egoic self-interest. Our ability to love unconditionally is a measure of our freedom, and vice versa.

20. Consider this Nasruddin story. Once there was a lot of smuggling going on between two adjacent countries, and the border guards had strict orders to search all valises before letting anybody through. Nasruddin was one of the people who frequently went through in his donkey cart with lots of suitcases, but no border guards ever found anything in spite of their suspicions. Years later, one guard met Nasruddin and asked him his secret. "We all knew you had to be smuggling something. But where were you hiding the things?" "I was smuggling donkeys," said Nasruddin. The guards never thought of going beyond the letter of their instructions.

21. A willingness to take risks often takes us beyond ego and allows our creativity to express itself.

22. The ego self is always defensive. Because it is centered around the past, it always justifies its past actions.

23. If you can tolerate unpredictability and uncertainty, you are better able to plunge into the quantum mode of living.

24. A creative new order can emerge only if you overcome the ego tendency to constrict your responses within the limits of the past.

25. The question is: Do you play only to win or to demonstrate your superiority, or are fun and relationships major satisfactions for you in games?

26. If you stay with uncertainty and don't capitulate to known, if unsatisfying, patterns in order to escape it, you can grow and begin to feel the vitality that signifies our quantum modality.

27. Relaxation in the middle of striving nurtures unconscious processing, which is very important for eventual breakthrough insight.

28. Commitment and motivation can not only fuel the strong will of the ego but also support a surrender to the new and unexpected.

29. Every time you are able to respect another being, regardless of objective reasons for rejecting him or her, your ego supremacy lessens a bit and your openness to the quantum expands.

30. Planning extensively for the future is to try either to mold it in the patterns of the past or to avoid quantum uncertainty.

31. Openness can be defined by the John Lilly (1974) dictum, "Expect the unexpected."

32. Talking about oneself often entails a lack of humility. There is a story about a guru whose disciple was so devoted to him that one day in an emergency he was able to walk on water in

his guru's name. When the guru found out, he began to tell others about this as a reflection of his greatness. One day, one of his listeners lost impatience and challenged him. "If your name is so great, why don't you show me that you can walk on water too while uttering your name?" The guru felt up to the challenge and tried to walk the river. Unfortunately he did not know how to swim, so he drowned.

33. The question is, do you let your conditioned beliefs restrict your experiences? Permitting yourself to acknowledge an ESP experience does not necessarily force you to a nonmechanistic worldview; and giving value to experiences that you do not understand with only past history just increases your freedom.

34. Same comment as the one just given. Think about it.

35. Myths and allegories are "histories of the soul"—the quantum self.

36. Technique, competition—these are common tendencies of the ego. Surrendering yourself to the dance will help you to experience openness.

37. Arbitrary consistency is death to the creative self.

38. Synchronicities often represent important nonlocal movements of consciousness.

39. Black and white classical logic is the ego's logic, but it is not the logic of our being.

40. Intensity is a key ingredient of creativity.

41. Resentment is a favorite ploy of the ego to escape the openness to the present moment, to what is.

42. Having a sense of purpose is a characteristic of creative people. However, seeing purpose in every little (non- creative) event can be one of the ego's well-laid traps.

43. There is a story in the Hindu tradition. A disciple, through a great amount of meditation and devotion, was granted the ability to walk on water. The next day, he saw his guru waiting for the ferry. He offered his hand to the guru and walked him on the water, so great was his power. When they went across, the guru gave him a quarter. "What is the quarter for?" he enquired, a little surprised. "Your power is worth a quarter, the price of the ferry ride," said the guru wryly. In spiritual traditions, pursuing paranormal power is discouraged because it interferes with creativity. And in case powers come uninvited, the creative thing to do is to use them for service and without fanfare.

44. Singing in the shower, or other such expressions, is suggestive of relaxed joy in the moment.

Some further comments. Even highly creative people, when they honestly appraise themselves with the help of such questions as those given earlier, find that they are very much in their ego. Although their ego tendency is to deny it, they merely maintain a small window in their ego habits that enables them to keep an open mind in a narrow area of expertise. Let me suggest, and both theory and empirical data bear me out, that perhaps even most creative people limit themselves in this way in their adult development. Something works for you reasonably well, but it can work even better. You may be at the height of creativity right now, but this does not necessarily last. Even Einsteins get stuck in old patterns, and the dwindling of creativity with age is fairly common—yet it is by no means universal. What secret do some people discover that enables them to be creative all their lives? If Rabindranath Tagore got his second creative wind at the seasoned age of 50, why can't all of us? If Linus Pauling did creative and original scientific research well into his 80s, should we not take heart?

If we look at the lives of some of these creative second-winders, we discover something interesting. Their creative lives are remarkably integrated between outer and inner, situational and fundamental creativity. But because of the polarity within which creativity expresses itself, most creatives have a tendency to emphasize one pole over the other. We tend to carve out a comfortable window for our creative expression and stay there. Hence, individual creative people can often be grouped, on the basis of their work, into four classes according to their tendencies: outer-fundamental, outer-situational, inner-fundamental, and inner-situational. This habit is hard to change. As we have seen in Chapter 19, entire societies customarily emphasize one pole over the other. This, then, is our personal challenge: to integrate the modes of creativity within us as appropriate.

> You ask, Are there ways to cleanse
> the impurities of my sattwa?
> to integrates the modes of my creativity?
> Say the wise, there are,
> but you have to know your patterns first.

21

WAKING UP TO OUR CREATIVE POTENTIAL: WHAT CAN WE DO?

The universe seems to be evolving in a way that promotes wider and wider expressions of the themes of consciousness in keeping with its purpose of manifesting these archetypal themes. We have a drive that pushes us in the same direction—*sattwa*, the drive of creativity.

But the ego—our conditioned self—thinks in symbols. The apparent locus of our thought patterns and behavioral organization, the ego itself is the symbol for the constellation of meanings an individual gleans from his or her personal history of experiences. When we consciously act in the world, it seems to be our ego acting. A most fascinating part of maturation is to experience the growing definition and power of this ego. And for some of us, this fascination forever dominates—and limits—our lives.

For others of us, however, an elusive something dances tantalizingly around the ego. When communing with nature in the woods, suddenly the ego-boundary begins to dissolve in a mysterious way. The self seems to remember. But almost as suddenly the thought occurs, "Ah, I am a part of this forest!" And this thought itself, a reassertion of ego-dominance, instantly shatters what is for most of us only a fleeting moment. We reflect, I had a spiritual experience.

While engaged in creative activities, we sometimes realize that our ego is not the source of our creativity. Thus Einstein says, "I did not discover relativity with rational thinking alone." Or Escher writes,

"While drawing I sometimes feel as if I were a spiritualist medium." Or Bach says, "It's God who makes the music." This realization that creativity is not a function of the ego leads creative people to wonder about their hidden source or fountain of creativity—their *quantum self.*

But the ego operates in symbols and classifications, so we create symbols, we externalize what is essentially internal, we act like the characters of *The Wizard of Oz.* The scarecrow doubted that he had a brain, the tin man bemoaned the lack of a heart, and the lion felt lacking in courage until the wizard conferred on them respectively, a diploma, a ticking clock, and a medal of courage—all external symbols.

But symbol collecting and manipulation are conditioned actions; we do them as habits. Like the inhabitants of T. S. Eliot's *Waste Land,* we become drained of the juice of life. How do we shift from the ego to the creative self—how do we revitalize our waste land?

In the myth of the *Holy Grail,* when Percival comes to the Grail castle where the king is maimed, his intuition is to ask the king, "What's wrong with you?" But he had previously been instructed that an aspiring knight does not ask questions. So he shies away from possible conflict, and indeed no movement occurs.

"Seek, and ye shall find," said Jesus. Ask your question, and the door to creative transformation will open as it did eventually for Percival, who patiently stayed with his question and conflicts for six years. When he returned to the Grail king, he asked his question, and the kingdom was revitalized.

The crippled Grail king is a metaphor for the psyche when the self is dominated by ego identity. Only by continuing to ask the appropriate questions and addressing our conflicts do we transform and move from ego-bondage to an identity with the creative self.

HOW CAN YOU PRACTICE CREATIVITY?

A master musician was once asked on a street in New York, "What is the way to Carnegie Hall?" The maestro replied, "Practice, practice, practice." But alas! Practice alone may land you a job in a Carnegie Hall orchestra, it may even enable you to write music as problem solving, but it is no guarantee of true creativity in music. This does not mean that practice is not important to creative acts, only that there is more to creativity than technical mastery in a field. In truth, such mastery is neither a necessary nor a sufficient condition for creativity.

So the question arises, is there any other kind of practice for creativity than achieving mastery in a field? For example, Carl Rogers (1959) said creativity requires keeping an open mind. An open mind is a prerequisite to the quantum modality of the self. Can you practice an open mind? If outer creativity and inner creativity were separate endeavors, the answer to such questions would have to be no. Practicing an open mind is against the grain of the ego. In fact, creativity itself is against the grain of the ego.

Fortunately, although it is convenient to classify creativity as outer and inner, we are whole—outer and inner creativity are not separate networks of enterprises. In fact, each can help the other. When the novelist Natalie Goldberg had writer's block, her Zenmaster told her, "make writing your Zen practice."

Using outer creativity to investigate inner reality is an age-old practice. In outer creativity, we create from the silence beyond the ordinary thinking mind. Because the objective of inner creativity is to act from silence, in general, one can see why outer creativity is good practice for the inner creative. Can inner creativity be a similarly useful practice in outer creativity?

Both inner and outer creativity are about freedom. Inner creativity is the way to access greater and greater freedom in one's actions; outer creativity is the expression in the outer world of one's inner freedom. Clearly, greater inner access to freedom should only enhance one's outer creativity.

Behaviorists deny any freedom at all in human lives—all one's actions, according to them, are manifestations of stimulus-response-reinforcement conditioning. This new science of creativity has a very different view. Freedom of choice is always available in how consciousness manifests the material world, if only one accesses and exercises it. In order to access freedom, one has to learn to go beyond one's conditioned modality, the ego.

The problem of creativity, both outer and inner, is the paradoxical role that the ego plays. One cannot be creative without a strong ego to handle the anxiety of creative uncertainty. At the same time, creativity requires that one continually takes the risk of changing the character of the ego. One becomes afraid: what if changing the ego affects that very strength that makes one creative!

But one can have a strong ego without identifying with it. One can have ego as function without a rigid identity structure built around it. The goal of inner creativity is to shift one's identity beyond ego to the level of what I (Goswami, 1993a) have called buddhi—a weighting of one's identity toward a greater role for the quantum self. In buddhi, the ego serves and implements the choices made by the quantum self, but one must guard against allowing ego reactions to obscure and subvert the quantum vision.

Until now—with a few exceptions such as William Blake, Walt Whitman, Rabindranath Tagore, and Carl Jung—inner creativity has been used primarily toward the journey to God or spiritual liberation from the world. But spirituality does not have to be world negating; we are the world, so why negate it? Let me propose that the practice of inner creativity be redirected toward a spirituality of joy in which the spiritual transformation is used in creative service, including outer creativity, to the world.

When I was young, I read a children's story by a Bengali writer, Shibram Chakraborty. It was about two characters named Harshabardhan and Gobardhan. The first name means one whose wealth is joy, but the second name is awfully funny to a child—it means one whose wealth consists of cow dung. The two brothers took a train to Delhi from Calcutta. Because they had never before been on a train and they were riding first class, they were quite enjoying themselves. There was only one other passenger in their small compartment, who was on the upper bunk; the brothers shared the lower bunk.

At a major junction where the train stopped for at least an hour, the brothers left the train to look around the station. Time passed quickly until suddenly the hour was up and the train whistled. The two brothers rushed and somehow found their way to what they thought was their compartment; but to their surprise, they found a different man on the upper bunk. Gobardhan asked, "Where are you going, sir?" The man's reply, "To Calcutta," startled him. When he expressed his surprise to Harshabardhan, Harshabardhan exclaimed, "Look at the marvel of modern science; while the lower bunk is going to Delhi, the upper bunk is going to Calcutta." When the brothers arrived at their destination, of course, they couldn't help but notice the similarity of "Delhi" to Calcutta, but they only felt superior that Delhi should "copy" Calcutta so exactly. Gobardhan scoffed, "Look, they even copied our bridge."

When I reflect on our divided self, I often puzzle at the marvel of the modern human. The purposive evolution of our self is pointed toward "Delhi," but losing ourselves in the ego, we inadvertently head back toward "Calcutta!" This dichotomy becomes the barrier to our creativity. Can you penetrate this illusory dichotomy once you have become entrenched in your adult ego?

In the *Tibetan Book of the Dead*, there is a scene that describes the journey of the soul through what the Tibetans call the "bardos." Most souls, it is said, follow a bow-shaped trajectory and promptly return to earth to be reincarnated. But every soul gets the opportunity to go to the clear light if only it recognizes it. I think this is a good metaphor for adult human life. We pretty much live adulthood in an ego pattern of endless, habitual repetitions. But at any point we can break through and change our patterns, we can begin to manifest our creativity.

In the Tibetan scenario, if the soul is ready for an early glimpse of its true nature, only a subtle hint is needed, the clear light is enough. So it is with geniuses; a childhood experience of nuance is enough. In the later parts of the journey through the bardos, the hints get heavier and heavier in the form first of good gods and then of violent gods. It is the same with us; adults entrenched in the ego often need the crisis of a traumatic change—losing a job or spouse or facing death—to turn to creativity. But it happens. It happened to me. At midlife, I lost my research grant, I divorced and remarried, all in the course of a couple of years. Turning to creativity was inevitable.

Let's consider five practices that can help you break through the patterns of your ego to allow more participation in your life by the quantum self. You can think of these practices as a purification of sattwa—your creative drive. You can also think of them as designed to awaken buddhi—a more integrated mode of being and identity from which to create, from which to fulfill your human potential. The practices are:

1. The practice of openness, awareness, and sensitivity.
2. The practice of concentration.
3. The practice of imagination and dreaming.
4. Working with archetypes.
5. The practice of ethics.

THE PRACTICE OF AN OPEN MIND, AWARENESS, AND SENSITIVITY

Underneath all our creative acts lies a paradox. How can we know and yet not know? A professor went to a Zen master to learn about Zen. The master offered the professor some tea. As the master was making the tea, the professor began to show off his erudition, expounding on his knowledge of Zen. When the tea was made, the master began pouring the tea into the professor's cup. He went on pouring even after the cup was full until the professor cried, "My cup is full." The Zen master simply said, "So is your mind with ideas of Zen. How can I teach you if your mind is so full with your own ideas?"

Like the cup of tea, a mind too full of past learning can receive nothing more. Such a mind tries to convince others of the truth of fixed opinions; it cannot learn anything new and cannot be creative. A creative mind is never full. A creative mind retains a certain amount of naivete.

The naive student often has an advantage, as in the following story about a crown prince in ancient India. The prince and his brothers were instructed by their guru (teacher) to learn the first book. The teacher was very satisfied with the performance of his students until he tested his prize student, the crown prince. When asked, "How many sentences have you learned?" the prince replied, "One, maybe two." The teacher became angry at the prince's apparent negligence and began to beat him with a cane. The prince stood, calmly absorbing the punishment, his face showing not the slightest trace of anger. The guru was surprised. Suddenly, he remembered that the first sentence the prince was supposed to "learn" was *never be angry.* Immediately, he realized that the prince had really learned the sentence. When he asked the prince if this was so, the boy said, "Teacher, please. I should say, I've almost learned that sentence, because when you first started beating me, I did feel angry for a moment." As the prince spoke, the teacher remembered the second sentence that the prince felt he had learned, *always tell the truth.*

You see, nobody told the prince that learning a sentence meant memorization. In more recent times, nobody told a supposedly retarded boy named Albert that the absolute nature of space and time was already known; so the child grew up with beginner's questions about space and time and eventually discovered their relativity.

But the situation is paradoxical for an adult. A creative person remains open to new possibilities and yet has convictions and visions. He or she not only has mastery but also has "beginner's mind" (Suzuki, 1984), the ability to look at a thing as if for the first time, suspending all prior knowledge about it:

We shall not cease from exploration
And the end of all our exploring
Will be to arrive where we started
And know the place for the first time. (Eliot, 1943, p. 59)

Buddhists and Jains in India sometimes debate about what it means to know everything, to be omniscient. The Jains tell a story of two artists competing for the king's favor. One artist has done one wall of the art gallery, and the king is very pleased. "How can you beat this?" he asks the second artist. "I can't. So I have painted exactly the same thing," replies the artist, opening the drapes on the opposite wall, and the king is amazed. Indeed, the same painting shows up in dazzling beauty. The trick, of course, is the mirror quality of the wall. So, say the Jains, Be like the mirror and reflect perfectly all knowledge. That is omniscience.

But the Buddhists see it differently. Why be burdened with all knowledge when you don't need it all the time? Let knowledge come to you as required.[1] That is omniscience to them. This kind of omniscience flourishes with emptiness of mind. That is the approach of creativity.

The creative person develops mastery but does not dwell in the information gained. If, after mastery is attained, we allow knowledge to come to us as prompted by the creative process, a new creative idea can surface occasionally instead of old knowledge. But how can you create this emptiness of mind?

The meditative practice for cultivating beginner's mind, or emptiness of mind, is called *awareness meditation*. As thoughts, feelings, etc. arise in awareness, watch their parade, but without attachment or interference. Start with 20 minutes a day of practice of this choiceless awareness, then make an effort to maintain awareness during the rest of everyday life. Let life become a yoga—a union of our two self-identities.

A powerful (and perhaps indispensible) practice for making life into yoga is self-observation, a radical, unflinchingly honest, yet nonjudgmental observation of your behavior with others and of your inner motivations, feelings, and thoughts. Initially, the pressure to change your reactions through willpower is strong, but it is counter-productive. The purpose is to unmask yourself. If you do this practice of self-awareness and observation sincerely, you gradually begin to identify specific rationalizations, justifications, and other defenses that shore up and armor your ego. With ongoing awareness, you can penetrate deeper and more subtle layers of defensive camouflage, a process that is by turns profoundly illuminating and acutely painful. To be most effective, and sometimes merely tolerable, do this practice with compassion for yourself, a compassion that, with advancing practice, will deepen and extend to others.

I have spoken of the importance of experiencing nuance, a special kind of sensitivity to primary quantum processes. If you watch your thoughts without attachment, defense, or interference, consciousness becomes empty, receptive to nuance, ready to resonate with the indwelling themes of the universe.

It happens. Subhuti, a disciple of Buddha, was meditating under a tree when flowers began to shower on him. "We are praising you for your discourse on emptiness of mind," voices said. "But I haven't spo-

---

[1] I heard this playful comparison of Buddhists and Jains from Professor Jaini of the University of California-Berkeley.

ken," said Subhuti. "You haven't spoken, and we haven't heard. This is true emptiness," said the voices. And the flowers showered.

When the mind becomes empty, when you transcend the ordinary mind of discourse, you become sensitive to the primary creative reality. Then the flowers shower, a nuance tunes you to the universe's purpose, and your creative life can bloom.

THE PRACTICE OF CONCENTRATION

The Nobel prize winner (twice) Marie Curie had such concentration in her youth that once her siblings made a wall of tables and chairs around her while she was working at her desk. Marie was completely oblivious of what was going on until she got up and the furniture crashed around her, to her huge embarrassment.

There is a similar story about the Indian physicist Meghnad Saha who, while working on a problem in astrophysics, once talked with a boy while walking home. Upon encountering his wife, he enquired who the pleasant boy was, and his wife tersely reminded him that the boy was his own son.

One morning Einstein told his wife, "Darling, I've got a wonderful idea," and disappeared into his study. It is said that he more or less stayed there for the next couple of weeks until his idea took form in the general theory of relativity.

Similar stories abound for creative people. Where do creative people get such concentration? More to the point, can you cultivate concentration? And finally, why is concentration important for creativity?

Cognitive research confirms that if you have a thought present in awareness, it interferes with any other thought while the repetition of the same thought is facilitated (Posner, 1980). Thus a burning question helps to maintain itself in cognition. This may be where creative people have their edge—they have burning questions about the world or themselves.

A meditation technique called concentration meditation provides a close equivalent to a creative burning question. This technique cultivates the concentration that creative people display in their process. Here is the technique in one Hindu version called *japa*. Choose a short word (a monosyllabic one such as the Sanskrit *rhim* or *om* works well) and repeat the word internally. When other thoughts interfere—as they will, especially in the beginning—and you become aware of it, firmly bring your attention back to your word (which is called a *mantra* in Sanskrit meaning protector of the mind). Start your practice with twenty minutes, gradually lengthening it.

It is possible with practice to so internalize the mantra that it seems to go on by itself. (That is, one day you will notice that the mantra is going on without any conscious effort.) This stage is called "*japa* without *japa*" and is similar to the unconscious processing of a burning question that leads creative people to their insights.

To be creative, says the philosopher Eric Fromm, "[one] has to give up holding on to himself as a thing and begin to experience himself only in the process of creative response; paradoxically enough, if he can experience himself in this process, he loses himself. He transcends the boundaries of his own person, and at the very moment when he feels 'I am' he also feels 'I am you,' I am one with the whole world."

It happens also in meditation. There are many cases of concentration meditation culminating in a special state of consciousness called *samadhi,* which the Hindu 2nd-century sage Patanjali empirically studied (Taimni, 1961). This is a state in which primary quantum process dominates awareness, and one recognizes the world in its true nature— neither objects nor oneself seem separate from consciousness. Many years ago, in 1976, I did the practice of japa for seven days and had such an experience. Here is what I later wrote about it.

> On a sunny November morning, I was sitting quietly in my chair in my office doing japa. This was the seventh day since I had started, and I still had a lot of energy left. About an hour of japa, and I got an urge to take a walk outside. I continued my mantra deliberately as I walked out of my office, then out of the building, across the street, and onto the grassy meadow. And then the universe opened up to me.
>
> . . . when meadow, grove and stream
> The earth, and every common sight,
> To me did seem
> Apparelled in celestial light,
> The glory and freshness of a dream.
> (Wordsworth, cited in Hutchinson & De Selincourt, 1967)

I seemed to be one with the cosmos, the grass, the trees, the sky. Sensations were present, in fact, intensified beyond belief. But these sensations were pale in significance compared to the feeling of love that followed, a love that engulfed everything in my consciousness—until I lost comprehension of the process. This was *ananda,* bliss.

There was a moment or two of which I don't have any description, no thoughts, not even feeling. Afterwards, it was just bliss. It was still bliss as I walked back to my office. It was bliss when I talked to our cantankerous secretary, but she was beautiful in the bliss, and I loved her. It was bliss when I taught my class, the noise, even the back-row kid who threw an airplane was bliss.

It was bliss when I came home and kissed Maggie and told her what happened. It was bliss to see her happiness. . . . It was bliss to do the chores, it was bliss to lie down by Maggie and watch TV, it was bliss to make love, and it was bliss to fall asleep. It was all bliss. (Goswami, n.d.)

But don't get too caught up in the idea of such exalted experiences; we cannot make them happen. (I did not make my experience happen! It happened. I have not been able to duplicate it since.) The purpose of concentration meditation from the point of view of enhancing creativity is best served by regular practice for a short period (twenty minutes is adequate) supplemented by an effort to bring the practice into everyday life situations as and when appropriate.

To be creative, you must distinguish between desire and will. They are related, but desire leads to a treadmill to nowhere, whereas will at the service of creativity holds the purpose of the universe. When you want to lose weight but also want sweet goodies, it is desire; conflict always accompanies desire. Desire is wanting to want. In contrast, when you really commit to something, the wanting becomes will (*samkalpa* in Sanskrit). This is where concentration meditation helps you. Look at the life of Van Gogh: it was will that guided him to paint *Sunflowers* in the blazing summer sun of southern France, no mere desire to do so would have sufficed.

Japa, and mantras, in general, focus on the auditory sense. For some people, visualization comes more easily. For them visualization is a powerful practice of concentration. You can visualize anything that engages your enthusiasm in some way: a flower, the face of a loved or respected one, an archetypal symbol such as a mandala. Initially, the image will be fragmentary; with practice, however, it stabilizes to such an extent that you can manipulate it. You can also invoke it at will. Again a time may come when the visualization is internalized; it may go on all the time while the practitioner is carrying out daily activities. Christian contemplatives practice holding the image of Jesus in their hearts. Brother Lawrence spent his life "practising the presence of God," and this transformed him. This kind of practice also can lead to exalted experiences.

Why is concentration important for creativity? Concentration can lead you to such states of absorption with the object that you can see the object in its suchness—that it is not independent from consciousness. Try to comprehend what the virtuoso pianist Lorin Hollander said about his childhood piano practice: "when I would play a note I would become that note." It is in the spontaneity of these states of quantum modality that creative ideas, insights, understandings, and visions crystallize. The novelist Gustave Flaubert had this to say:

> When I wrote about Emma Bovary's poisoning [in Madam Bovary] I had the taste of arsenic so strongly in my mouth, I was so thoroughly poisoned myself, that I gave myself two bouts of indigestion, one after another, two very real bouts since I vomited up my entire dinner. (quoted in Briggs, 1990, p. 201)

However, neither exaltation nor a creative absorption state can be forced, thus it is fruitless to make such experiences the objective of concentration practice. The great guaranteed virtue for the creative person of being able to concentrate on an object—for example, of being able to visualize an object and manipulate the visualization—is the handle it gives imagination.

THE PRACTICE OF IMAGINATION AND DREAMING

In perception, an external stimulus produces a brain image for which we find a correlated mental state that gives it meaning. In imagination, we start with a mental state and find a match of it in the physical (for example, representing a thought by language). In visualization, we find a match of what we are imagining with not only language but also a visual representations in the brain repertoire, so we see a visual image even though there is no external object. With some control of concentration, the power to imagine images, visual or thought, that have never been known becomes unleashed. Now we are making new maps in the brain of creative mental states of primary awareness using the brain's chaos dynamics. "Genius is the capacity to treat objects of the imagination as real, and even to manipulate them as such" (Novalis, quoted in Cobb, 1992, p. 140).

Now you can understand what Coleridge meant when he distinguished between fancy and imagination; fancy is but a frivolous expression of the intellect, the playful doodling of the ego. But imagination, said Coleridge, springs "from elemental parts of the spirit [archetypes] shared by all."

But creative imagination is difficult in ordinary ego awareness; it is difficult to be open to the primary awareness of the quantum self.

In our ego mode, we make known images from our past experience. But if we are not wedded to the ego, as in a dream state, we may easily fall into the quantum self. Then we may be able to explore truly creative imagery, manifesting the unknown. This is when we begin to see things in their archetypal suchness, which creative ideas represent.

When we dream, our normal ego-defensiveness relaxes, allowing us to dip into the unknown in ways that the conscious, ego-dominated mind never permits. In dreams, the unconscious is the major player; largely, for many people, that means the personal unconscious—those Freudian repressions. But for someone with a healthy ego, or for one who has awakened into buddhi, the unconscious that comes into play in dreams is often the collective unconscious.

Jung (1971b) stressed the archetypal content of creative dreams. The archetypal content of dreams in connection with creative acts is revealed in such incidents as the experience of the inventor Elias Howe when he was in the final stage of designing the first sewing machine. In his dream Howe was captured by savages whose leader demanded that he finish his machine or be executed. He then noticed that the spears of his captors had eye-shaped holes (a well-known archetypal image) near the points. Waking from the dream, he realized instantly that the key to his sewing machine was a needle with a hole near the point.

The case of pharmacologist Otto Loewi is interesting because his brilliant idea for experimentally demonstrating that nerve impulses are chemically mediated came from a dream, but with a quirk. The first time he dreamed it, he wrote it down when he awoke momentarily, but the following morning he could not decipher his own handwriting. Fortunately, the next night, he dreamed the same idea once more. This time he was careful to write it down legibly.

Can you manipulate dream imagery? In effect, this would amount to knowing that you are dreaming. In esoteric literature, this practice of cognition while dreaming is called dream yoga. Dream yoga combines the creative potency of the dream state, the lessening of ego-boundaries, with the ability of conscious imagination. The English romantic poets discovered the potency of some sort of dream yoga—going in and out of dream and waking consciousness.

> Was it a vision, or a waking dream?
> Fled is that music:—Do I wake or sleep?

wrote John Keats in his *Ode to a Nightingale*. Why does this ode touch us? Precisely because "we don't know where we are in it" (Atchity & Atchity, 1990).

Lucid dreaming, in which you are aware that you are dreaming, is the same state as practiced in dream yoga. In a way, Kekule's snake dream (see chapter 4) is an example of lucid dreaming. After his experience, Kekule became greatly enthusiastic about creative dreaming. "Let us learn to dream," he wrote. And let's follow it up with the East Indian sage Patanjali's advice, "meditate on knowledge that comes during sleep [dream]."

There is new research that suggests that how we participate in our dreams depends on our self-development (Wolf, 1994). In particular, some researchers think that lucid dreaming—when we consciously reflect on the fact of our dreaming—may signal the beginning of a passage to higher states of conscious awareness.[2]

The neurophysiologist John Lilly has advised programming the "biocomputer" before going to sleep. Asking your quantum self for a dream with vague guidelines related to your quest (much like a prayer) is a good idea—it works.

Somewhere between sleep and alertness, the brain waves change from the more commonplace beta (high frequency) and alpha (frequency between 7 and 14 hertz) waves to theta waves (frequency 4 to 7 hertz). There is some evidence that creativity may be enhanced when the brain goes into theta waves (Goleman, Kaufman, & Ray, 1992). The physician Elmer Green had a breakthrough in his research in a drowsy state of theta-wave dominance. It is said that Thomas Edison sat in his comfortable chair to doze off with metal balls in his hands, and two metal pans positioned to catch the balls in case they fell. Just as Edison would doze off, the balls' falling into the pans would make a racket, waking him, and he often had good insights in that semi-stupor between sleep and waking.

In passing, let me also mention the use of drugs. Can drugs, especially psychedelic drugs, enhance creativity, as the creativity researcher John Gowan (1974) has suggested? Gowan was much discredited for his view, but I think it is a legitimate question. Psychedelic drugs lead us also to an altered state in which the ego-boundaries are considerably enlarged; in that sense, they are similar to dream states.

Can we learn to control these altered states enough to take advantage of the loosened restrictions on our imagination and, perhaps, increased access to the quantum modality? The difficulty in using such states for creativity is that creativity is the marriage of both heaven and earth, both ego and quantum modalities. Unfortunately, according to published reports, our ego functioning seem to be disrupted in these

---

[2]Details can be found in Wolf (1994).

drug-induced altered states. Moreover, whereas there is no identifiable problem of dream addiction, there is such a problem with drugs; this, of course, is antithetical to seeking freedom in the quantum modality, so their negative potential should not be underestimated.

WORKING WITH ARCHETYPES

Jung emphasized the importance of working with some of the archetypes of the collective unconscious that seem particularly important in the way the unconscious drive of creativity expresses itself.

You can easily understand the repression of certain archetypal themes in the collective unconscious that try to express themselves in creativity. For example, a male would tend to suppress mental states that pertain to the experiences of a female body, for which he has no context. The anima is the female archetype in men—the possibility waves of the male mind that corresponds to the "female" in males that are suppressed because the male (physical) form and conditioning (both genetic and environmental) are not inherently appropriate for their expression. The animus, likewise, is the suppressed "male" possibilities in women. In men's conditioned modality, only the conditioned male patterns collapse, while the female patterns are suppressed. But creatively, a man can access "female" qualities if consciousness so chooses. The same can be said of a woman; creativity can release her suppressed "male" qualities.

But why should a man engage his creative drive to experience the patterns of the other sex? A woman mystic of India, Meera Bai, went to Brindaban, the birthplace of Krishna, a spiritual Mecca of India, in search of a guru. But when she wrote to a venerable guru asking him to accept her, he refused because "she was a woman." She wrote back, "I thought that in Brindaban everyone is a woman, that the only man is Krishna." The guru was very impressed with this reply and accepted her as his disciple. The deep meaning of what Meera Bai wrote is, of course, that to be an inner creative we must all approach the inner quantum self with a receptivity that is a core quality of the female experience. In actuality, this receptivity is essential for insight in both outer and inner creativity. Thus a man could be amply rewarded for making conscious his unconscious feminine qualities.

Likewise, a woman needs to integrate her animus because it enhances her capacity for preparation, perseverance (will), and production—the three Ps—essential in the creative process. In the movie *Wolf*, the heroine drifts along in life until she discovers (with crucial help from the men of the movie, both the protagonist and the antagonist) the warrior inside her, her animus, symbolized by the werewolf. Of course, very appropriately, the men, too, had lost their "werewolves," their power; they were victims of the mediocrity of modern enterprises. They had to recover their werewolves themselves before they could serve the heroine.

Both the animus and the anima integration can be much facilitated by working with the opposite sex in a committed relationship. This is a unique opportunity for an "I-thou" relationship. Here, thou is your own anima or animus, but embodied in your partner. Your dreams may be particularly powerful allies as you integrate these important archetypes.

Another important archetype for creatives to investigate is that of the hero. In a sense, every creative act is the culmination of a hero's journey: the hero embarks on a quest, strives and endures, has insight, and then returns with the accomplished product—you can easily see the stages of the creative process here. In the *Iliad*, Zeus pulls all things to himself with a golden cord; similarly, the hero archetype attracts all of us. India has a different metaphor for the cord of inner creativity—the sound of Krishna's flute. But whether you have heard the flute or felt the pull of the cord, the result is the same; you set sail on an irreversibly creative journey.

To integrate the hero, you must shun the ego and yield, during moments of intuition or insight, to the bidding of the archetype in your transformational journey. (This is parodied by the heroes and heroines of the *Iliad*, who are manipulated by the gods like puppets.) Even so, between intuitions and insights the ego has its role to play, and the archetype is not outside us.

The movie *Accidental Tourist* is a good depiction of a modern hero's journey. The hero here, Macon Leary, has the same problem as the heroine in *Wolf*; he has lost his internal warrior, his werewolf. He shuns anything that is potentially painful, physical or emotional, and thereby has abandoned creativity entirely. In order to return to the hero's journey, Macon has to be reinitiated. The job falls to a female, naturally, Muriel Pritchard, who has the energy of the East Indian goddess Kali, the cleanser. Some cleansing happens, Macon makes a guarded start back toward life but, still reluctant to face pain, returns to his wife when she beckons, even though the marriage doesn't work any more. In the highly symbolic end, Macon is running around Paris, suitcase in hand and pain in his back, searching for a taxi, until he drops his baggage, both physically and symbolically. On his way to the airport—sans his suitcase, his emotional baggage—he sees Muriel (who has followed him to Paris) on the sidewalk, and his frozen face gives way to a warm smile (acted wonderfully by William Hurt). Macon's creativity has broken through, he has rediscovered love.

All great creatives are heroes personified when they are within the stages of a creative act. The inner creative whose buddhi is awakened and who has integrated the hero archetype is the hero personified at all times; without much effort she or he lives on the razor's edge. In India, they call such a person an avatara.

CREATIVITY AND MADNESS: WORKING WITH THE SHADOW ARCHETYPE

Psychoanalytical theorists of creativity, beginning with Freud, make a considerable connection between creativity and neurosis, even madness. For Freud, both schizophrenics and creative people partake of what Freud called "primary process thinking," hence the connection.

Indeed, primary-awareness processes reflect the quantum modality from which creative people draw their insights. The question has been raised, Do schizophrenics also enter the quantum modality? Are they frustrated or short-circuited creatives? My view is, no; psychopathology is related to the repression dynamic of the personal unconscious—a below-par functioning of the ego due to repressed mental states—whereas creativity involves the universal quantum self that transcends the ego.[3]

But in the popular mind, the strange associations that mental patients sometimes make seem to be similar to those of creative people. "The lunatic, the lover and the poet,\ Are of imagination all compact," wrote William Shakespeare. Carl Jung wrote of a mental patient suffering from paranoid dementia who thought of the world, in a way similar to the great philosopher Schopenhauer, as his picture book. To thicken the plot, many exponents of inner creativity (the East Indian Ramakrishna is a prime example) have referred to themselves as "mad." And now, even quantum physicists have begun investigating whether both creative people and schizophrenics use "quantum logic" to arrive at their bizarre associations (Oshins & McGoveran, 1980).

Fortunately, careful experimentation by the psychologist Albert Rothenberg (1983) seems to rule against any relationship between creative and schizophrenic thinking. In his experiment, Rothenberg gave word-association tests to four different groups: (a) a group of eighteen psychiatric patients at the Austen Riggs center; (b) a group of 12 Nobel

---

[3]This position is compatible with the chemical basis of some schizophrenia.

laureates; and (c) and (d) two groups of undergraduates designated as "high" and "low" creatives, respectively. What Rothenberg found in schizophrenics' thinking that was very different from that of the creatives is a relative inability to think in opposites (creative people, of course, excel in oppositional thinking).

But still, there are just too many instances of creative people gone crazy, even committing suicide under the spell of their craziness. The list is long: Van Gogh, Virginia Woolf, and Friedrich Nietzsche are some of the most famous. Why?

I think that the craziness of creative people (and mystics, too) comes from getting lost in the twilight zone of what Jung called the *shadow archetype*. Creative people confront an apparent fragmentation of the psyche, but the fragmentation is between the ego and the quantum self. (For schizophrenics, on the other hand, the conditioned psyche is perhaps fragmented into multiple ego structures that are separated by processes of the personal unconscious.) When creative people turn inward to find a new transformed center for their actions (of outer and inner creativity) that is weighted more heavily toward the quantum self, they may find a barrier, the shadow—an amalgam of their collective and personal repressed material, repressed to satisfy the demands of form and conditioning. You have to "lighten" the shadow (make it conscious) in order to recover from the fragmentation and become whole.

But the journey into the shadow to meet and integrate the archetypes of creative freedom is fraught with difficulties mounted by the conditioned ego and fueled by repressed personal material. This is mythologized beautifully in the story of Orpheus. Orpheus was a musician whose music charmed even animals. But when the love of his life, Eurydice, is claimed by death, Orpheus enters Hades in search of her, his anima. Orpheus finds Eurydice and is allowed to lead her back to light and life, but on one condition. He must not look back while she follows him out of Hades. The story ends sadly because Orpheus cannot handle the creative uncertainty; he loses faith and looks back, succumbing to his past conditioning, whereupon Eurydice forever dies to him.

Creative people who go crazy or commit suicide perhaps replay the Orpheus myth. But some of them do successfully make the journey back from the encounter with their shadow and then write about it, transforming the myth. This is what gave us Dante's *Divina Comedia*. Dante's Beatrice, his retrieved anima, actually leads him to fulfillment.

It's a Cinderella story. So long as Cinderella, the one who grew up among cinders, stays in the background, nobody gets Prince Charming. But when Cinderella attends the ball with the help of a magic wand (quantum leaps), she is united with Prince Charming, and creativity can flourish.

When you work with your shadow, you are cleansing your ego in order to increase your openness to the quantum self. Until your ego functions in a strong and aware fashion, you cannot handle the anxiety that accompanies the creative encounter with the quantum self and thus to be open for transformation.

Why do some mystics such as Ramakrishna call themselves crazy? Because mystics, too, have to do ego cleansing before they can move into deeper realms of inner creativity. Ramakrishna was crazy with his devotion to Kali. Who is Kali—the naked, dark goddess—in Hindu mythology? She is the cleansing goddess.

PERSONAL CRISIS, CREATIVE ETHICS, AND THE OPPORTUNITY FOR TRANSFORMATION

The creativity researcher Michael Piechowski (1993) has studied a few cases of inner creativity in some detail. Let's consider one of these cases. Etty Hillesum was a young Jewish woman living in Amsterdam during World War II. Although fully aware of the growing menace of Nazism, she nevertheless focused her life on spiritual growth. Even though her life was busy, she sought to give it a deeper meaning, to reach what was truly essential in herself, which she intuited to be present but locked away. In 1941, when she was 27, she started a diary. She describes her inner struggles to fight restlessness of spirit, inner chaos, depression, despair, and physical pain. Often these inner battles were "short but violent" but each made her feel "a little stronger." At some point during her struggles, she realized that to hate the Germans for their persecution of the Jews was to become like them.

This fundamental conflict between the (outer) behavioral ego self and the inner creative quantum self along the path of self-inquiry is beautifully depicted in the opening chapter of the *Bhagavad Gita*: when the hero Arjuna refuses to fight his kinsmen, Krishna, his friend and teacher, tries to inspire him to fight. It may seem strange for a religious book to encourage war until you realize that the conflict in question is the perpetual conflict in the psyche that results from the false identification with the outer self (the ego). And you can never resolve the conflict without engaging creatively with it. So Krishna appeals to Arjuna's inner self and free will, because the resolution of the conflict can come only from the creative impulse resting in the inner self.

Creative ethics is generated by the resolution of the crisis of confrontation between your ego and quantum self identities. The creative resolution of ethical conflicts is the basis of inner psychic transformation in moral exemplars. Etty Hillesum is one example; Eleanor Roosevelt, Gandhi, Martin Luther King, etc. are more famous examples. Moral exemplars are a subclass of self-actualizing people about whom Abraham Maslow (1968) said, "they do right and do not do wrong." To do right, in this case, means to move away from selfish involvements and ego-defensiveness and, instead, to be of service to others.

But moving away from selfishness is not an easily accomplished task—it calls for unrelenting inner work. Eleanor Roosevelt described it as "knowledge of yourself, a knowledge based on a deliberately and usually painfully acquired self-discipline." It is this honest self-observation that sorts out the dynamics of one's behavior. The resulting recognition of selfish motives better enables us to make ethical choices (Picchowski & Goswami, 1991).

Creative ethics as a process of inner transformation answers the question with which Immanuel Kant struggled for many years, Why be moral? Those who do not run away from inner conflicts but engage in the journey of self-knowledge see moral duties as categorical imperatives. They become moral because, wanting to know their own self-nature, there is no alternative to creative ethics, it is imperative. But moral duties are not categorical imperatives to the vast majority of people locked in their behavioral ego-identity. Does it affect their creativity? I think it does.

THE PRACTICE OF ETHICS

The question is, Is the purpose of the universe ultimately ethical? Confusions arise because we see around us "good" people who are not particularly creative; conversely, we see "immoral" people flourish in creativity. Similarly, we ask, Why do bad things happen to good people? and Why are bad people not punished for their evil deeds?

The confusion can be resolved when we realize that the price for immanence is a certain conditioning that cannot be avoided. Matter has inertia; if you get in the way of a moving truck, you will be crushed. Similarly, your life experiences condition you (Easterners call it *karma*), begetting you a certain amount of suffering, even if you are good or creative. Likewise, if "bad" people have accumulated good karma in their past, they may seem to escape the consequences of their current evil deeds. But such events are no reflection on the fundamental ethical nature of a universal purpose—to know itself in immanence via creativity.

So then, creativity—both outer and inner—goes hand in hand with a fundamental idealist ethics in which the ethics of living is firmly planted in the respect and facilitation of everybody's access to his or her creative quantum modality (Goswami, 1993b). Essentially, the practice of idealist ethics proceeds in three stages. In the first stage, we practice action without coveting the fruit of the action. In the second stage, we practice selflessness by serving others in a context of compassionate love. These stages involve disidentifying with the ego and cannot be fully accomplished without waking to buddhi. In the third stage, we practice appropriate action until it springs spontaneously from our quantum modality.

The practice of the first stage is very important if you want to liberate yourself from the reward-punishment cycle of action that often inhibits creativity. Research shows that children and young adults become less creative in reward-punishment environment (Amabile, 1990). Yet this behaviorally moralistic gospel dominates most of our social structures. The practice of non-attached action frees you from this cycle, allowing you to pursue your personal burning questions without socially conditioned incentives or fears.

Manifesting the joy of consciousness revealing itself to itself is a universal purpose. This joy is an expression of selflessness, which you approach when you appreciate otherness—that equality of another person in her or his essence and creativity. Then you are able to discover love in its archetypal content. It is this love that is the most exalted expression of creative work: great literature, great art, great music, even great science all have one thing in common—they excel in love.

The third stage—living in appropriate action—is very rare in currently evolved humanity. What is appropriate action? Perhaps the meaning is already clear to your intuition. The Eastern concept of karma—the perpetuation of cause-effect dynamics in conditioned existence—is also useful here. When your acts don't further increase your own or others' karma, you approach acting appropriately. And if your acts help reduce the karmic suffering of somebody, you are involved in appropriate action. Such action requires a deep, insightful responsiveness. Essentially, it means to live like a verb without identifying with the subject (or the object), to live in perpetual being, or in radical present-centeredness. What is the meaning of creativity in such an exalted mode of living? Creativity is no longer special: All is creative, all is rooted in the total freedom of the quantum modality of being.

THE CHANGING VIEW OF LIFE

A young king wanted to know the purpose of life—what is it all about? His library had many books in it, and no doubt the information was all there. Unfortunately, the king had work to do, enemies to conquer, and so on. Thus, he ordered the learned people of the library, the magi, to consolidate all the knowledge on this question about the meaning of life. And then he set out to conquer his enemies.

East and west, north and south, when all enemies were vanquished many years later, the king returned. Meanwhile, his learned employees had compiled a 100-volume encyclopedia about the purpose of human life. Sighed the king upon seeing the size of the project, "I am never going to find the time to read so much. Condense all this to one volume," he ordered.

It took another 10 years, but it was done. Then there was a rebellion, and the king was too busy to read even the one volume. He squelched the rebellion but was mortally wounded. On his deathbed, the king requested that all the knowledge be summed up for him in one sentence. The magi pondered the whole night. The next morning, in his last hour, they told the king the essence of their synthesis of human wisdom on the subject: Man (or woman) is born, suffers, and dies.

Traditionally, religion has taken this view of life—life is suffering. And don't look at materialism for meaning, either. Materialists consider life to be a dance of atoms. The more we explore the universe, the more it appears to be meaningless, lamented the Nobel laureate physicist Steven Weinberg (1979).

But we have seen in this book that the idealist synthesis finally recovers the meaning of life—it is creativity. Idealist science would have led to a different one-sentence summary: *Man (or woman) is born, is creative (which sometimes involves suffering, but so what?), and dies.*

> You wannabe creative?
> Creativity costs.
> Your sattwic account grows
> at the expense of your tamasic account,
> or didn't you know that?
>
> But if you truly bankrupt conditioned mind—
> > cultivate awareness
> > practice concentration,
> > release your imagination,
> > integrate your archetypes,
> > couple your creativity with ethics—
> What happens?
> Find out. What have you got to lose?
> Only slavery to the known.

Restore creativity to a healthy balance.
Then only will conditioning and ego
stay in the bounds of simple function.
And when you transcend all the drives—
of creativity, of libido, and of conditioning—
you become a hero-avatara.

22

TOWARD A CREATIVE SOCIETY

During the time of the Italian renaissance, Duke Frederico da Montefeltro was building a palace but was at a loss as to what to do with the great mass of earth excavated. An abbot is said to have found a solution. Why not dig a hole to dump the excavated earth into? To which the duke laughed and pointed out that there would still be the problem of disposing of the excavated earth from the hole. But the abbot did not give up. Make the hole so big that it can hold both, he said (Grudin, 1991).

This abbot would have been quite popular today—witness the kind of solutions that we often accept in treating some of our most gigantic problems: environmental destruction, deficit reduction, health care, urban unrest, and so forth. It seems much less daunting to dig a hole or to form a committee to study a problem than to find a creative solution that may threaten the existing norms of society.

I expect you see the similarity between social inertia and the ego's; it is tempting to define a social ego. Society manifests structure and stability, creativity manifests change. Can the two, stability and change, coexist constructively, each yielding to the other as needed?

In a society as individualistic as the United States, creativity unfortunately is looked on not as a social endeavor but as an extremely personal one. But creativity on a large scale is needed to break up social inertia. Such creativity must somehow act through both the individual and the collective, as in a renaissance. There are, of course, historical examples of such renaissance periods: Pericles's Greece, the Italian renaissance, and the nineteenth-century Bengali renaissance in which Rabindranath Tagore flourished. How do renaissances work?

285

I suspect they occur through nonlocal correlation en masse. Society embodies interactions among its members; thus many brain-mind complexes in a particular society may become correlated under certain circumstances in the presence of a shared clear intention. This nonlocal correlation, under the tremendous pressure of social need, may elicit creativity en masse, a renaissance.

Can societies engender en-masse creativity in normal times? Societies must change the way they harvest personal creativity in order to solve the problems of their own inertia. This would be simple if the benefits of creative activities that lead to monumental societal changes were recognized immediately and seen as part of the process of societal development. The difficulty is that creative people and their acts of creation often are years ahead of prevailing social contexts, whereas short-term (often personally profitable) perspectives and the tendency to maintain stability and the status quo guide powerful influences in society. There are several steps that can lead to a solution.

Societies can teach and exemplify an intrinsic respect for creativity. They can eliminate barriers and nonsolutions (such as solving problems by digging holes) against creativity. Societies can hold social institutions accountable for their true purpose, namely, to serve the well-being, including the purposiveness, of the society—both its individual members and the collective. The society must be ethical, in practice as well as theory, tangibly supporting "liberty and justice for all."

Let's look at these steps one by one. First, can society develop such a healthy respect for creativity that it continues to nurture creativity beyond dependency on creativity's immediate romantic appeal? The way to develop such respect is to make creativity a pivot in the fundamental education of all citizens.

TEACHING CREATIVITY IN SCHOOLS

What is the primary problem with creativity in schools? It is that learning, any learning, is conditioning—the antithesis of creativity. But we can minimize the negative effect of the mind's conditioning on creativity by overtly encouraging students to keep an open mind and not to be satisfied with only their conditioned responses. Furthermore, we can teach them to discriminate between tasks for which rote learning is appropriate and sufficient and those that require a more creative engagement.

In addition, what can we do specifically to enhance creativity in the education of young people? Although a paradigm/context-shifting creative act cannot be manufactured at will, understanding and creative learning are somewhat less demanding acts of creativity. Can these be taught?

The answer is no but, fortunately, with a caveat. Knowing the target answers to carefully constructed problems, the teacher can skillfully guide students and mediate the creative learning process of breaking through to understanding or to a creative learning of new contexts.

How about situational creativity—at least the problem solving part that involves an artful, heuristic reshuffling of existing contexts? A heuristic is a method for which we can give an algorithm only after we have found the solution. We can encourage students to develop heuristics for problem-solving in specially created, ambiguous situations for which the teacher already knows at least one workable heuristic. This is where pedagogy comes in, and its role in education has proven value.

A dilemma of teaching heuristic problem-solving skills is that straightforward algorithmic approaches, to which most academic problems yield, take up most of the teaching time. The psychologist Shawn Boles (1994) suggested that we teach students by presenting them randomly distributed, short opportunities to practice heuristics and, in particular, teach them to recognize when a heuristic approach is necessary. The 9-point problem of Chapter 5 can be used, for example. When the student experiences anger, boredom, or other frustrations and tries to escape the problem, a wise teacher can point out that those are the signals that the problem requires more than a solution in terms of known algorithms.

The low probability of a creative response is a special problem in creativity. Persistence reduces this problem by increasing the number of collapses of the mind's quantum state relative to the same question, thus increasing the chance to realize a new response. Accordingly, we must encourage our students to be persistent. One shortcoming of modern schooling is the negative connotation of failure. We should encourage children to recognize interim failure as an inherent component of creativity and of eventual success. "Give me a fruitful error any time, full of seeds, bursting with its own correction," said Vilfredo Pareto. "You can keep your sterile truths to yourself."

One high-school English teacher who understood this point was trying to stimulate her disadvantaged students to read Shakespeare. One day she asked the class about the meaning of a particular passage in *The Taming of the Shrew*. After a long silence, a usually nonparticipating student attempted an answer, but it was wrong. The teacher, however, was so pleased with his unexpected attempt that without thinking she reached in her pocket, came up with a dollar bill, and gave it to the student. When another student complained about rewarding a wrong answer, the teacher explained, "Sometimes it takes a lot of wrong answers before you get the right one." Her class later unanimously voted for more Shakespeare.[1]

---

[1] I read this story in a *Reader's Digest* article.

Acceptance of failure without stigma in a context that encourages persistence can open students to further risk-taking (and eliminate much cruel teasing of slow learners). A risk-taking attitude allows children to wander from homeostasis and promotes the onset of quantum leaps, creating open minds for inner listening (destructuring) as well as for new orders of restructuring. There is some evidence that many creative adolescents come from home environments supportive of risk taking (Dacey, 1989). Women, perhaps, are discouraged from creativity by society's pressures to stay near homeostasis (Helson, 1990).

The creative necessity of destructuring and restructuring in learning needs to be emphasized along with the value of preserving homeostasis. In Hindu terminology, Vishnu is the god of preservation while Shiva is the god of destruction and recreation. Societies as a rule worship Vishnu; but the demand of creativity is not met until a society learns to acknowledge Shiva's role as well. (After all, destructuring occurs, anyway—witness inner-city devastation and its criminal exploitation. Accepting its natural inevitability in systems that don't work may promote more effective and conscious destructuring, thereby reducing violent forms.) Traditionally, our culture suppresses emotions. Teachers need to develop constructive ways to acknowledge emotions, to elicit their information content, and to appropriately guide students in responding to negative ones. Teaching students restructuring skills and engaging them in restructuring efforts in their communities, whether school or neighborhood, will increase their learning success as well as preparing them for more effective and happy lives.

Americans are just beginning to explore multiculturalism, the respectful valuing of other cultures and the recognition that single-language expressions within a multicultural society unnecessarily limit our creative potential. Multiculturalism helps to put sociocultural conditioning in perspective. For example, consider requiring all children in the early grades to learn a second language. This provides an illuminating window on another culture because language embodies cultural values and ways of thinking. In fact, language should be taught explicitly as an exploration of culture. Another advantage to studying culture through language is that understanding the humor of a culture is a powerful way to understand its values.

Along with multiculturalism, we must emphasize multiple ways of processing intelligence. Current school curricula overemphasize linguistic and logical-mathematical intelligence processing to the neglect of visual-spatial, musical, and kinesthetic processing. A more comprehensive approach not only will help students with different types of intelligence in their creative learning but also may greatly facilitate the creative journey of adults at a later age. (It should also lead to physically and psychologically healthier, more balanced "whole" persons by facilitating mind-body integration.)

In the seventies, new educational systems were developed to incorporate some of the ideas above. However, they made one major mistake. The mistake was to disregard or undermine the importance of the ego modality in a creative act. New math (emphasizing the ideas of set theory) is best presented in tandem with conventional teaching of arithmetic and algebra, as clumsy as that may look. Creativity is the play of Shiva and, therefore, often looks chaotic. If we learn to accept and permit the tangled interplay of both the ego and quantum modalities of the students in our classrooms, our whole educational process will take a quantum leap. Additionally, many of these approaches will enhance the self-esteem of students who don't "fit" the current classroom model, thus sparing such students needless suffering and increasing their ability to make positive contributions to society.

A word about cost. We must become willing to pay for the kind of education that can produce adults who are competent to deal creatively with the challenges of a rapidly changing, technological world in which complex economic and political interactions make us all near neighbors. Too many of our students receive too much of their "education" from media which is more intent on entertaining than on informing. This contributes to the 1996 World Competitiveness Yearbook ranking of the United States as only 15th among 46 countries in education and training.

It is also tempting to speculate about the connection between our reluctance to fund education at a level that will ensure our goals and students' reluctance to appear brainy to their peers (Steinberg, 1996). Optimal funding of education would add muscle to the rhetoric about education. Tax-paying parents would be likely to expect more of their children who would begin to take more seriously their job as students (compare the four hours weekly spent on homework by U.S. students with the four hours daily spent by students in many other industrialized countries). And students would feel less need to play dumb.

INTUITION, IMAGINATION, AND INSPIRATION

Because the probability of having a new component in the quantum mind's superposition of possibilities is better with an unlearned stimulus (one to which we have not previously been exposed), confronting ourselves with unlearned stimuli often elicits creativity. Thus reading about a new idea can trigger a shift of contexts in our own thinking, even about an unrelated matter. Especially valuable in this perspective are unlearned stimuli that are ambiguous, such as surrealistic paintings or even inkblots, as in Rorschach images; such things stimulate imagination. But education in schools usually proceeds in an unambiguous, linear, and unimaginative fashion. Can we, in addition, emphasize the value of ambiguity and imagination? In other words, let's encourage kids to act the cartoon character Calvin some of the time.

Our scientific culture, with its materialist emphasis, has often generalized the experimental value of (prediction and) control. Whereas experimental control is necessary as an amplification device to evaluate variables and more clearly see the object or process under study, it becomes counterproductive when used inappropriately. Specifically, it is detrimental to creative processes such as imagination and intuition. These human activities require a surrender of control, a radical receptivity to the nonlocal domain of human experience. (In general, the currently popular refrain, "Take control of your life," should be replaced by another, "Exercise your choice in your actions.")

Because nonlocality is an essential component of the quantum modality, we can enhance the probability of students' creative acts by giving value to nonlocal knowing—intuition—in addition to locally and continuously learned knowledge. An important way to foster nonlocality in creativity is dialog. Etymologically, dialog comes from two Greek words—*dia*, meaning through, and *logos*, meaning word—through the word. As David Bohm said, "dialog can be considered as a free flow of meaning between people in communication" (Bohm & Peat, 1987). But the comprehension and communication of meaning, which often transcends the ordinary context, involve nonlocal consciousness and require sensitivity to the quantum modality. By learning to dialog, students can learn to be sensitive to the quantum self.

Brainstorming—a free-flowing exchange of ideas among participants to solve a problem—can also be useful. With some practice of listening in silence, the communication in a brain-storming session can extend beyond local interactions and the locally learned biases of the students involved, and the probability is that the outcome will be greater than the sum of the parts.

We must never underestimate the role of inspiration. Inspiration comes from relaxation, meditation, and communion with nature. Efficiency-minded curricula have hardly any room for such nonstructured activities.

When I was a child, I didn't go to school (until age eleven, when I entered the eighth grade). My parents taught me at home for roughly two hours a day, including homework. So I had a lot of time by myself in our backyard, which was a jungle, of sorts, full of mango, leechi, and jackfruit trees, cranberries, and other lush vegetation. There was also a pond where I skipped stones; I liked watching their wakes as they danced over the water. But mostly, I reenacted the great epic stories of the *Mahabharata*, which I studied sometimes with my parents but mostly on my own. This was my nuance, my initiation to the subtle world, my secret source of inspiration.

Can we create opportunities for inspiration in the life of every schoolchild? We rightly worry about providing breakfast for their physical bodies, but their mental bodies starve from the lack of inspiration from the quantum self. Let's face it; those Nintendo games that many children play so early in their lives may be exciting, but they are not inspirational. If anything, they probably are anti-inspirational.

Our present education system is overly reliant on artificial problem solving—solving problems with no real-world counterpart. Since such problems are not significant in terms of universal purposiveness, solving them does not engage our drive toward creativity and is only superficially helpful to creativity. Our education must incorporate a confrontation with real-life problems. Indeed, research finds that real-world problem solving is a good indicator of creativity in high school students (Okuda, 1992).

Furthermore, the current system of education teaches problem solving at the same level as the problem. This is particularly so because the problems are artificial, not real-world ones. Real-life problems often demand solutions that require changing the existing context of the problem. Students need inspiration, imagination, and intuition to go beyond the known context.

Also, importantly, we must encourage students to develop a few burning questions, a network of personal enterprises that inspire. Presently, students are urged to understand systems of knowledge *per se* rather than the reality that systems of knowledge describe. ("Research" papers, for example, often consist of paraphrased passages from library sources; seldom is critical analysis or independent thinking truly required.) Instead of studying the moon directly, students learn to study the fingers that point to the moon. This is true even of experimental science, although to a lesser extent.

(Encouraging students to develop a network of enterprises of their choosing will require the inclusion of parents in children's education and much creative parenting. Parents can help teachers discover the individual interests of students which the teachers then can accommodate in the classroom curricula.[2])

---

[2]This point is strongly made by Leonora Cohen (private communication).

Let's remember that all self-conscious beings, and students are no exception, have an inner connection to the world which is them. By studying nature directly, students will learn to explore this inner connection, and surely this will lead to burning questions much faster than learning knowledge systems alone. A map is not the territory and is not as interesting as the territory.

"The world is open before us, everything is still to be done, and not to be done over again," said the immortal Picasso. "Why hang on hopelessly to everything that has fulfilled its promise" (quoted in Zervos, 1996)? Picasso was chiding young painters, but his admonishment applies to all young learners.

> You've taught your child the three R's.
> Where would they be if you hadn't?
> But have you remembered the three I's—
> imagination, intuition, and inspiration?
> Their mastery of the three R's has cultivated will.
> Without the three I's, how will they learn surrender?

THE ROLE OF TEACHERS

"Why waste time learning," asks the cartoon character Calvin, "when ignorance is instantaneous." Ultimately, creative learning by students demands creative teaching by teachers. So teachers must be given more freedom in regard to such aspects of schooling as efficiency, testing, and short-term results. This requires a major depoliticization of education. Like race liberation and women's liberation, we need teachers' liberation.

Currently, teachers are straight-jacketed in either of two roles. The Korean-Japanese eco-philosopher Tae-Chang Kim puts it this way: teachers have to conform either to a sculptor image or to the image of gardener. In a rigid society, teachers are expected to be authoritarian, sculpting the minds of their students with proven facts of knowledge. This was the teaching style in the United States in the 1950s and 1960s. In the style of a liberal society, teachers are caretakers of the garden in which students learn for themselves. Do you recognize the teaching style of the 1970s?

Kim suggests that teachers adapt a third image—that of mediator and co-creator. A good teacher can effectively mediate the creative encounter of the ego and the quantum self that every student needs to experience. An example is the use of heuristics, discussed earlier. But even mediation is not enough; teachers have to participate in their students' projects and become co-creators with them.

Teachers must be secure enough in their own knowledge base to learn from their pupils if they are to be co-creators. The poet Rabindranath Tagore, at age six or thereabouts, had a confrontation with his English teacher. The teacher pronounced "pudding" to rhyme with "budding". Tagore's family was Westernized and had pudding regularly at home, so naturally Rabindranath knew how to pronounce the word. But when he pointed out the correct pronunciation, the teacher took it as an affront to his authority. One thing led to another, and the upshot was that Tagore never returned to formal schooling.

In order to succeed as co-creators with their students, teachers also need to be dedicated to creative becoming. Static ego-homeostasis is for the sculptors and gardeners, not for the teacher who is committed to co-creating. Creative becoming uses methods of inner creativity to surrender the ego to the quantum-self identity. Quantum self-identity is essential because co-creation involves quantum nonlocality to which we are privy only in our quantum-self identity.

THE SOCIETAL BARRIER AGAINST CREATIVITY

When we erect a barrier against somebody's creativity or contribute to any inhibition of creativity, it shows our ignorance. It is to act like the proverbial fool who saws off the branch of the tree that supports him/her. When an entire society, out of the ignorance of its members, puts up barrier after barrier against creativity, soon the very foundation of the society becomes shaky, and the society becomes moribund.

To put it differently, changes happen anyway. If we cannot align our changes to the universal purpose that creativity enables us to see, then the changes of decay rule. This is entropy, and it stinks from the death smell of the society that succumbs to it. We need to balance the progress of entropy. Periodically, we need to go back to basics and to redefine the very fundamentals on which society is based so that they continue to reflect the particular context in which we live. This redefinition requires creativity.

As an example, take the United States. This society was defined by the U.S. Constitution; by the Bill of Rights; by democracy and capitalism, its mainstays for growth; by the mystique of an individualistic know-how and can-do; and by a deep sense of spiritual values. These marvelous ingredients have carried the society through thick and thin. Why? Because during a crisis, for example, the Civil War or the Depression, a redefinition has always been possible (Hoeller, 1992). Creativity has always been available.

But one cannot take creativity and the redefinition it generates for granted. After the Vietnam war, in contrast, instead of a redefinition, the society as a whole did the great ostrich maneuver, sticking its head in the sand of denial. This time, shackled by systems of knowledge based on a worldview that is oppositional to creativity, it has been difficult to dig ourselves out.

I submit that a major source of entropy in our society is the heavy weight of accumulated "knowledge" that we call the social sciences. These "sciences" must be redefined.

THE PURPOSE OF SOCIAL SCIENCE

The reader may have noticed one big omission in our discussion of various creative endeavors; we have not discussed creative acts in what is called the social sciences. The reason for the omission is that the nature of the social sciences is more complicated than either the sciences or the arts and humanities. But finally, we have a useful context for talking about creativity in the social sciences.

First, what is a social science? Fields such as economics, political science, sociology, social psychology, anthropology, and history are collectively called social sciences because these fields pertain to human societies and cultures rather than to nature (which the natural sciences investigate). Practitioners who want their fields to be as objective as natural science have insisted on calling them science, even though they deal with subjects, humans. An idealist revolt in these fields emphasizes multicultural, multilingual, and polythematic answers to problems (see, e.g., Bella, 1991).

A behavioral/cognitive-science view—that the human being is a determined machine—certainly justifies these disciplines in an objective study of human societies. Unfortunately, behaviorism leaves out the creative aspect of the human being and therefore the creative aspect of human societies. In other words, the so-called social sciences, insofar as they put their entire emphasis on objectivity, are doomed to be incomplete.

We need to free the social sciences from this behavioral-mechanistic half nelson and to redefine them within the monistic worldview of idealist science. Accordingly, social sciences must have a clearly acknowledged subjective component. Whereas the objective, behaviorist aspects of the social sciences can profitably use the quantitative methods of science, the subjective component must use the process of creativity. The purpose of such an idealist social science will then clearly be recognized as a creative purpose—to manifest the themes of consciousness such as love, beauty, compassion, and so on.

The psychological drives—tamas, rajas, and sattwa—affect not only individual people but also the societies the people comprise. Tamas at the societal level is social inertia—the tendency to maintain the status quo even in the face of environmental changes. Rajas at the societal level helps maintain healthy homeostasis via adaptation. It enables us to adapt old learned contexts to new environmental situations and to initiate changes when new contexts of living are discovered. But it is sattwa that introduces the critical new meanings and contexts.

The objective, behavioral component of social science is most useful once the society has arrived at a homeostasis; the behavior of societies during these periods approaches the lawfulness of natural science. But objectivity and law-like disposition are of little help during the creative changes from one homeostatic level to another. It is here that the social sciences must be open to a subjective thrust, to creativity. They must give up any notion of the fixity of their laws.

Can you imagine the excitement of pursuing political science if the objective of this science was clearly seen to be congruent with that of creative freedom—namely, to help us not only at times of homeostasis but also with political transition and evolution that can open new vistas of freedom?

Can you imagine what happens if we rewrite our economics or business texts with the well-being and service of people in mind? At first glance, this may seem to be antithetical to capitalism. But is it?

Capitalistic economics is ordinarily seen to be compatible only with a sociobiological picture of us—namely, that we are fundamentally competitive consumers in the service of self-interest (alas! too many of us conform to this view). If this is *all* of our nature, then the most we can hope for is the ethics of the greatest good for the greatest number (Bentham, 1976; Mill, 1973), which favors the rich and creates a large middle class that shares the glory of the rich through trickle-down economics. But we are the whole, we are the world, and the "greatest good for the greatest number" ethic is a limited ethic. This is becoming increasingly clear in the problems almost every capitalistic society is having in constructively integrating its minorities and diversities.

No, I do not think that capitalism is incompatible with the idealist worldview. But we do need to revise capitalism to bring it into accord with a new idealist ethics. A first step toward this is to redefine our index of well-being from one that measures the gross national product to one that measures the number of people directly related to creative work. An important goal of a creative society is to create a wealth of jobs that are primarily or secondarily connected with creativity (see also Schumacher, 1975).

Materialism has a very old history. What we do today in the name of progressive economics has been done before. A philosopher in ancient India named Charvaka proclaimed, "Live happily all your life." And the recipe he gave was, "Borrow and drink ghee [clarified butter]." Forget about drinking ghee, that's cultural. But aren't we emulating Charvaka's economics with a capitalist economics that is based on depleting finite resources of the entire planet, borrowing from future generations? In materialism, there is no responsibility to future generations. But in idealist thinking, in Native American economics, for example, consideration is given to seven future generations. Fortunately, here again tides are turning, and idealist economics is beginning to appear in the literature.

CREATIVITY IN ECONOMICS AND BUSINESS

Adam Smith, the founder of capitalist economics, thought that economic growth occurs from investment in factories and farms. Later, John Maynard Keynes propounded consumer spending as the drive for economic growth. But gradually, a third idea, the importance of creativity and innovation in economic growth, is gaining ground.

The Berkeley economist Paul Romer, for example, clearly recognizes that not just any investment drives economic growth, nor does increasing investment in what we already have (bigger is not necessarily better). What fuels real capital creation is innovative, creative ideas: steam engines, automotives, computers, lasers, and the like.

Creativity in business begins with this recognition that innovative ideas create capital. However, recognition of creativity does not alone make an idealist economics or business community. Very important is the redefinition of economic growth. Currently, most economists give undue importance to the gross national product as virtually the sole indicator of economic growth. But ultimately, economic growth is for the well-being of the members of society. Does GNP adequately measure well-being?

If a materialist society were truly possible, the answer might be yes. But materialism is an incomplete description of human nature. When the role of subjective experiences in society is acknowledged, other indicators must be sought; for example, the satisfaction of the creative urge of the individual. Such indicators may not be as quantitative as GNP, but that makes them no less relevant or important.

So creativity in business involves working toward the well-being of employees and, ultimately, of the entire society (extending to the environment and the world at large). As authors Willis Harman and John Hormann (1990) point out, creative businesses need to be places that bring together employees whose personal visions coincide with the visions that the businesses fulfill. This is possible only when a business's vision involves products that are meaningful to the society (and, ultimately, consistent with the creative purpose of the universe).

What about profit, the penultimate concern of a materialist approach to business? Profit is not incompatible with a meaningful vision based on a useful, creative idea that attracts capable people under an effective, visionary leader.

The author Alvin Toffler has popularized the idea, based on the notion that businesses increasingly recognize the interconnectedness of the organizations of the world, of a third wave of change in the way business operates. The creative Japanese businessman Katsuhiko Yazaki (1994) implores businesses also to recognize our interconnectedness with future generations. Businesses, says Yazaki, can be built with a long time-scale in mind to serve not only the present generation but future generations as well. Yazaki discusses means and examples of how businesses can work against perpetuating the four faces of egoism: economism (overreliance on economic expansion), nationalism (the tendency to overemphasize national boundaries or spatial limits), scientism (overreliance on rational classical science for guidance), and now-ism (forgetting the nonlocality of time).

Of course, in idealist science, this interconnectedness stems, ultimately, from nonlocal oneness in space and time. When we deeply recognize that we are the world, that our personal well-being coincides with the well-being of everyone else on the planet—past, present, and future—then a third wave will indeed wash through society, and business will truly become a creative venture like the arts and the sciences. That will be a huge step toward an ethical society.

THE ETHICAL SOCIETY

The basic idealist ethics is a subjective ethics as opposed to the objective one of the greatest good for the greatest number (Bentham, 1976; Mill, 1973). The fundamental ethical principle that each one of us must understand and live by is that of the preservation and enhancement of our and others' access to the quantum modality. This must include even the outsiders of a particular society, because ultimately there is no outsider. Such an ethics upholds both freedom and creativity.

Admittedly, such an ethics needs practice at the individual level, and only a creative understanding enables us really to live it. But a society that is committed to such an ethics is also committed to creativity. Somebody said that to be creative one has only to involve oneself with creative work. Creativity will follow. The same might be said about an ethical society. We must commit ourselves to the ethics, then we will become ethical by being ethical.

A passing comment. In our materialist society, legalism has increasingly replaced ethics. In an ethical society, law is still necessary; it protects the innocent from crimes committed by unconscious people driven by blind and often pathological ego. But the ethical society deals with such people in a very different manner. Rather than categorically demanding punishment, it builds in opportunities for growth and penance. The living ethics for a society is not a set of "do"s that are rewarded and "don't"s that are punished but continuing opportunities for a creative encounter in a transformative framework.

HARMONIC CREATIVITY

Material-realist science is a science of half-truths because its ontology—material supremacy—is only half true. Sociobiology (Wilson, 1975), a model of social behavior based on Darwin's theory of evolution (a half-truth in view of recent developments[3]), is also half true. Darwin said that biological evolution proceeds via competition for survival—only the fittest survive. Sociobiologists say that human beings are fundamentally competitive because of their biological survival instinct.

Does this competitive model of ourselves hold for creative people? If you look at current mainstream trends, you might say yes on the basis of your observations. There is much evidence of intense competition among creatives in many fields.

In science, there is ugly competition for research funds. Exaggeration, student exploitation, even data-falsification—you name it, big-time science has it. When scientists are forced to collaborate, as in some of the high-energy physics projects that sometimes require as many as four-hundred physicists and technicians to work together, the backbiting and posturing that go on seem to confirm the sociobiological theory. Even when scientists collaborate on a small scale, collaboration is often competitive and does not last. Physicists Richard Feynman and Murray Gell-Mann, both later to win Nobel prizes, collaborated in the late fifties to discover a new law of elementary-particle interaction, only to become bitter enemies within a few years. There are many such examples.

But to say that competition is our only nature is a half-truth. If we look at creative endeavors over a long time-scale, the evidence more

[3]Darwin's theory, even as extended (neo-Darwinism), cannot accommodate such phenomena as punctuated equilibrium (see Eldredge & Gould, 1972) and Gaia (Lovelock, 1982); see also Goswami (1994).

clearly shows that human creativity is not a lonely mission but a collaborative and cooperative movement of consciousness.[4]

When I started working on the idea of consciousness collapsing the quantum possibility wave back in the early 1980s, there was much opposition from my colleagues, who thought I was wasting my time. But strangely, I had my personal supporters. Maggie, of course, thoughtfully participated in many long discussions of my half-formed ideas. There was also an enthusiastic group of "new-agies" who were available as intelligent sounding boards. And mystics helped me to delve into consciousness.

My experience is not isolated. Recently, historians of science have discovered that Einstein himself, during the early 1900s, benefited from much nonacademic cooperation from his friends. He, too, had a sympathetic and capable wife with whom he could discuss ideas. Who knows how much the theory of relativity owes to Einstein's discussions with Mileva Einstein, herself a physicist?

In times of scientific revolution, collaboration and cooperation, not competition, are the general rule. When quantum physics was replacing classical physics in the 1920s, there were many collaborative groups. Especially famous is the Copenhagen school that included such luminaries as Niels Bohr and Werner Heisenberg.

In the arts, there are many stories of mutual support among artists to bring about paradigm changes. The impressionist artists are one example; the beatnik poets are another and the existentialist creatives of France yet another example of such cooperative movements.

One can make a good case that, during renaissance periods, collaboration and cooperation are significant. How can individuals, without the urgency of a renaissance, bring themselves to more cooperation?

Let's return to the difficulty of individual collaboration. An attribute of the creative encounter is the switch from the simple hierarchy of the ego to the tangled-hierarchical quantum self; therefore, it makes sense that collaborative creativity between two people demands a tangled-hierarchical relationship between them. Unfortunately, the tendency of the ego is just the opposite, to make a simple hierarchy of every relationship. A dominating ego degrades attempts at collaboration into power plays. The way out is for individual creatives to integrate inner creativity into their practice of outer creativity. The less you identify with the ego and the more your being is defined by the quantum self, the more you are able to engage in a tangled-hierarchical relationship with another, making true collaboration possible.

---

[4]Aptly pointed out by social theorists of creativity; see Gardner (1993).

When you integrate the inner quantum- and the outer ego-levels of being, the world becomes your family, and you see yourself as a co-creator with everyone else. Then a harmonic convergence of everyone's creativity can take place.

IN CLOSING

In the Sisyphus myth, the Greek king Sisyphus was given the option of immortality in the afterworld, but he chose an apparent punishment—to push a large stone up a hill, only to have it roll down again once he reached the top. What's the point, one wonders, of this repetitive labor? We assume, of course, that the stone always falls back down the same slope of the hill on which it was lifted. But suppose the stone falls down the opposite slope and, the next time, Sisyphus does not push it up to the previous peak but to a new peak.

This then would describe the creative journey of humankind; in this journey we join the quest for immortality in immanence. And yes, we (consciousness) have chosen it over immortality in transcendent potentia. It is a great journey, the great play of the revelation of consciousness to itself. Every peak opens a new vista from which consciousness looks. Yes, creativity is no easy matter; it is like pushing a boulder uphill. But we choose it over the comfort of death in the ego homeostasis, and we do it because at the end of the agony, ecstasy awaits. We are all invited to share that ecstasy. The next hill of our collective creative journey, an unprecedented harmonic convergence of creativity, is ahead of us. It is our task to make it to this new peak, and we will.

> Ah! how wonderful creativity is,
> savoring the joy of the world
> from our creative peaks.
> Want the view permanently?
>
> There is one little condition,
> the world-joy-club membership fee.
> We—you, too—must leap beyond the personal
> to engage co-creatively with all.
>
> Then we will all dance
> to the music of harmonic creativity,
> together on our nonlocal dance floor.
> Then reigns love—eternally.

REFERENCES

Aldridge, J. W. (1992). *Talents and technicians*. New York: Macmillan.

Amabile, T. (1990). Within you, without you: The social psychology of creativity and beyond. In M. A. Runco & R. S. Albert (Eds.), *Theories of creativity*. Newbury Park, CA: Sage.

Anderson, S., & Hopkins, P. (1991). *The feminine face of god*. New York: Bantam.

Arnold, J. (1959). Creativity in engineering. In P. Smith (Ed.), *Creativity*. New York: Hastings House.

Aspect, A., Dalibard, J., & Roger, G. (1982) Experimental test of Bell inequalities using time-varying analyzers. *Physical Review Letters, 49*, 1804-1807.

Atchity, K., & Atchity, V. (1990). Dreams, literature and the arts. In S. Krippner (Ed.), *Dreamtime and dreamwork*. Los Angeles: Tarcher/Perigee.

Aurobindo, S. (1955). *The synthesis of yoga*. Podicherry, India: Sri Aurobindo Ashram.

Banerji, R. B. (1994). *Beyond words* [Preprint]. St Joseph's University, Philadelphia, PA.

Barron, F. (1955). The disposition toward originality. *The Journal of Abnormal and Social Psychology, 51*, 478-485.

Barron, F. (1968). *Creativity and personal freedom*. London: Van Nostrand.

Barron, F. (1969). *Creative person and creative process*. New York: Holt, Rinehart, Winston.

Bass, L. (1975). A quantum mechanical mind-body interaction. *Foundations of Physics, 5*, 155-172.

Bateson, G. (1980). *Mind and nature*. New York: Bantam.

Bella, R. N. (1991). *The good society*. New York: Vintage Books.

Bentham, J. (1976). *The works of Jeremy Bentham* (J. Bowing, Ed.). St. Clair Shores, MI: Scholarly Press.

Bergia, S. (1979). Einstein and the birth of special relativity. In A. P. French, (Ed.), *Einstein: A centenery volume* (pp. 65-89). Cambridge, MA: Harvard University Press.

Blake, W. (1981). *Poetry and prose*. Berkeley: University of California Press.

301

Blood, C. (1993). *On the relation of mathematics of quantum mechanics to the perceived physical universe and free will* [Preprint]. Camden, NJ: Rutgers University Press.

Bly, R. (1992). *Iron John.* New York: Random House.

Boden, M. (1990). *The creative mind.* New York: Basic Books.

Boden, M. (1994). What is creativity? In M. Boden (Ed.), *Dimensions of creativity.* Cambridge, MA: MIT Press.

Bohm, D. (1951). *Quantum theory.* Englewood Cliffs, NJ: Prentice-Hall.

Bohm, D., & Peat, F. D. (1987). *Science, order, and creativity.* New York: Bantam.

Bolen, J. S., Walker, A., & Allende, I. (1993). The storyteller as shaman. *Magical Blend, 39,* 8.

Boles, S. (1990). A model for routine and creative problem solving. *Journal of Creative Behavior, 24,* 171-189.

Boles, S. (1994). *Developing a taxonomy for teaching routine and creative problem solving abilities* [Preprint]. Eugene: Oregon Research Institute.

Briggs, J. (1990). *Fire in the crucible.* Los Angeles: Tarcher.

Brook, P. (1968). *The shifting point.* London: Methuen Drama.

Brown, G. S. (1977). *Laws of form.* New York: Dutton.

Chung-yuan, C. (1970). *Creativity and taoism.* New York: Harper and Row.

Clark, D. (1971). *Einstein: The life and times.* New York: Avon.

Cobb, N. (1992). *Archetypal imagination.* Hudson, NY: Lindisfarne Press.

Cohen, L. M. (1985) *Toward a theory of gifted eduation.* Unpublished doctoral dissertation, Temple University, Philadelphia.

Cohen, L. M. (in press). World views: A conceptual lens for looking at theories of creativity and giftedness. *Journal for the Education of the Gifted.*

Csikszentmihayi, M. (1990). *Flow: The psychology of optimal experience.* New York: Harper Collins.

Dacey, J. S. (1989). Discriminating characteristics of the families of highly creative adolescents. *Journal of Creative Behavior, 23,* 263-271.

Dantes, L. (1990). *The unmanifest self.* Boulder Creek, CA: Aslan Publishing.

Dass, R. (1977). *Grist for the mill.* Santa Cruz, NM: Unity Press.

Davis, G. A. (1975). In frumious pursuit of the creative person. *Journal of Creative Behavior, 9,* 75-87.

De Bono, E. (1970). *Lateral thinking: Creativity step by step.* New York: Harper and Row.

Eberhard, P. (1978). Bell's theorem and the different concepts of reality. *Nuovo Cimento, 46B,* 392.

Eccles, J. C. (1986). Do mental events cause neural events analogously to the probability fields of quantum mechanics? *Proceedings of the Royal Society of London, B227,* 411-428.

Edwards, B. (1989). *Drawing on the right side of the brain.* Los Angeles: Tarcher.

Einstein, A. (1979). *Autobiographical notes.* La Salle: Open Court Publishing.

Eliot, T. S. (1943) *Four quartets.* New York: Harcourt, Brace, Jovanovich.

Elredge, N., & Gould, S. J. (1972). Punctuated equilibrium. In T. J. M. Schopf (Ed.), *Models in paleontology.* San Francisco: Freeman.

Ernst, M. (1960). Inspriation to order. In B. Ghiselin (Ed.), *The creative process* (pp. 64-67). New York: Mentor.

Fabun, D. (1968). *You are creative.* New York: Macmillan.

Feldman, D. (1980). *Beyond universals in cognitive development.* Norwood, NJ: Ablex.

Feldman, D. (1986). *Nature's gambit.* New York: Basic.

Fodor, J. A. (1981). The mind body problem. *Scientific American, 244,* 114-123.

Freeman, W. J. (1991, February). The physiology of perception. *Scientific American,* pp. 78-85.

Freud, S. (1961). *Introductory lectures on psychoanalysis, vol XV of the standard edition.* London: Hogarth

Freud, S. (1963). *Introductory lectures on psychoanalysis, vol. XVI of the standard edition.* London: Hogarth.

Friedman, A. I., & Donley, C. C. (1985). *Einstein as myth and muse.* Cambridge, UK: Cambridge University Press.

Gallup, G. (1982). *Adventures in immortality.* New York: McGraw-Hill.

Garcia, J. D. (1974). *Psychofraud and ethical therapy.* Ardmore, PA: Whitmore.

Gardner, H. (1993). *Creating minds.* New York: Basic Books.

Gell-Mann, M. (1994). *The quark and the jaguar.* New York: Freeman.

Getzels, J. W., & Czikszentmihalyi, M. (1976). *The creative vision: A longitudinal study of problem finding in art.* New York: John Wiley.

Gibran, K. (1971). *The prophet.* New York: Knopf.

Gleick, J. (1987). *Chaos.* New York: Viking.

Goleman, D., Kaufman, P., & Ray, M. (1992). *The creative spirit.* New York: Dutton.

Goswami, A. (1988). Creativity and the quantum theory. *Journal of Creative Behavior, 22,* 9-31.

Goswami, A. (1989) The idealistic interpretation of quantum mechanics. *Physics Essays, 2,* 385-400.

Goswami, A. (1990) Consciousness, quantum physics, and the mind-body problem. *Journal of Mind and Behavior, 11,* 75-96.

Goswami, A. (1993a). *The self-aware universe: How consciousness creates the material world.* New York: Tarcher/Putnam.

Goswami, A. (1993b). An idealist theory of ethics. *Creativity Research Journal, 6,* 185-196.

Goswami, A. (1994). *Science within consciousness: Developing a science based on the primacy of consciousness* [Research Report]. Sausalito, CA: Institue of Noetic Sciences.

Goswami, A. (1996a). Creativity and the quantum. *Creativity Research Journal, 9,* 47-61.

Goswami, A. (1996b). *Physics of the soul: Death and reincarnation in the quantum world.* (in press).

Goswami, A. and Burns, J. (1993). *Quantum theory and the self.* Unpublished manuscript. Eugene: University of Oregon.

Gowan, J. C. (1974). *Development of the psychedelic individual.* Buffalo, NY: Creative Education Foundation.

Gowan, J. C. (1977). Some thoughts on the development of creativity. *Journal of Creative Behavior, 11*(2).

Green, E. (1977). *Beyond biofeedback.* New York: Dell.

Grinberg-Zylberbaum, J., & Ramos, G. (1987) Patterns of interhemispheric correlations during human communication. *International Journal of Neuroscience, 36,* 41-54.

Grinberg-Zylberbaum, J., Delaflor, M., Attie, L., & Goswami, A. (1994, December). Einstein-Podolsky-Rosen paradox in the human brain: the transferred potential. *Physics Essays, 7,* 422-428.

Gruber, H. (1978). Darwin's "tree of nature" and other images of wide scope. In J. Wechster (Ed.), *On aesthetics in science.* Cambridge: MIT Press.

Gruber, H. (1981). *Darwin on man* (2nd ed). Chicago: University of Chicago Press.

Gruber, H., & Davis, S. N. (1988). Inching our way to Mount Olympus: The evolving systems approach to creative thinking. In R. J. Sternberg (Ed.), *The nature of creativity* (243-270). Cambridge: Cambridge University Press.

Grudin, R. (1990). *The grace of great things: Creativity and innovation.* New York: Tickner and Fields.

Guilford, J. P. (1959). Traits of creativity. In H. H. Anderson (Ed.), *Creativity and its cultivation* (pp. 142-161). New York: Harper.

Guillaumont A., et al. (Trans.) (1959). *The gospel according to Thomas.* San Francisco: Harper & Row.

Hadamard, J. (1939). *The psychology of invention in the mathematical field.* Princeton, NJ: Princeton University Press.

Haefel, J. W. (1962). *Creativity and innovation.* New York: Van Nostrand Reinhold.

Hampden-Turner, C. (1981). *Maps of the mind.* New York: Collier.

Harman, W., & De Quincey, C. (1994). *The scientific exploration of consciousness: Toward an adequate epistemology* [Research Report]. Sausalito, CA: Institute of Noetic Sciences.

Harman, W., & Hormann, J. (1990). *Creative work: The constructive role of business in a transformative society.* Indianapolis, IN: Knowledge Systems, Inc.

Harman, W., & Rheingold, H. (1984). *Higher creativity.* Los Angeles: Tarcher.

Hawking, S. (1990). *A brief history of time.* New York: Bantam.

Helson, R. (1990). Creativity in women: Outer and inner views over time. In M. A. Runco & R. S. Albert (Eds.), *Theories of creativity.* Newbury Park, CA: Sage.

Herbert, N. (1986). *Quantum reality.* New York: Dutton.

Herbert, N. (1993). *Elemental mind.* New York: Dutton.

Hesse, H. (1973). *Siddhartha.* London: Pan Books.

Hoeller, S. (1992). *Freedom.* Wheaton, IL: Theosophical Publishing House.

Hofstadter, D. R. (1980). *Goedel, Escher, Bach: The eternal golden braid.* New York: Basic Books.

Holton, G. (1973). *Thematic origin of scientific thought.* Cambridge, MA: Harvard University Press.

Holton, G. (1979). What precisely is thinking? Einstein's answer. In A. P. French (Ed.), *Einstein: A centinery volume* (pp. 153-166). Cambridge: Harvard University Press.

Humphrey, N. (1972). Seeing and nothingness. *New Scientist, 53,* 682.

Hutchinson, T., & DeSelincourt, E. (1967). *Wordsworth: Poetical works.* London: Oxford University Press.

Jung, C. G. (1971a). In J. Campbell (Ed.), *The portable Jung.* New York: Viking.

Jung, C. G. (1971b). *Man and his symbols.* New York: Dell.

Jung, C. G., & Pauli, W. (1955). *The nature and interpretation of the psyche.* New York: Pantheon.

Kazantzakis, N. (1965). *Report to Greko.* New York: Simon and Schuster.

Koestler, A. (1964). *The act of creation.* New York: MacMillan.

Kornfield, J. (1993). *A path with a heart*. New York: Bantam.

Kraft, D. C. B. (1996, Spring). Shadows in the mirror. *Quest*, p. 51.

Kuhn, T. S. (1970). *The structure of scientific revolutions*. Chicago: University of Chicago Press.

Lamb, D., & Easton, S. M. (1984). *Multiple discovery*. Trowbridge, UK: Avebury.

Langley, P., Simon, H. A., Bradshaw, G. L., & Zytkow, J. M. (1987). *Scientific discovery. Computational explorations of the creative process*. Cambridge, MA: MIT Press.

Lawrence, D. H. (1971). *A selection from Phoenix*. London: Penguin Books.

Libet, B. (1985). Unconscious cerebral initiative and the role of conscious will in voluntary action. *The Behavioral and Brain Sciences, 8*, 529-566.

Libet, B., Wright, E., Feinstein, B., & Pearl, D. (1979). Subjective referral of the timing for a cognitive sensory experience. *Brain, 102*, 193.

Lilly, J. C. (1974). *Programming and metaprogramming in the human biocomputer*. New York: Bantam.

Lockwood, M. (1989). *Mind, brain, and the quantum*. Oxford, UK: Basil Blackwell.

Lovelock, J. E. (1982). *Gaia: A new look at life on earth*. Oxford: Oxford University Press.

Mackinnon, D. W. (1962). The personality correlates of creativity: A study of American architects. In G. S. Nielsen (Ed.), *Proceedings of the Fourteenth Internatinal Congress of Applied Psychology* (Vol. 2, pp. 11-39). Copenhagen: Munskgaard.

Magallon, L. L., & Shor, B. (1990). Shared dreaming: Joining together in dreamtime. In S. Krippner (Ed.), *Dreamtime and dreamwork*. Los Angeles: Tarcher/Perigee.

Malraux, A. (1951). *The voices of silence*. New York: Doubleday.

Malville, K. (1975). *A feather for Daedalus*. Menlo Park, CA: Cummings.

Mansfield, R. S., & Busse, T. V. (1981). *The psychology of creativity and discovery*. Chicago: Nelson-Hall.

Marcel, A. J. (1980). Conscious and preconscious recognition of polysemous words: locating the selective effect of prior verbal context. In R. S. Nickerson (Ed.), *Attention and performance VIII*. Hillsdale, NJ: Erlbaum.

Maslow, A. (1968). *Toward a psychology of being*. New York: Van Nostrand Reinhold.

May, R. (1976). *The courage to create*. New York: Bantam.

McCarthy, K. (1993). Indeterminacy and consciousness in the creative process. *Creativity Research Journal, 6*, 201-220.

McCarthy, K., & Goswami, A. (1993). CPU or self-reference?: Discerning between cognitive science and quantum functionalist models of mentation. *Journal of Mind and Behavior, 14*, 13-26.

Margulis, L. (1993). Reflection. In C. Barlow (Ed.), *From Gaia to selfish gene*. Cambridge, MA: MIT Press.

Merrell-Woll, F. (1973). *Philosophy of consciousness without an object*. New York: Julian Press.

Miller, A. I. (1989). Imagery and intuition in creative scientific thinking: Albert Einstein's invention of the special theory of relativity. In D. B. Wallace & H. E. Gruber (Eds.), *Creative people at work* (pp. 171-188). New York: Oxford University Press.

Mill, J. S. (1973). On liberty and utilitarianism. In *The utilitarians*. New York: Anchor.

Mishlove, J. (1993). *The roots of consciousness*. Tulsa, OK: Council Oak Books.

Mitchell, M., & Goswami, A. (1992). Quantum mechanics for observer systems. *Physics Essays, 5,* 526-529.

Monod, J. (1974). *Chance and necessity*. London: Collins.

Moss, R. (1981). *The I that is we*. Berkeley, CA: Celestial Arts.

Moss, R. (1984). *Radical aliveness*. Berkeley, CA: Celestial Arts.

Nagendra, H.R. (Ed.). (1993). *New horizons in modern medicine*. Bangelore, India: Vivekananda Rendra Yoga Research Foundation.

Nicolis, G., & Prigogine, I. (1990). *Exploring complexity: An introduction*. New York: Freeman.

Nikhilananda, Swami (Trans.). (1964). *The Upanishads*. New York: Harper and Row.

Okuda, S. (1992). *Journal of Psychoeducational Assessment, 9,* 45-53.

Orlov, Y. (1981). A quantum model of doubt. *Annals of the N.Y. Academy of Sciences, 373,* 84-92.

Oshins, E. (1983). Errata to a quantum model of doubt. *Annals of the N.Y. Academy of Sciences, 410,* 361-363.

Oshins, E., & McGoveran, D. (1980). . . . .thoughts about logic about thoughts. . .: the question schizophrenia. In B. H. Banathy (Ed.), *Systems science and science* (pp. 505-514). Louisville: Society for General Systems Research.

Overton, W. (1976). The active organism in development. *Human Development, 19,* 71-86.

Pasricha, S. (1990). *Claims of reincarnation: An empirical study of cases in India*. New Delhi: Harman Publishing House.

Peace Pilgrim (1982). *Peace Pilgrim: Her life and work in her own words*. Santa Fe, NM: Ocean Tree Books.

Penrose, R. (1991). *The emperors new mind*. New York: Penguin.

Penrose, R. (1994). *Shadows of the mind*. Oxford, England: Oxford University Press.

Piaget, J. (1977). *The development of thought: Equilibration of cognitive structures*. New York: Viking.

Piechowski, M. M. (1993). Is inner transformation a creative process? *Creativity Research Journal, 6,* 89-98.

Piechowski, M. M., & Goswami, A. (1991). *Personal crisis, creative ethics, and the opportunity for transformation*. Unpublished manuscript.

Poincare, H. (1924). Mathematical creation. In G. B. Halsted (trans.), *The foundations of science*. New York: Science Press.

Plato. (1980). *Collected dialogs*. (E. Hamilton & H. Cairns, eds.). Princeton, NJ: Princeton University Press.

Posner, M. (1980). Mental chronometry and the problem of consciousness. In P. Jusczyk & R. Klein (Eds.), *The nature of thought: Essays in honor of D.O. Hebb*.

Preston, J. H. (1960). A conversation with Gertrude Stein. In B. Ghiselin (Ed.), *The creative process*. New York: New American Library.

Prior, H. W., Haag, R., & O'Reilly, G. (1969). The creative purpose: Training for novel behavior. *Journal of Experimental Analysis of Behavior, 12,* 653-661.

Rabi, I. I. (1975, October). Profiles—physicists, I. *The New Yorker Magazine*, October 13.

Ramana, Maharshi. (1978). *Talks with Sri Ramana Maharshi*. (T. N. Venkataraman, ed.). Madras, India: Jupiter Press.

Ray, M., & Myers, R. (1989). *Creativity in business*. New York: Doubleday.

Rogers, C. R. (1959). Toward a theory of creativity. In H. H. Anderson (Ed.), *Creativity and its cultivation*. New York: Harper.

Rothenberg, A. (1976). The process of Janusian thinking in creativity. In A. Rothenberg & C. R. Hausman (Eds.), *The creavity question* (pp. 311-326). Durham, NC: Duke University Press.

Rothenberg, A. (1983). Psychopathology and creative cognition. *Archives of General Psychiatry, 40*, 937-942.

Rothenberg, A., & Hausman, C. R. (Eds.). (1976). *The creavity question*. Durham, NC: Duke University Press.

Rumi. (1988). *The branching moments* (J. Moyne & C. Barks, trans.). Providence, RI: Copper Beech Press.

Russell, B. (1965). *How I write*. In *Portraits from memory and other essays*. London: Allen and Unwin.

Sawyer, K. (1992). Improvisational creativity: An analysis of jazz performance. *Creativity Research Journal, 5*, 253-263.

Schmidt, H. (1993). Observation of a psychokinetic effect under highly controlled conditions. *Journal of Parapsychology, 57*, 351-372.

Schumacher, E. F. (1975). *Small is beautiful*. New York: Harper and Row.

Searle, J. (1987). Minds and brains, without programs. In C. Blakemore & S. Greenfield (Eds.), *Mindwares* (pp. 209-234).

Simonton, D. K. (1984). *Genius, creativity, and leadership*. Cambridge, MA: Harvard University Press.

Simonton, D. K. (1988). *Scientific genius. A psychology of science*. New York: Cambridge University Press.

Skinner, B. F. (1971). *Beyond freedom and dignity*. New York: Knopf.

Shevrin, H. (1980, April). Glimpses of the unconscious. *Psychology Today*, p. 128.

Sperry, R. (1983). *Science and moral priority*. New York: Columbia University Press.

Stapp, H. P. (1977). Are superluminal connections necessary? *Nuovo Cimento, 40B*, 191-99.

Stapp. H. P. (1982). Mind, matter, and quantum mechanics. *Foundations of Physics, 12*, 363-398.

Stapp, H. P. (1993). *Mind, matter, and quantum mechanics*. New York: Springer.

Steinberg, L. (1996). *Beyond the classroom*. New York: Simon and Schuster.

Stevenson, I. (1974). *Twenty cases suggestive of reincarnation*. Charlottsville: University Press of Virginia.

Stuart, C. I. J. M., Takahashy, Y., & Umezawa, M. (1978). Mixed system brain dynamics, *Foundations of Physics, 9*, 301-329.

Suzuki, S. (1984). *Zen mind, beginnner's mind*. New York: Weatherhill.

Tagore, R. N. (1913). *Collected poems and plays*. London: Macmillan.

Tagore, R. N. (1931). *The religion of man*. New York: MacMillan.

Tagore, R. N. (1976). *Later poems of Rabindranath Tagore* (A. Bose, trans.). New York: Minerva.

Taimni, I. K. (1961). *The science of yoga*. Wheaton, IL: Theoseosophical Publishing House.

Tardif, T. W., & Sternberg, R. J. (1988). What do we know about creativity? In R. J. Sternberg, (Ed.), *The nature of creativity* (pp. 429-440). Cambridge, UK: Cambridge University Press.

Torrance, E. P. (1988). The nature of creativity as manifest in its testing. In R. J. Sternberg (Ed.), *Current psychological perspectives* (pp. 3-75). Cambridge, UK: Cambridge University Press.

Van Gogh, V. (1937). *Dear Theo* (I. Stone, ed.). New York: New American Library.

Varela, F. J., Thompson, E., & Rosch, E. (1991). *The embodied mind*. Cambridge, MA: MIT Press.

Vaughan, F. E. (1979). *Awakening intuition*. New York: Doubleday.

Von Neumann, J. (1955). *The mathematical foundations of quantum mechanics*. Princeton, NJ: Princeton University Press.

Wagner, R. (1911). *My life*. London: Constable.

Walker, E. H. (1970). The nature of consciousness. *Mathematical Biosciences, 7*, 131-178.

Wallas, G. (1926). *The art of thought*. New York: Harcourt, Brace, and World.

Walters, J., & Gardner, H. (1986). The crystallizing experience. In R. J. Sternberg & J. E. Davidson (Eds.), *Conceptions of giftiftedness*. Cambridge, UK: Cambridge University Press.

Weinberg, S. (1979) *The first three minutes*. New York: Bantam.

Weisberg, R. W. (1993). *Creativity. Beyond the myth of genius*. New York: Freeman.

Wertheimer, M. (1959). *Productive thinking*. New York: Harper and Row.

Whitman, W. (1972). *The leaves of grass*. New York: Avon.

Wigner, E. P. (1962). In I. J. Good (Ed.), *The scientists speculates*. Kingswood, Surrey, UK: The Windmill Press.

Wilber, K. (1977). *The spectrum of consciousness*. Wheaton, IL: Theosophical Publishing House.

Wilson, C. (1957). *The outsiders*. New York: Dell.

Wilson, E. O. (1975). *Sociobiology: The new synthesis*. Cambridge, MA: Harvard University Press.

Wolf, F. A. (1981). *Taking the quantum leap*. San Francisco: Harper and Row.

Wolf. F. A. (1984). *Starwave*. New York: Macmillan.

Wolf, F. A. (1994). *The dreaming universe*. New York: Simon and Schuster.

Wolfe, T. (1960). The story of a novel. In B. Gheislein (Ed.), *The creative process*. New York: New American Library.

Woodman, R. W. (1981). Creativity as a construct in personality theory. *Journal of Creative Behavior, 15*, 43-66.

Wordsworth, J., Abrams, M. H., & Gill, S. (1979). *The prelude, 1799, William Wordsworth*. New York: Norton.

Wotiz, J. H., & Rudofsky, S. (1984, August). Kekule's dreams: Fact or fiction? *Chemistry in Britain*, pp. 720-723.

Yazaki, K. (1994). *Path to Liangzhi: Seeking an eternal philosophy*. Kyoto: Future Generations Alliance Foundation.

Yeats, W. B. (1960). Three pieces on the creative process. In B. Ghiselin (Ed.), *The creative process*. New York: New American Library.

Zervos, C. (1960). Conversation with Picasso. In B. Ghiselin (Ed.), *The creative process*. New York: Mentor.

Zolla, E. (1981). *Archetypes*. London: Harcourt Brace Jovanovich.

AUTHOR INDEX

/UBJECT INDEX

A

Accidental Tourist, The, 277
Ah-ha insight (*see* insight)
Akbar, 242
Algorithms, 11, 20, 42
Alice in Wonderland, 39
Allen, W., 10
Amadeus, 24
Anima, 226, 276ff
Animus, 226, 276ff
Archetype, 36, 80, 120, 225, 247, 276ff
Archimedes, 10, 153
Arjuna, 220, 248
Arthur, 2
Artistic creativity (*see* creativity, in arts)
Asimov, I., 77
Association, in thought awareness, 103
Atman, 58, 96

Atoms, 11-12
Avatara, 243
Awareness
    and meditation, 266ff
    primary, 97, 148
    secondary, 98, 148
    and unconscious, 92-93

B

Bacon, 21, 65
Bach, J. S., 182, 264
Balzac, H., 182, 185
Barashnikov, M., 46
Barret, E., 151
Barriers to creativity, 216
Beatles, 182
Beauty, 81ff
Beethoven, L. van, 178, 246
Behaviorism, and creativity, 215ff
Bell, A. G., 41-42
Bhagavad Gita, 233, 241-242, 280

313

LaVergne, TN USA
28 October 2009
162357LV00002B/1/A